The Commercialization of News

in the Nineteenth Century

The Commercialization of News in the Nineteenth Century

Gerald J. Baldasty

The University of Wisconsin Press

The University of Wisconsin Press
2537 Daniels Street
Madison, Wisconsin 53718

3 Henrietta Street
London WC2E 8LU, England

9   8   7   6   5   4

Printed in the United States of America

Library of Congress Cataloging-in-Publication Data
Baldasty, Gerald J.
   The commercialization of news in the nineteenth century   /
   Gerald J. Baldasty.
   240 pp.   cm.
   Includes bibliographical references (p. 000) and index.
   ISBN 0-299-13400-8 (cloth)   ISBN 0-299-13404-0 (paper)
   1. Press—United States—History—19th century. 2. Journalism—
Economic aspects—United States—19th century. 3. American
newspapers—Economic aspects—History—19th century. I. Title.
PN4888.C59B34   1992
071'3' 09034 —dc20   92-10590

For Richard J. Baldasty
and
Don R. Pember

Contents

Tables and Figures

Tables

Figures

Acknowledgments

I am indebted to many for their assistance during this project: the University of Washington for a year-long sabbatical leave from teaching, during which time I wrote the first draft of the manuscript; and the University of Washington Graduate School Research Fund for a grant that allowed me to complete ongoing research on the political press.

Space precludes thanking everyone who helped me, but, to mention a few, I am indebted to the late William E. Ames, Edward P. Bassett, the late Philip W. Blumstein, Richard F. Carter, Herbert Costner, Glenda Pearson, Carla Rickerson, and Roger A. Simpson, all of the University of Washington, Tim Gleason, University of Oregon, Carolyn Stewart Dyer, University of Iowa, and Ted Curtis Smythe, California State University–Fullerton, for their ideas, suggestions, and support. John E. Bowes, University of Washington, helped me with the research design and data analysis on political affiliation and always served as a friendly but sharp critic. I'm also indebted to Pat Dinning, Trudy Flynn, Jodi Naas, Karen Nagai, and Kelly Vigdal. As staff members of the University of Washington School of Communications, they covered for me when I was preoccupied with this project and graciously helped with many small but significant details. Others who helped at various stages of this project include David Beck von Peccoz, Vikki Haag, Susan Henry, Philip Jerry, Mike Jordan, and Jeff Rutenbeck.

Anna McCausland and Ruth Kirk, of the University of Washington Interlibrary Borrowing Services, often were my lifeline to research sources. Words cannot adequately express my thanks for their hard but often unheralded work.

James L. Baughman, University of Wisconsin–Madison, Hazel Dicken-Garcia, University of Minnesota, Linda Lawson, Indiana University, Richard Kielbowicz, University of Washington, Thomas Leonard, University of California–Berkeley, David Paul Nord, Indiana University, Don Pember, University of Washington, and Don Ritchie, assistant Senate historian, all read at least one version of the manuscript and offered cogent criticisms. Carol Smith, University of Kentucky, gave invaluable suggestions for revisions. She gave freely of her time and ideas. Randy Beam, University of Oregon, provided superb advice, edited the manuscript, and served as a valuable critic.

Don R. Pember, my colleague in the School of Communications at the University of Washington, and Richard J. Baldasty, my brother, provided assistance of far greater value than they will ever realize. For their ideas and for their never-wavering support, this book is dedicated to them, with my deepest gratitude.

The Commercialization of News

in the Nineteenth Century

Introduction

In 1801, Federalists in New York City established the *Evening Post* to espouse their cause, attack the Jefferson administration, and serve as the political mouthpiece of Alexander Hamilton. The first issue of this four-page daily newspaper included attacks on the Jeffersonians, essays on American politics and on the press, notices of an upcoming city charter election, accounts of foreign events, reports on shipping, and news about the Philadelphia theater.[1] One Jeffersonian referred to the *Evening Post's* editor, William Coleman, as "the Field Marshall of the Federal Editors." Many Americans saw "Hamilton's Gazette" as one of the nation's leading antiadministration papers.[2]

At century's end, the now 12-page paper still carried news about politics, but it was no longer a party organ. In 1897, in just one day's issue of the newspaper, the reader could find articles on sports, lectures, murder, road improvements, books, business, auctions, stocks, European money markets, theater, fashion, literature, crime, accidents, parks, and New York real estate, as well as accounts of various local happenings and a calendar of upcoming events.[3]

This change in the *Evening Post* exemplifies the transformation of American journalism in the nineteenth century. Early in the century, newspapers were usually small-circulation, four-page weeklies or dailies. Their content was dominated by politics and advocacy, reflecting their close ties to political parties and interest groups.

By the 1890s, newspapers (particularly in the metropolitan areas) were large-circulation, 8- or 12-page dailies that usually eschewed close political affiliation. Newspapers still dealt with politics, but now they did so from a position of some autonomy. More important, they devoted much of their attention and space to other topics, providing a diverse mix of local, regional, and national news and features on dozens of topics—business, crime, accidents, fires, divorce, suicide, labor, education, religion, sports, inventions, disease, weather, books, theater, music, fashion, and recipes, to list a few. They even serialized fiction.

Just how much newspapers had changed in one century is underscored by the fact that the content of the *Evening Post*, even after its metamorphosis to a general-interest newspaper, was more restrained than that of its competitors in New York City. By 1900, sensational mass-circulation newspapers dominated in New York City, with their screaming headlines, lurid stories of illicit love, suicide, and graft, and jumble of puzzles, contests, comic strips, and fiction. When the *Evening Post* began publication in 1801, its competitors were other small-circulation newspapers that paid little heed to events beyond politics and business.[4] In 1900, all those other newspapers were gone, and the *Post* was part of a substantially different newspaper market.

What had happened that so changed the American newspaper? How had the vision or definition of the press in American society changed? The answer is a complex one, embracing far-reaching changes not only in the press but also in American society itself. Technological innovation, the rise of a market economy, the broad sweep of industrialization, greater leisure time and literacy, the rise of great cities, to name just a few factors, helped reshape the American newspaper. Within the newspaper industry itself, particularly after the Civil War, new ideas about the role of the press in society broadened the purview of the press and the content of newspapers.[5]

This book focuses on just one part of the changing newspaper in the nineteenth century by looking at the thrust toward commercialization of the news. In the early nineteenth century, editors defined news as a political instrument intended to promote party interests. By century's end, editors defined news within a business context to ensure or increase revenues. News had become commercialized.

This book explores the commercialization of news. It traces changes in society and the press that gave rise to news values that exalted profit-making at the expense of older notions of news as political information or persuasion. In a broad sense, then, commercialization here refers to the process by which news values were redefined to include this concern for the bottom line and to the evolution of news as a commodity to be shaped and marketed with an eye for profit.[6]

The commercialization of news in the nineteenth century was the result of changes in three important areas of the newspaper: its finances, the vision of what the press could and should do, and the exigencies of day-to-day operations.

The intimate connection between finances and content figures prominently in the changing nature of the press during the century and was central to the rise of commercialized news. Political parties in the antebellum era provided a measure of financial stability to many newspapers. In return, the papers ardently supported their party.

Similarly, when advertisers replaced political parties as the key constituent (and chief financial angel) of the press, the press came to support them, too. These two constituencies, first political parties and later advertisers, were instrumental in defining news. Both helped shape news to reflect their own needs and interests.

Besides this simple interplay of money and content, there was the more subtle interplay between vision (how newspaper producers saw their own role, saw their readers) and content. Rather simply put, partisan editors viewed their readers as *voters*. They geared their content primarily to such an audience.[7] By century's end, editors and publishers saw their readers not only as voters but also as *consumers*, so they produced content that went far beyond the world of politics and voting. This vision of a "commercialized reader," if you will, naturally fueled commercialized news.

Beyond finances and vision came the practical exigencies of the publishing business. In 1830, a journeyman printer could start a weekly newspaper in a small town with $500.[8] Even in the larger urban areas, the financial barriers to the market were relatively low. In 1835, with only $500 capital, James Gordon Bennett established his *New York Herald* in a basement office furnished with a few packing cases covered with planks.[9] Costs grew enormously during the century. Increasingly mechanized production systems (steam-powered presses, Linotypes) meant more capital was needed to start a newspaper. Operating costs grew, too. Staff size grew with the rise of reporting as an occupation and the increasing departmentalization common to big-city newspapers. Another expense accrued through use of the telegraph, because papers came to rely more and more on that for news.[10] Charles A. Dana, editor of the New York *Sun*, estimated that starting a new daily in New York City in 1840 would have cost between $5,000 and $10,000 and, in 1850, as much as $100,000.[11] Costs soared after the Civil War, driving start-up expenses closer to $1 million in New York City.[12] Again, all this emphasized the business aspects of the newspaper, which in turn propelled the commercialization of news.

In detailing the commercialization of news in the nineteenth century, this book concentrates on three phases of the press: (1) the partisan newspapers of the Jacksonian era (circa 1825–35), (2) transitions in the press and in American society in the middle decades of the century, and (3) the business environment of news and newspapers in the last two decades of the century.

The highly political Jacksonian era represents what was probably the high tide of the partisan press. During the 1820s and 1830s, subsidies and patronage at the local, state, and federal levels systematically provided financial stability for the press, and partisan newspapers flourished.[13] The middle decades of the century saw changes in American life that propelled changes in American journalism. And newspapers across the nation—from small-town weeklies to large metropolitan dailies—all manifested the commercialization of news in the latter two decades of the century.

The process of commercialization is best understood by noting the contrast between the Jacksonian era partisan press and the commercialized press of the late nineteenth century. Chapter 1 details the operations of the Jacksonian political press, and in a sense provides the baseline for this study. Chapter 2 shows the rise of a new environment for journalism with the concomitant decline of partisan journalism in the middle decades of the century. Chapters 3, 4, and 5 detail the operation of the press in the latter decades of the nineteenth century. Chapter 3 details *external* pressures on the press and on news engendered by the rise of advertising. Chapters 4 and 5 document the business orientation *within* the newspaper industry, and show how this orientation helped commercialize the news.

The press is not monolithic, and so its variety demands attention. In this book, three general categories of newspapers are examined: newspapers in *metropolitan* areas such as New York, Boston, Chicago, Pittsburgh; newspapers in *small cities and large towns* such as Albany, New York, Salem, Oregon, and Mansfield, Ohio; and newspapers in *small towns* such as Haverhill, Massachusetts, and Drain, Oregon.[14]

Comparisons often invite oversimplification, and it is important not to exaggerate or oversimplify the characteristics of the press at either end of the century. Not all newspapers in the 1820s and 1830s, even at the height of the partisan press era, were partisan. In the larger cities, literary and commercial papers had flourished since the eighteenth century. Indeed, in cities such as New York, newspapers that could be more appropriately seen as political-commercial-literary hybrids existed. The New York *Evening Post*, for example, under the editorship of William Cullen Bryant and William Leggett in the early 1830s, was part of the radical wing of the Jacksonian Democratic party, fervently endorsing the bulk of Jackson's political agenda. It also devoted a good deal of attention to literary work (including Bryant's own verse) and business news.[15] The 1830s and 1840s witnessed a great surge in the number of temperance, religious, and other ostensibly nonpartisan papers.[16] Not all ostensibly partisan newspapers devoted all their attention to politics. Vivid stories about death from rabies, accounts of executions, tales of love gone wrong, and book reviews were found in many partisan newspapers of the 1830s. Nonetheless, partisan content dominated pre–Civil War American newspapers. The 1850 U.S. census estimated that 80 percent of newspapers were partisan, and Michael McGerr estimates that 95 percent of newspapers at that time were partisan. Financial subsidies, from politicians on the local, state, and federal levels, nurtured this broad network of political newspapers. Many editors were also political activists, organizing party meetings, drafting party platforms, and recruiting candidates. This partisanship was most evident in Washington, D.C., and in state capitals. But it appeared elsewhere, too, in the great metropolitan centers such as New York or Boston as well as in large towns like Macon, Georgia, and small towns like Lyons, New York. The state of Georgia had 11 newspapers in 1830, and all were embroiled in political fights.[17] Some of the largest antebellum political-commercial newspapers, such as the New York *Courier and Enquirer*, were deeply involved in the political battles of that era.[18]

Commercialization of news led to a deemphasis on politics and advocacy. Not all late nineteenth-century newspapers avoided politics, however. Indeed, even what is arguably the most commercialized newspaper of the era, William Randolph Hearst's *New York Journal*,[19] gave substantial coverage to the city's 1897 mayoral election and consistently made clear its political preferences in the paper's main news columns.

Nonetheless, a commercial vision guided the late nineteenth-century press, a vision fundamentally different from that of the partisan press. In 1898, an *Evening Press* editorial writer argued that partisan newspapers were just bad business because they could not be "fair and truthful."[20] That a newspaper such as the New York *Evening Post*, established to promote Alexander Hamilton and the Federalist party, could disdain partisanship as bad business, indicates that something had clearly changed. Commercial concerns now propelled American newspapers.

In analyzing the commercialization of news, a variety of sources was useful. Newspaper content was important, and this study is based on a general reading of hundreds of newspapers across the century and on a quantitative content analysis of nine newspapers in the antebellum era[21] and of 16 newspapers in the late 1890s.[22] The content analysis scheme is in appendix 1.

To help explain content changes, this research relied upon manuscript collections, government reports, late nineteenth-century trade journals (in the newspaper and advertising industries), newspaper trade association proceedings, newspaper directories, and nineteenth-century periodicals. The trade association proceedings and the industry trade journals are of particular importance, because they so fully describe business concerns and issues of the late nineteenth century and because they are one of the few indicators of business operations. Very few newspaper business records exist for the nineteenth century.

This work explores the character of the American press in the nineteenth century, thus complementing or extending ideas developed in particular by Hazel Dicken-Garcia's *Journalistic Standards in Nineteenth-Century America*, Carolyn Stewart Dyer's "Political Patronage of the Wisconsin Press, 1849–1861," and John Nerone's "Mythology of the Penny Press."[23] Dicken-Garcia examines nineteenth-century press criticism, showing how perceptions and expectations of the press changed during the century. Dyer shows the enduring importance of the partisan press throughout the antebellum era; highly partisan newspapers were an important part of American journalism on the eve of the Civil War. Nerone disputes the notion that the penny press was the single great turning point in nineteenth-century journalism. While recognizing the importance of the penny press, I attempt to show in this book that changes in the press during the nineteenth century were part of a larger process of political and social change.

This book also examines the changing definition of news. A variety of authors have already explored this area, concentrating primarily on the post-1960 era.[24] These authors conceptualize news as a social construct rather than an undistorted reflection of what occurs in the world. News was a manufactured product in the nineteenth century as well, reflecting the financial requirements of the newspaper organization, the vision of its producers, and the day-to-day exigencies of production. The changes in definitions of news clearly reflect the changing economic base of the press from a political one to a commercial one. When news is seen, quite properly, as a manufactured product, it becomes even more compelling to examine the assumptions or agendas behind it. Some of the canons of modern journalism, such as objectivity, are derived, at least in part, from commercial considerations.

This work also deals with the implications of commercialization itself. As William Leiss and his colleagues have noted, commercialization has been based on "increasing readerships and lower costs" per reader and on a level of autonomy within the press vis-à-vis government: "This creation of a press independent of political party or party factions, and of a specific circulation base of loyal subscriber-supporters, a press free to find its own niche purely in terms of its market success in winning and holding readers, is the final and most important step in the long process of commercializing the press."[25] Autonomy from government, increased readership, and lower per capita costs are clearly the benefits of commercialization in the newspaper. But there are trade-offs. Commercialization imposes the imperative that newspapers must entertain their readers. When entertainment is paramount, difficult issues or current events that are not inherently interesting or entertaining may well get short shrift. Witness the blight of lowest-common-denominator and least-offensive programming in television.[26]

All this matters because traditionally the press has certain responsibilities in a democratic society. In 1888, Charles A. Dana, the New York *Sun* editor, called the press the bulwark of national liberty and a powerful agent in the public debate that is central to self-government: "It takes men when their information is incomplete, when their reasoning has not yet been worked out, when their opinions have not yet been fixed, and it suggests and intimates and insinuates an opinion and a judgment which often times a man—unless he is a man of very great force of character and intelligence—adopts as something established and concluded."[27] But will a vision of news as a money-making commodity always square with broader societal interests and needs? Can news be, simultaneously, both a commodity and a vital source of information in a democratic society? When commercial considerations dictate the general news process, the press will serve democracy only when such service is financially profitable.

Chapter One

American Political Parties and the Press

In the early 1830s, members of the Antimasonic party in Plymouth, Massachusetts, spent nearly two years trying to start a newspaper to promote their party and candidates. Few in number and lacking major financial resources, they struggled to raise enough money to buy a press and type, ensure 200 subscribers, and find a competent printer-editor who shared their views. Several times, they almost gave up. They persevered because a newspaper was the key to reaching voters and ultimately to winning elections. The appearance of *We The People and Old Colony Gazette,* just two weeks before the 1832 election, was a major organizational victory for the Antimasons. It enabled them to compete with other parties for voters.[1]

Such an ordeal in starting a newspaper was perhaps unusual in the Jacksonian era, when newspapers often seemed to spring up overnight to espouse political causes. Nonetheless, the Plymouth experience demonstrates the intimate relationship between party and press in the late 1820s and 1830s. American political parties saw the press as a vehicle to inform, propagandize, and exhort voters. William Henry Seward, one of the organizers of the Antimasonic party in the late 1820s, said that the press was the *only* channel to the people; without it, a party "never can gain the public favor."[2]

Jacksonian Era Politics and Press

The close relationship between party and press wasn't new in the 1820s. The two had supported one another since the early days of the American Revolution. The relationship became more emphatic and extensive, however, in the 1820s and 1830s, when growing interest in presidential elections and changes in the political process dramatically increased voter participation.

After 1800, presidential politics had lapsed into somnolence, because presidents chose their successors and the congressional caucus rubber-stamped that choice. In 1824, however, the incumbent James Monroe refused to anoint a successor, and the ensuing factionalism discredited the caucus. In the first major battle for the presidency in a generation, no one obtained a majority of the electoral college votes, pushing the election into the House of Representatives. Amid charges, countercharges, and histrionics, the House elected John Quincy Adams, the runner-up in the popular vote, prompting charges of corruption by the supporters of Andrew Jackson, who led the popular vote.[3]

The result, other than mutual recrimination, was the formation of national political organizations to contest the *next* presidential election. No sooner had the House voted than the next campaign began. The Jacksonians pioneered in this organizational work.

The growth of national political activity paralleled several changes in politics at the state level. The number of statewide (as opposed to county) elections dramatically increased. Earlier in the century, voters elected only state legislators, who in turn elected governors and other state officials. In 1800, presidential electors were subject to statewide popular vote in just two states; by 1832, all but South Carolina had adopted the popular vote for the position of presidential elector.[4] Consequently, state political party organizations came into being in the late 1820s and early 1830s to nominate candidates and organize campaigns in statewide elections.[5]

More candidates were elected, rather than appointed, to office by the 1820s and 1830s. State constitutional revisions in the 1820s and the 1830s made many county-level positions, such as sheriff and clerk, subject to popular vote. Thus the populace elected more officials, while parties faced a greater task of recruiting, nominating, and supporting candidates.[6]

There were more people voting in the Jacksonian era. The population grew rapidly, doubling every 20 years. Suffrage requirements loosened by the 1820s, so that all adult white males could vote.[7] By 1826, 21 of the 24 states had adult white male suffrage or small poll taxes that were tantamount to adult white suffrage. Voter participation grew nationwide throughout the 1820s, rising from 9 percent of adult white males in 1820 to 57 percent by 1828.[8]

A ban on self-promotion by candidates made political organization all the more difficult. The era of stump speeches, press conferences, and public debates among candidates had not yet arrived. Tradition dictated a disinterested approach. As Robert V. Remini notes, the "accepted decorum of presidential candidates" was to keep "aloof from the campaign." When Andrew Jackson attended a party barbecue in Lexington, Kentucky, the Washington, D.C., *National Intelligencer* commented, "We do not recollect before to have heard of the President of the United States descending into the political arena."[9] One newspaper writer said that presidential candidates ". . . ought not to say one word on the subject of the election. Washington, Jefferson and Madison were as silent as the grave when they were before the American people for this office."[10] Even on the state and county level, candidates generally were expected to refrain from self-promotion.

Americans simply distrusted the man who grasped for office. The ideal official was one who answered the call to office by those who knew him best—his neighbors. Self-promotion meant that a candidate lacked the fame or support that came from his own qualifications. One Jacksonian condemned the "lust for office," calling it "a crying evil." He argued that "place should be sought by no man, and it is tolerable and honorable only when we are called to it by the unsolicited suffrages and spontaneous preferences of the people and their representatives."[11]

Voters at political rallies in Nash and Beaufort counties, North Carolina, vowed that they would not support any candidate who stooped to electioneering.[12] When one congressional candidate in Massachusetts wrote an anonymous essay on his own behalf, self-promotion became a major campaign issue once his authorship was disclosed. Opponents dredged up that indiscretion for at least a decade.[13] One of his critics noted that "New Englanders hold no fellowship with 'stump orators' and do not like to hear a man sound his own Trumpet or sing his own praise."[14] A Pennsylvania editor sought biographical information from a gubernatorial candidate in the early 1820s but promised he would never divulge the source lest the candidate appear to be campaigning for himself.[15]

This style of electioneering worked only when electoral units were small (e.g., township or county) and voters knew the candidates personally. But the structural changes in politics in the 1820s upended this quaint local system. The ban on self-promotion quieted candidates, but it left all organizational tasks—recruitment, nomination, and campaigning—to the parties.

In most states, a state central committee and a network of county committees carried on this organizational work. These committees wooed voters with conventions, campaign songs, parades, and barbecues. The 1840 William Henry Harrison Log Cabin campaign is the most vivid example of such spectacles.[16]

The single most important link between party and electorate, however, was the partisan newspaper.[17] Newspapers *alone* were not sufficient; even the best newspaper could not sell a poor candidate. But political newspapers, as a link between party and electorate, were vital. They helped the party mobilize voters and were an extremely efficient way to reach a dispersed rural population. Political parties did not have a paid staff to send out to court voters, and even if they had, travel was difficult and slow. Farmers, laborers, merchants, and other voters simply could not attend many party meetings or rallies. But the newspaper took the party's views, arguments, and candidates to them. Newspapers circulated widely not just to individual subscribers but also to taverns and crossroads stores, so they were accessible to nonsubscribers, too.[18] Some newspapers and towns established reading rooms so that the public could peruse papers from around the country.[19]

- Parties also valued newspapers because they weren't as ephemeral as rallies and speeches. Newspaper essays could be read, discussed, and debated a week, a month, or more after publication. And people read these papers. Tocqueville noted Americans' near-addiction to newspapers. Russel B. Nye wrote of the "compulsive reading habits" of nineteenth-century citizens. "Addicted" to print, Americans had a higher literacy rate (90 percent among whites) than England or the Continent.[20]

The regular publication schedule of most newspapers—daily in metropolitan areas and many state capitals, weekly elsewhere—meant that a party could constantly reiterate its views and support its candidates. Newspapers also provided the foundation for a national political network particularly as the number of newspapers grew (to 1,200 in 1833)[21] and as postal laws encouraged the free exchange of newspapers among editors throughout the country. This free-exchange system facilitated the circulation of newspapers throughout the nation, providing knowledge about partisan allies and an infusion of propaganda and enthusiasm.[22] The most widely circulated newspapers of the 1820s and 1830s were those in Washington, D.C., but other newspapers, such as the *Albany Argus* (New York), circulated throughout the country.[23]

For readers, the political newspaper served as a reliable source of party news and views. Editors frequently were part of a party's hierarchy (e.g., a member of a county central committee) and could speak for the party. Francis Preston Blair and the Washington, D.C., *Globe* represented the national Jacksonians in the early 1830s. The

Albany Argus was the voice of Martin Van Buren's political machine (the Regency), while the *Albany Evening Journal* represented Thurlow Weed and the New York Antimasonic party. In metropolitan areas, editors such as Henry Laurens Pinckney of the *Charleston Mercury* and Charles Gordon Greene of the *Boston Morning Post* served as spokesmen for their parties.[24] This pattern is repeated again and again, both in capital cities and in smaller towns.

Newspapers were ideal for organizing grass-roots political support, particularly for new political parties or groups supporting a certain candidate or program. The Antimasons, a third-party movement in the late 1820s and early 1830s, relied extensively on the press simply because they had few other means of reaching the public. The first New York State Antimasonic convention, in 1829, concluded with a report that stressed: "Free presses constitute the means upon which the country must rely to uproot and overthrow Free Masonry. They enlighten and stimulate public opinion."[25]

Many believed that newspapers really could sway voters. One Antimasonic editor in upstate New York refused to give up the fight in the early 1830s, even after his party had lost several key elections. "Constant dropping will wear away stones," he told his brother. "A perpetual exhibition before the public eye" and "the constantly repeated exposition" of Antimasonry's goals and policies "will eventually succeed in winning over the people."[26] Others believed in the efficacy of political newspapers. James Gordon Bennett wrote in his diary, "It only requires a circulation of newspapers in the West to kill anti-masonry . . ."[27] When John C. Calhoun broke with President Jackson, he believed he would be publicly vindicated through the press. "Let the press direct the public indignation against the continuance of this profligate intrigue," he told one ally.[28] When President Jackson opposed the rechartering of the Second Bank of the United States, the bank's president, Nicholas Biddle, turned to a press propaganda campaign to win public support for his bank. Biddle believed that a "direct appeal to the reason of the country" could "resist the pressure of the authority of great names and the force of party discipline" and thus restore public confidence in the bank.[29] That appeal would be through the press—"the channel of communication between the Bank and the country."[30]

The political profile of the press varied from place to place and from newspaper to newspaper. Politics was most clearly the mission of the press in Washington, D.C., and in state capitals, where newspapers served as the flagships for their state party organizations. In the small cities and towns, partisan newspapers flourished as part of county-wide political organizations.

In metropolitan areas, however, papers were concerned with both politics, which accounted for about half of their content,[31] and business, which accounted for about a quarter of their content.[32] They also had substantially more advertising than did their nonmetropolitan counterparts.[33]

Even with this relative emphasis on business, many metropolitan newspapers were still highly partisan.[34] The *Boston Morning Post,* the *Boston Daily Advertiser,* and the *Charleston Mercury,* were clearly recognized as party organs. Other newspapers, such as the New York *Courier and Enquirer* or the *Charleston Courier,* had close ties to political parties but were relatively independent of party control.[35] And still others were less partisan. The *Savannah Republican* or the *New York Journal of Commerce* regularly took political positions but devoted themselves primarily to business.

(Metropolitan newspapers represented only a small portion of United States journalism in the 1820s and 1830s. According to the 1830 census, only 8.8 percent of the nation's population lived in "urban" areas [i.e., with a population of 2,500 or more].[36] Only 4.1 percent of the population lived in cities with a population of 25,000 or more.[37] Most of the population—and most of the political newspapers—were outside metropolitan areas.)

Establishing and Maintaining Party Presses

Because newspapers were so vital to party success in the Jacksonian era, politicians worked hard to establish and maintain, primarily through subsidies, reliable party organs in every hamlet, town, or city of the nation.

Establishing Newspapers

Party organization in the Jacksonian era usually began with the formation of a central committee to coordinate party activities. The next task was to establish political newspapers.

The Jacksonian coalition provided the model in newspaper establishment. Shut out of the presidency in 1824–25, the Jacksonians turned to establishing newspapers to contest the 1828 election. Robert

Remini contends that "perhaps the single most important accomplishment" of Jackson's allies in Congress in the middle 1820s was the "creation of a vast, nationwide newspaper system."[38]

The most important newspaper for the Jackson campaign was the *U.S. Telegraph* in Washington, D.C., established in 1826 to lead the fight against the administration.[39] Jackson's friends arranged for a loan for Duff Green, the editor who took over the paper in 1826.[40] During the 1828 campaign, Green issued a special paper (an extra), circulating 40,000 issues weekly throughout the country in the months before the election.

Even after Jackson's victory in 1828, party activists established newspapers while new party battles emerged and party lines were redrawn. In 1832, Jacksonians established the *Carolina Watchman* in Salisbury, North Carolina, to counteract the shift of the other Salisbury newspaper from supporting Jackson to supporting John C. Calhoun.[41] In the early 1830s, new Jackson papers appeared in Milton, Roanoke, and Elizabeth City, North Carolina; Peterson and Trenton, New Jersey; Logansport, Indiana; Springfield, Illinois; Lebanon, Ohio; Worcester, Massachusetts; Norfolk, Virginia; and Juniata, Harrisburg, Pittsburgh, Philadelphia, and Lancaster, Pennsylvania.[42]

Among Jackson's opponents, the Antimasons were the most active in the establishment of political newspapers in the late 1820s and early 1830s. The Antimasons had no choice but to establish newspapers. Most older party papers spurned the Antimasons. The older party organizations included many Masons; consequently their newspapers refused to deal sympathetically with Antimasonic principles or policies. In 1826, only two or three newspapers in New York State championed the Antimasonic cause. By the end of 1827, the Antimasonic party had 22 papers in New York; by 1832 they had 70.[43] By 1832, Antimasons had established 32 newspapers in Pennsylvania, 5 in Massachusetts, and 1 each in Vermont and New Hampshire.[44] The party also tried to establish a newspaper in Washington, D.C., that year to support its first (and last) presidential candidate, William Wirt. Both the candidate and the project failed.[45]

In the South, particularly in South Carolina, political activists established newspapers as part of the fight over state rights in the 1820s and 1830s. Extreme state rightists established the Charleston *State Rights and Free Trade Evening Post* in 1829 to counteract the more moderate political agenda of the older, established Charleston papers.[46] Outside Charleston, extreme state rightists helped establish newspapers in Greenville (the *Sentinel*), Abbeville (the *Whig*), Georgetown (the *Winyaw Intelligencer*), Yorkville (the *Banner*), and Camden (the *Camden and Lancaster Journal*).[47]

When retiring editors sold their newspapers, they and the politicians allied with them tried to keep these papers in the party fold. When Charles McDowell announced his plan to sell the *Bedford Gazette* (Pennsylvania), he promised to sell to a loyal Democrat. When S. C. Stambaugh left the Harrisburg *Pennsylvania Reporter*, he assured his readers the paper was in "safe hands."[48] When John Brazer Davis wanted to sell the *Boston Patriot*, the National Republican party helped find a new editor.[49]

Politicians and parties discarded disloyal or unreliable editors. In South Carolina, when the Jacksonian coalition divided in the late 1820s over the tariff and state rights philosophy, moderates such as Charles F. Daniels, editor of the *Camden Journal* (South Carolina) found that some of his old supporters (including U.S. senator S. D. Miller) deserted him.[50] The Jacksonians broke ties to the New York *Courier and Enquirer* in 1832 when the paper endorsed the rechartering of the Second Bank of the United States, despite Jackson's hatred of that institution. Jacksonians had long been fairly tolerant of the maverick nature of *Courier and Enquirer*, but its support for the bank cut its ties to Jackson. Jacksonians dropped their subscriptions and withdrew patronage.[51]

Similarly, the Jacksonians broke with southern political newspapers (and ended financial subsidies) that opposed the president in the nullification controversy in late 1832 and early 1833. Jacksonians dropped the *Augusta Chronicle* (Georgia) and the Milledgeville *Georgia Journal*.[52]

At times, parties had such direct and powerful control over newspapers that they could replace recalcitrant editors. When the editor of the *Albany Argus*, Isaac Q. Leake, refused to support the Regency's presidential candidate in 1824, he was hurried into retirement and replaced by Edwin Croswell.[53] When Luther Tucker of the *Rochester Daily Advertiser* wanted to support Andrew Jackson in 1828, his coeditor balked. The Regency helped Tucker buy out his partner.[54] In Lynn, Massachusetts, Jonathan Buffum, owner of the Antimasonic *Lynn Record*, fired his half-hearted Antimasonic editor.[55] In Albany, New York, the Antimasons forced Solomon Southwick out as editor of the *Albany Observer*, because he was simply unwilling to work within the party.[56]

When editors owned their own printing establishments, they could not be dislodged easily if they proved unreliable or disloyal. In these cases, political parties usually started a new newspaper to compete with the older one. When Jacksonians decided that Duff Green's *U.S. Telegraph* was disloyal, they helped establish the Washington *Globe,* edited by Francis Preston Blair.[57]

Financial Subsidies

Financial subsidies to the partisan press were common and vital. For editors, the subsidies often provided financial stability in a notoriously unstable business. One historian has noted that approximately two-thirds of all newspapers established in North Carolina between 1815 and 1836 failed within a few years of their establishment.[58] The *Fayetteville Observer* (North Carolina), in 1834, reported that seven newspapers had failed during the preceding 12 months.[59] Many subscribers simply did not pay for their newspapers. In 1832, one North Carolina editor estimated that only 10 percent of his 600 subscribers had paid for the paper.[60] In 1844, the *Carolina Watchman* had about 800 subscribers, but a tenth were eventually dropped for delinquency.[61] Editors frequently had to beg their readers for payment.[62]

Outside the metropolitan areas, when newspaper subscribers paid, they usually bartered farm products or other goods.[63] Although editors were happy to be paid at all, bartered goods didn't provide the cash to pay for paper, ink, presses, and types.[64]

The importance of financial subsidies varied from paper to paper. Carolyn Stewart Dyer's pioneer work indicates that patronage could constitute half or more of a newspaper's income. Dyer deals only with Wisconsin, but there is evidence elsewhere that patronage was important to most newspapers. Editors vied with one another for contracts, and when they lost them they faced hardship or failure. For small rural papers, these subsidies provided *cash.* Even small amounts of cash were valuable. One weekly editor in upstate New York highly prized a patronage contract that paid only $3.50 per year.[65] Thurlow Weed found that the income of two or three dollars a week from a patronage job was a great help in supporting his family in the early 1820s.[66]

Partisan subsidies were important for larger papers, too. Donations by wealthy members of the National Republican party in Massachusetts provided the financial underpinning for the *Boston Daily Advertiser* in the early 1830s.[67]

Federal Patronage of the Press

Government printing contracts were the major source of patronage in the Jacksonian era. The federal government—the executive branch, both houses of Congress, and the Supreme Court—used printers for a variety of jobs, such as printing the proceedings of Congress or producing stationery for executive departments. Partisan editors were the key beneficiaries of these contracts. From 1819 to 1846, each house of Congress elected a printer to publish its proceedings, debates, and laws. These lucrative contracts ran for two years with profit margins running from 20 to 55 percent.[68] Editors used the profits to maintain their political papers and to undertake other partisan activities, such as publishing campaign newspapers.

The other key congressional subsidy to political newspapers was the extensive use of the franking privilege in the late 1820s and 1830s. Senators and representatives could send newspapers or pamphlets free of charge through the postal system if they signed their names to these items. During campaigns, franking was an important subsidy to political newspapers, because it allowed them to circulate through the postal system at no cost. Remini wrote that franked newspapers cost the federal government about $40,000 a year and that "hundreds of newspapers circulated freely throughout the country."[69]

Other federal subsidies nurtured the partisan press, too. Throughout the 1830s, executive branch expenditures on printing increased steadily, rising from $110,004.24 during the Twenty-second Congress (1831–33) to $174,244.00 during the Twenty-sixth Congress (1839–41).[70] Under Jackson, the preponderance of the executive patronage went to Jacksonian newspapers in Washington, D.C. (primarily the Washington *Globe*), in metropolitan areas (Louisville, Boston, and Philadelphia), and in state capitals (Boston, Concord, and Columbus).[71]

Jackson also appointed editors to a relatively large number of salaried political posts. Some of Jackson's closest advisers were either editors or former editors. The Kitchen Cabinet included Blair, Amos Kendall, former editor of the *Argus of Western America* (Frankfort, Kentucky), and Isaac Hill, former editor of the Concord *New Hampshire Patriot*. The most common patronage job for editors was postmaster. Milton Hamilton notes that 22 editors served as postmasters in New York State in 1830.[72] In all, about 50–60 editors around the country actually received patronage jobs.[73]

State Patronage of the Press

State governments and party organizations also subsidized Jacksonian era newspaper editors. Dyer found four major sources of state patronage: printing contracts, publishing official notices and laws, providing newspapers to members of the legislature, and appointive patronage jobs (such as clerks or watchmen).[74] These subsidies varied from state to state. Some legislatures provided rather healthy profits to printers, while others were more frugal. The experiences of three states—New York, Pennsylvania, and Georgia—illustrate the state patronage system.

In New York, state printing contracts were the centerpiece of press patronage into the 1840s. Throughout the 1820s and for most of the 1830s, Martin Van Buren's political machine controlled this patronage. The Regency's editor, Edwin Croswell of the *Albany Argus,* received much of the funding. From 1827 to 1832, Croswell averaged $15,700 in state printing contracts annually.[75] Regency patronage also went to loyal party newspapers throughout the state. In all, about 40 newspapers received patronage, usually for printing state notices and laws. The sums paid to country printers in New York State were not big. Most ranged from $20 to $50 a year; the largest was about $150.[76] The state also paid for two or three newspaper subscriptions for each legislator.[77]

In Pennsylvania, the state printing contracts amounted to about $15,000 a year in the 1830s. They were divided among three printers: one printed the *Journal of Proceedings* in English; another, the *Journal of Proceedings* in German; and a third, a compendium of laws passed. These contracts generally went to editors in Harrisburg, the capital.[78] Pennsylvania legislators also received two or three daily newspapers (the number varied during the 1820s and 1830s).[79] And the governor frequently gave patronage appointments to editors. The stipends for these positions varied, but some were quite lucrative.[80]

As in other states, the Georgia legislative printing contracts were the most important aspect of state subsidies to the press. Throughout the late 1820s and early 1830s, the Troup party controlled the state legislature and awarded printing contracts to the Milledgeville *Georgia Journal,* the party's chief paper in the capital.[81] Georgia editors—especially those associated with the leading newspapers in the state capital—also benefited from patronage appointments, serving as secretary to the governor or in various paid advisory posts.[82]

The patronage practices in these three states appear common else-where. Most states awarded legislative printing contracts to subsidize editors. In Virginia, for example, Thomas Ritchie of the *Richmond Enquirer* held the state printing contracts throughout the 1820s and 1830s, earning an annual stipend of $2,600. Additional printing orders (for an extra session of the legislature, for example) could double the amount he was paid.[83] North Carolina's legislature was not as generous as other states, paying only $900 a year for printing session laws, journals, and bills. Nonetheless, editors still vied for the patronage.[84]

Patronage of the Press on the Local Level

In New York, Georgia, and Pennsylvania, newspapers in the state capitals were the major recipients of state financial subsidies. Other editors received funds from the state, but those amounts were generally not large. Dyer's study of the Wisconsin press indicates that state patronage provided major support for newspapers in Madison, the state capital, and for the financially troubled newspapers on the sparsely settled frontier counties (where local subsidies would have been scarce). Many local newspapers received patronage from city or county governments. Printing contracts from the sheriff, for instance, were important, for they could constitute half of a weekly newspaper's annual income.[85] Other local governmental units also supported the press with printing and advertising contracts. The advertising alone for Dauphin County (Harrisburg), Pennsylvania, in 1830 amounted to $118.[86] And the printing and advertising for Philadelphia County totaled $340.50 in 1828.[87]

Some local newspapers drew support from government at all levels. The *St. Lawrence Republican* in upstate New York received patronage from the federal government (from the customs house and post office), from the state government (for advertising), and from the county government.[88]

Other Patronage

Although the largest subsidies came through government contracts, control over those contracts rested with political parties. When parties controlled the contracts, their editors benefited through patronage. But even when parties lacked such political control, their editors often received financial aid from the party faithful. Funds might be less ample, but they existed. Throughout the country, political parties and

Table 1.1. Percentage distribution of contents, by category, among nine antebellum newspapers, 1831–32

	Five metropolitan newspapers	Four nonmetropolitan newspapers
Politics	50.5	69.6
Crime and courts	2.5	2.3
Accidents	3.6	4.8
Society and women	2.5	1.4
Leisure	2.8	5.0
Business and labor	22.9	2.3
Religion	0.6	4.2
Science and education	1.7	1.2
History	0.3	0.0
Weather	0.5	0.6
Other	0.8	1.7

Note: Figures are median percentages of column inches for each content category. See appendix 2, tables A2.1 and A2.2, for a fuller presentation of the data.

interest groups used gifts, donations, loans, and sometimes even outright ownership of newspapers to assure that the party's views were advanced.[89]

Partisan Content: Wooing and Mobilizing the Voters

Newspapers of the Jacksonian era were opinionated, politically biased, one-sided, argumentative, and frequently strident. As table 1.1 shows, content was primarily political in nature—a mix of reports on political events, political essays, and other political exhortations or propaganda. Editors debated with one another over the political issues and candidates as if the fate of democracy and of the nation itself was at stake.

The partisanship of the nonmetropolitan newspapers is clearest. Those newspapers devoted more than two-thirds of all content to politics. Politics dominated the metropolitan press as well, constituting half of all content. Three of the metropolitan newspapers studied here—the *Boston Daily Advertiser,* the *Charleston Mercury,* and the New York *Courier and Enquirer*—were leading political organs in their respective cities and states.[90]

Newspapers became the symbol of party strength, and the leading cities and towns of the nation all had rival political newspapers in the late 1820s and 1830s. In the early 1830s, Charleston, South Carolina, had five major political newspapers—three supporting the Unionist party and two supporting the nullifiers. Columbus, Ohio, had newspapers representing the Jacksonians, National Republicans, and Antimasons. This kind of competition existed in cities and towns across the country. Even Boston, where voters overwhelmingly favored the National Republican party in the early 1830s, had both Jacksonian and Antimasonic daily newspapers, in addition to three National Republican dailies. In New York State, 65 percent of county seats had rival newspapers in 1830. Editors without competition at home usually found a rival nearby. When the *Lyons Countryman* (New York), an Antimasonic newspaper, failed in late 1831, the editor of its crosstown Jacksonian rival, the *Lyons Western Argus,* turned to fighting the Antimasonic editor of the *Penn Yan Enquirer.* The Jacksonian editor in Cortland, New York, debated not only his home-town rival but also two anti-Jackson newspapers in a town four miles away.[91]

Such competition probably was inevitable, given the belief that newspapers were necessary for the success of any political party. The presence of one party's paper in a town dictated that opposing partisans maintain a newspaper if those partisans wanted an active political presence. In Greenville, South Carolina, the popularity of the moderate, pro-Union *Greenville Mountaineer* propelled the establishment of a nullification newspaper in the early 1830s. Similarly, unionists contemplated establishing a newspaper at Beaufort, South Carolina, primarily because nullifiers had just done so.[92]

The patronage system served to *guarantee* this competition and diversity in the press. With three major sources of funding in most states and on the national level (the two houses of the legislature and the executive branch), competing newspapers all could receive subsidies simultaneously. During the last two years of the John Quincy Adams administration, federal patronage went to the three major political newspapers in the nation's capital: the executive patronage went to the *National Journal,* Adams' official organ; the House printing contracts went to Joseph Gales and William Seaton of the *National Intelligencer,* and the Senate printing contract to Duff Green of the *U.S. Telegraph.* Consequently, during the 1828 presidential campaign, federal patronage funds were supporting two papers that advocated the reelection of Adams and one newspaper that advocated the election of Andrew Jackson.[93]

Patronage also nurtured competition and diversity on the state level. In Boston, subsidies went to all the leading newspapers. Federal funds sustained the *Boston Morning Post,* the Jacksonian newspaper. The editors of the Boston *Columbian Centinel,* a National Republican journal, held the state printing contracts. Funds from the party faithful went to the other three major political papers in the city: the *Boston Daily Courier* (representing the old Federalist wing of the National Republican party), the Antimasonic *Boston Daily Advocate,* and the National Republicans' *Boston Daily Advertiser.*[94]

Editors saw their readers as *voters* and provided content that would woo them to a particular party and then mobilize them to vote. There was no room for indecision or neutrality in the press. The *Louisville Public Advertiser* condemned a purportedly neutral Indiana paper: "We do not know how it is in Indiana, but, in this State, people have more respect for an open, independent adversary than for dumb partisans or shuttlecock politicians, who are considered too imbecile to form an opinion, or too servile to express an opinion when formed."[95] The Washington, D.C., *U.S. Telegraph* condemned a purportedly neutral Baltimore paper, noting that the neutrality was probably indicative of a complete lack of principle and an abundance of opportunism.[96]

In a comment quite typical of the age, a Jacksonian editor in upstate New York commented on a newspaper he had received through the mail, noting that it was

. . . precisely what we most of all things abhor and detest, to wit, a neutral paper. It pretends to be all things to all men. Now we would wish to be civil to the editor, but we can never consent to an exchange with any such paper, for we verily think they should all, one and all, be thrown out of the pale of the press. If we are asked why, we answer that the Editor must be doing violence to his opinions, or else he had none to abuse; and in either case, he is hardly entitled to the common civilities of his typographical brethren.[97]

It wasn't just the love of a good fight that led editors to advocacy; they also saw themselves as having a *duty* to debate. The editor of the *Greensborough Patriot* (North Carolina) noted that editors had a responsibility to the public "because Public Opinion is measurably formed from the Tone of the Press."[98] A. W. Thayer, editor of the *Essex Gazette* in Haverhill, Massachusetts, maintained that an editor was a "political preacher" and "a sentinel placed in his country's watch tower."[99]

Editors proudly announced their political affiliation. Indeed, that political affiliation was part of their appeal for subscribers, because editors who intended to establish a paper first issued a prospectus to obtain subscribers. The prospectus for the *Carolina Watchman* in Salisbury, North Carolina, promised to support the Jackson administration and to oppose internal improvements, the tariff, and extreme state rights agitation. Such declarations clearly defined that newspaper in terms of both national and state politics.[100] In his prospectus for the *Boston Morning Post*, Charles G. Green promised that he would urge that the tariff be modified, would call for the abolition of imprisonment for debt, and would give "a candid and temperate support to the National Administration."[101]

The mainstay of the newspaper advocacy was the partisan essay, with often sharp and vituperative commentary. Marmaduke Slade, editor of the *Macon Advertiser* (Georgia), attacked northerners who supported the protective tariff, saying, "They have mistaken our moderation for pusilanity and our devotion to the Union for a craven dependence upon their physical strength."[102] He criticized southerners who were willing to compromise on the tariff issue as "submissionists."[103] The Columbus, Georgia, *Democrat* expressed the hope that Georgians would "not be gulled on the present occasion" by the "nullification demagogues" who try to lure Georgians into "schemes of violence and revolution."[104] The editor of the *Macon Telegraph* urged Georgians to reject the "nullification kisses" of the "South Carolina python."[105]

The era's political essays could be lengthy. After Andrew Jackson vetoed the recharter of the Second Bank of the United States in 1832, Francis Preston Blair's Washington, D.C., *Globe* presented a multipart series of essays defending the veto. Before the 1832 election, Gales and Seaton of the Washington *National Intelligencer* presented nine essays ("The Ancient Mariner" series) detailing the heinousness of Jackson's first term as president.[106]

The object of these essays was to convince the reader-as-voter. Consequently, it was the argument presented rather than its timeliness that was of crucial importance. When President Jackson vetoed the bill to recharter the Second Bank of the United States, the editors of the *National Intelligencer* at first provided only a brief notice of the veto. Ten days later, after a good deal of thought, the editors finally analyzed and condemned the veto message itself. In such essays, the motive was to present a compelling and convincing argument to the voters, not to recount events quickly.

The give and take of political debate and competition was a central ingredient of the press. As one Pennsylvania editor noted:

When an editor firmly supports his principles in politics, and his preference as to men, he meets with rubs, as a matter of course, from those who espouse different principles and prefer other men; but whether he wins or loses in the contest, no reasonable man quarrels with him for the part he has taken. Those who take an active part in the strife of politics, generally consider that they give back to their adversaries as good as their adversaries sent them—and at the close of the contest, the account is about square between them.[107]

These "rubs" dealt with the key issues of the day, ranging from national economic and trade policy to local political issues and candidates. In the late 1820s and early 1830s, Essex County, Massachusetts, had newspapers that represented two factions of the National Republican party and the Jacksonian Democrats. These papers were engaged in a constant debate with each other over local and national issues, including the tariff, Andrew Jackson, and the Second Bank of the United States, as well as national and local elections.[108] Newspapers throughout the country—and particularly in the South—divided and fought over tariff policy and the novel constitutional theory that individual states could nullify laws deemed unwise.[109] A good deal of debate and discussion naturally surrounded the political campaigns of the era[110] and the protracted debate over the Second Bank of the United States.[111]

Although national issues were important considerations throughout the era, many newspapers were concerned primarily with local issues. American political parties in the age of Jackson were essentially not *national* parties but a coalition of local and state political interests. So local issues often dominated, both in politics and in the political press. In North Carolina, debates centered on legislative representation;[112] in Virginia, on the state constitutional convention in 1830–31;[113] in Massachusetts, on licensing laws and separation of church and state;[114] in Georgia, on the local parties (Troupites versus Clarkites) and on national Indian policy;[115] in South Carolina, on nullification, the state's own nullification convention and ordinance;[116] and in New York, on the state's banking system, its canal system, local competition between parties, and the potential for an amalgamation between the National Republicans and the Antimasons.[117]

All these debates, whether national or local in nature, eventually came to fruition on election day. Above all else, Jacksonian-era newspapers were devoted to winning elections. Editors tried to involve

their (male) readers in the party itself. Newspapers carried announcements of forthcoming conventions and meetings from the local to the
state level. In 1828, the *Louisville Public Advertiser* urged attendance at
a political barbecue "at which the principles involved in the present
struggle will be freely discussed."[118]

Newspapers routinely informed readers about party meetings and
conventions and urged attendance. The Springfield, Massachusetts,
Hampden Intelligencer announced one party meeting and added, "We
trust it will not be necessary to again urge the necessity of a punctual
attendance on this occasion."[119] In September 1832, the Boston *Columbian Centinel* urged National Republicans "in every county and
town throughout the state" to prepare for the forthcoming election.
"All must get going." The paper urged voters to hold organizational
meetings to support the party ticket and to encourage voting.[120]
Newspapers also printed party tickets, identifying and endorsing various candidates.[121]

Obviously, not all readers attended such meetings, and consequently
newspapers devoted a lot of space to the proceedings and discussions
of party meetings, reporting speeches and resolutions. Papers often
printed the formal addresses to the electorate that were produced by
the end of the conventions. Papers produced column upon column of
reports on these political happenings, ranging from the county level
to the national conventions first held in 1831 and 1832. The *Albany Argus*
printed proceedings of county party meetings and of a Young Men's
Democratic-Republican meeting in late 1831.[122] The *Charleston Mercury*
printed proceedings of various nullification meetings throughout
South Carolina in 1831 and 1832,[123] while the Milledgeville *Federal Union*
reported antinullification meetings throughout Georgia.[124]

The key to success, of course, was voter turnout, and Jacksonian-
era editors worked hard to exhort their readers to vote for the party.
In early 1831, just before the New Hampshire state elections, the
editor of Concord's Jacksonian *New Hampshire Patriot* reminded his
readers that "one week from tomorrow, you will again be called on to
exercise one of the most valuable privileges and dearest rights, sacred
to us by our republican institutions—that of electing our rulers." The
editor warned his readers that only "eternal vigilance" would win the
day.[125] In 1832, the Worcester *Massachusetts Spy* told its readers: "Go
to the polls and see that your neighbor goes, and there vote for the
men who have always been faithful to you and your interests—who
have stood by you, through good report and through evil report, and
will not abandon you in the hour of peril. Go to the polls . . . Hearken
not to those who would create divisions among you."[126]

The Limits of the Partisan Press

Such advocacy precluded an objective discussion of other parties or other issues. Newspapers did not try to be all things to all people, and they did not seek to cater to every interest. In the 1820s, the nascent Antimasonic party found that the existing partisan newspapers would not publicize its views. Antimasons complained bitterly about what they saw as hostility to their views on the part of the established partisan press.

Within the context of an advocacy press system, however, such exclusion made sense. The intent of an editor was to woo and to mobilize the voters, and neutrality or evenhandedness (admitting that the opposition might be right, for instance) certainly did not constitute effective campaigning. Evenhandedness or objectivity was not so much bad as inappropriate.

Other limits to press content existed, too. The political system itself, circa 1830, included only a third or so of the nation (the vote was denied to all but adult white males), and partisan newspapers thus dealt with a world of relatively elite men. These partisan newspapers seemed dedicated to upholding the political world as they knew it. They did not accept challenges to that status quo without reluctance if not actual hostility. They were, as a Pennsylvania editor noted, ready to meet "with rubs" during the course of political debate and battle and to give as good as they received,[127] but primarily with others who were part of that two-party electoral system. Little sympathy existed for those, such as abolitionists, who sought to disrupt the political status quo. When an angry mob in Alton, Illinois, killed abolitionist editor Elijah P. Lovejoy in 1837, newspapers from *both* major American political parties quickly blamed Lovejoy for his own death. Jacksonian and Whig newspapers in Missouri and in Washington, D.C., all condemned the "dislocating doctrines" of abolitionism and argued that Lovejoy, by insisting upon the right to publish whatever he chose, had caused his own death.[128]

Editors as Political Activists

The precise nature of political roles varied from editor to editor, from state to state, depending on factors such as the editor's personality or ambition. No single model for political activism existed. Some editors were de facto county or state directors of their parties, while others were political lieutenants rather than party leaders. Whatever the position, a common pattern existed: editors did much more than edit newspapers. They were extensively involved in politics outside of their newspaper offices. They served as central committee members, public speakers, and organizers of meetings and conventions.

The central committee (national, state, county, or even township) was the key organizational structure in Jacksonian-era political parties. These committees coordinated the day-to-day operation of the party, organized meetings and conventions, drew up lists of nominees, and promoted voter turnout. Thomas J. Lemay and Alexander J. Lawrence, editors of the Raleigh, North Carolina, *Star,* both belonged to the state central committee supporting the Jackson-Barbour ticket in 1832.[129] Three of the eight members of the Pennsylvania Antimasonic State Central Committee were editors.[130] David C. Miller, editor of the Batavia, New York, *Republican Advocate,* was a member of the first Genesee County Antimasonic Central Committee. James Percival, editor of the *Livingston Register* in Geneseo, New York, helped organize the town's first Antimasonic meeting in early 1827 and served on the county central committee for three years. E. J. Fowle, editor of the *Yates Republican* in Penn Yan, was a founder of the local Antimasonic party and served for five years on his county's central committee.[131] J. A. Hadley, editor of the *Lyons Countryman* (New York), was on the three-member Wayne County Central Committee and also served on the Wayne County Young Men's Central Committee.[132] In early 1831, another member of the Wayne County Central Committee, Myron Holley, became joint proprietor of the *Lyons Countryman* with Hadley. Holley continued to publish the paper and serve on the county central committee after Hadley retired.[133] Beriah B. Hotchkin, who served as editor of several Antimasonic newspapers in New York,[134] was a member of the New York Antimasonic Young Men's State Central Committee.[135] In Virginia, Thomas Ritchie, editor of the *Richmond Enquirer,* was on each of the six state central committees between 1824 and 1844; many considered him to be the key political leader in Virginia.[136] Elsewhere in the country—in New Hampshire, Massachusetts, Pennsylvania, New Jersey, and South Carolina—editors were members of party central committees.[137]

At times, editors were members of other party committees. They served as poll watchers (called committees of vigilance). Others served on committees of correspondence, writing letters to other partisans in efforts to coordinate political activity.[138]

Editors also performed some of the campaign tasks that candidates, by tradition, avoided. Benjamin Hallett, editor of the Antimasonic *Boston Daily Advocate,* spoke throughout Massachusetts in the early 1830s, urging party unity and promoting candidates.[139] Samuel A. Towne, editor of the Abbeville, South Carolina, *Whig,* delivered a partisan oration for Abbeville's Fourth of July celebration in 1832.[140] William Gilmore Simms, editor of the *Charleston Courier* in the early 1830s, addressed the Union and State Rights party in 1831.[141] And John Hemphill, editor of the *Sumter Gazette* (South Carolina) gave a partisan oration on the Fourth of July in 1832 to the unionist celebration in Sumter.[142]

Many editors attended party conventions as delegates and platform writers. M. D. Richardson, editor of the Sumter, South Carolina, *Southern Whig,* helped organize pro-Union (moderate state rights) meetings in the early 1830s and helped draft various resolutions adopted at those meetings.[143] Charles W. Gill, editor of the *Cortland Advocate* (New York), organized a public meeting to protest the Senate's rejection of Martin Van Buren as minister to England.[144] Gill also was a delegate to his county's convention in 1832 and helped draft the convention's resolutions.[145] T. C. Strong, editor of the Geneva *Independent American* was a delegate to the New York State Antimasonic convention from Orleans County.[146]

All the National Republican editors from Boston (from the *Columbian Centinel,* the *Boston Daily Courier,* and the *Advertiser* and *Independent Chronicle*) were delegates to the Massachusetts State National Republican Convention in 1832.[147] Joseph T. Adams, one of the editors of the Boston *Columbian Centinel,* was secretary at a Boston ward meeting of the National Republican party.[148] Across Massachusetts, editors attended party meetings as delegates.[149]

The two leading political editors of the Jacksonian era were Francis Preston Blair, of the Washington, D.C., *Globe,* and Duff Green of the Washington, D.C., *U.S. Telegraph.* Both worked extensively to promote presidential candidates and to coordinate partisan activities nationwide, issuing campaign extras and directing grass-roots organizations.

Green's greatest efforts were on behalf of John C. Calhoun in the early 1830s. Green developed a fairly elaborate strategy to get Calhoun elected president in 1832. He tried to deemphasize extreme state rights issues—specifically nullification, which was so closely tied to Calhoun and unpopular in the North.[150] He nurtured grass-roots political support primarily by establishing pro-Calhoun newspapers in Pennsylvania and Virginia so that the South Carolinian could win the Democratic presidential nomination.[151] And he hoped to win the Antimasonic party nomination for Calhoun for president.[152] When it became apparent by the spring of 1832 that Calhoun could not win any party's presidential nomination, Green supported an anti-Jackson coalition (endorsing no candidate, but just arguing against Jackson) and issued a *Telegraph* extra that assailed the Jackson administration's record.[153]

While Green was working to promote the political fortunes of John C. Calhoun in the early 1830s, Francis Preston Blair was trying to keep the 1828 Jacksonian coalition in line behind the president. Blair's loyalty to the president had been apparent from the first issue of his newspaper in late 1830, and the editor never faltered in his belief that Old Hickory's policies were best designed to keep the country and its citizens free.

Although Blair's prominence derived in large part from his ownership and editorship of the *Globe*, he was much more than just an editor. As William E. Ames writes, ". . . he was primarily a politician who edited a newspaper in order to advance his political party."[154] During his years with the *Globe*, politics and journalism were one and the same. He was interested in the occupation of journalism only as it promoted the political goals that he supported.[155]

As Ames notes, Blair followed the basic patterns of political activism pioneered by Duff Green, and he expanded upon them, emerging as a key confidant and political adviser to President Jackson and the key link between the president and many members of the party.[156]

Blair's political role within the administration was well recognized. Jacksonians in the states turned to Blair with their requests for political appointments,[157] and for help in solving their problems with the federal bureaucracy, particularly with the postal system.[158] Blair helped establish Jacksonian newspapers, loaning $200 to one editor to start an administration newspaper in Raleigh, North Carolina.[159] Other Jacksonians also turned to Blair for help in establishing papers loyal to the president.[160]

In 1832, Blair's major work during the election campaign was the publication and distribution of 30 weekly issues of *Globe* extras "so that the people may know and appreciate the measures and principles which guide Gen. Jackson in the administration of government." These were printed over the course of the six months preceding the election.[161] Blair was highly successful in distributing the extra. One Antimasonic editor in western New York said that "thousands and tens of thousands of extra sheets of this vile electioneering print" are being distributed "to the remotest corners of the Union."[162] Supporters of the Second Bank of the United States lamented the success of the *Globe*. One friend told bank president Nicholas Biddle that "the interior is inundated with official Globes and Jackson papers."[163]

Other issues of *Globe* extras appeared during the battle of the removal of the federal deposits from the Second Bank of the United States (in 1834) and during the presidential campaigns of 1836 and 1840.[164]

Elsewhere in the nation, in cities as well as in small towns, editors served as key political activists. The *Boston Statesman* was the center of the Massachusetts Jacksonian party in the late 1820s.[165] John Brazer Davis, a National Republican editor in Boston, worked to organize not only his own state's allies but also National Republicans throughout the country in the early 1830s.[166] Edwin Croswell of the *Albany Argus* (New York) was prominent in almost all Regency organizational efforts in the 1820s and 1830s,[167] just as Thurlow Weed of the *Albany Evening Journal* dominated Antimasonic party efforts.[168] In South Carolina, Henry Laurens Pinckney was not only editor of the *Charleston Mercury* but also a major political leader in the state legislature in the 1820s and early 1830s.[169] Many of these editors did not seek political office; they seemed content to work as party functionaries. Some were party kingpins, such as Thurlow Weed; others had far less power. All were political activists.

Conclusions

In *The Second American Party System*, Richard McCormick writes that Jacksonian-era political parties had two prime goals: first, to gain power, and second, to keep it. To those ends, American political parties devoted great effort to organization and electioneering. In that activity, newspapers and editors figured prominently.

Politicians and political activists saw newspapers as central to their hopes for electoral success. Martin Van Buren, the foremost political organizer of his day, never forgot that victory at the polls depended on reaching the electorate through political newspapers. Without such newspapers, he said, "we might as well hang our harps on willows."[170]

Van Buren was not alone in this belief. Each party wanted a newspaper in every hamlet, town, and city of the nation, ready to argue and advance party policies and candidates. Politicians and political activists worked hard to assure that the press would serve their needs. They shaped the press, recruiting editors, writing for newspapers, providing information and advice to editors. They also provided money to editors, subsidizing businesses that were often precarious financially.

This financial support, derived from the vision that politicians had of the press, clearly sustained the press. It gave political interest groups great power vis-à-vis the press. Indeed, disloyal editors were replaced, or their crucial subsidies were cut off. More often than not, however, partisan enthusiasms were not impressed upon unwilling editors. Editors themselves were party zealots, eager for patronage, but also eager for party debate and advocacy and for the power that came with victory.

Within this context, news dealt with politics: congressional and state legislative proceedings, partisan essays, profiles of candidates, and reports on party meetings. Despite the emphasis on political victory, these editors and politicians created a press that openly and loudly debated the day's public measures. There's no evidence that these editors engaged in debate because they idealized the *process* of debate. Rather, they engaged in debate in an effort to win elections.

The relatively small financial needs of the press fit well the largesse of the patronage system: a minimal amount of money could go a long way. The sums of money from political patronage in the early nineteenth century were not large, but editors of small rural newspapers found that even two or three dollars cash was a boon. For the newspapers in state capitals, such as Albany, the amounts were much larger. Few editors would become rich or even financially comfortable through the patronage system; for most it was merely a life-sustaining subsidy.

Newspapers were relatively cheap to establish, so political activists started newspapers to advance their beliefs and the candidates of their choice. New parties, such as the Antimasons, established scores of newspapers in the late 1820s. When a political newspaper proved disloyal or unsatisfactory, partisans would establish a new paper to replace it.

Patronage tied press and party together in an intimate fashion in the early nineteenth century. Patronage served as a kind of umbilical cord to the press, and many editors may well have been wary of taking unorthodox or maverick positions vis-à-vis their party for fear of losing that patronage. The extent of self-censorship is difficult to gauge. Certainly it limited press content. Party editors did not detail their opponents' views in any evenhanded way. They skirted discussions that would undermine the power of their political parties.

On balance, what seems more significant is that many editors were themselves party activists or leaders—members of the central committees that set the policies that they later promoted in their newspaper columns. These editors were the party strategists who created coalitions, chose party tickets, and guided campaigns. Parties were not, in a sense, dictating to newspapers; rather newspapers had been integrated into the party apparatus.

Chapter Two

New Directions in American Journalism

When Francis Preston Blair died in 1876, newspapers noted the tremendous changes in journalism in the preceding generation. The *Chicago Tribune* called Blair a leading Jacksonian partisan editor, and said that his death "recalls other and almost forgotten times in American politics."[1] The *New York Times* reported that political newspapers "were the fashion" in the 1840s, when every party looked to its recognized newspaper for "wisdom and guidance. . . . Independent newspapers were rare and of little account."[2]

The change in journalism in just one generation was both rapid and extensive. During Blair's tenure at the Washington, D.C., *Globe* (1830–45), the vast majority of American newspapers had been political organs, dedicated to party advocacy and to wooing the voters on election day. In 1876, both the *Chicago Tribune* and the *New York Times* discussed Blair and political journalism almost as ancient artifacts, relics of a distant era when editors were "naturally" politicians, when the *Globe* served as the "mouthpiece" of Andrew Jackson, and when "that headstrong leader was in the height of his power."[3]

In one generation, many American newspapers distanced themselves from politics and political parties and began to serve broader interests within society. The *Chicago Tribune*, just three days before it carried the Blair obituary, analyzed not the *political* role of the American newspaper but its *commercial* role as an advertising vehicle. According to the *Tribune*, a newspaper of "value" would circulate to "*the class who have the means to buy, and whose approbation constitutes that which is called reputation in business.*"[4]

While newspapers such as the *Tribune* continued to take political positions and endorse candidates, editors and publishers in the latter half of the nineteenth century saw the press in a way far distant from the vision held by Blair. Editors and publishers proclaimed an independence from politics and offered wide-ranging content designed to appeal not just to voters but also to any and all potential readers. And they saw advertising as an important component of their newspapers.

Within another 20 years, by century's end, editors and publishers would come to disdain the political press of the antebellum period. By 1900, newspapers not only often avoided political advocacy but sometimes even scorned it as "billingsgate."[5] One writer argued that the passing of antebellum "personal journalism" meant that the public was better served and better informed. He noted that "the newspaper is a business enterprise, founded primarily to make money."[6] Another writer in 1900 noted that "times have changed and so have the newspapers." Previously, partisan editors "felt it their first and highest duty to be an organ and mouthpiece for some political party," making "saints" of their party's candidates and "devils" of the opposition's. "Now newspapers are conducted on business principles and large ones are owned by corporations."[7]

The shift away from the partisan press in the nineteenth century reflected changes both in journalism and within American society. Those changes, for the press, included a shift in its financial base, a new vision (by newspaper owners and Americans at large) about the role of journalism in American society, and increasingly complex and expensive day-to-day operations. Broader social trends, including changes in literacy, urbanization, improvements in technology, the impact of economic change and related entrepreneurial activities, the dislocation and centralization of the Civil War, and the demands of industrialization, influenced the press and its content.[8]

Although all these factors merit attention, the focus here is on four broad aspects of American life and journalism that speeded the change in the American newspaper during the nineteenth century:

First, the nature of politics within American life changed. The national fascination with things political began, ever so subtly, to decline after the 1840s. Politicians became less dependent on the press. More important, they provided less financial support to the press while seeking other means to reach the electorate. The intimate link between party and press that had been so fundamental to the Jacksonian-era partisan press declined in the middle decades of the century.

Second, new visions arose about what journalism could and should do. The rise of the penny press, as limited geographically as those cheap and lively papers were, provided the basis for the press as a servant of business rather than of politics.

Third, urbanization created the need for a press that not only served the male political world but also reported on the wider world. Newspapers, particularly in the metropolitan areas, tried to make sense of urban life and to link its disparate parts.

And fourth, advertisers became the key constituency of the press when newspapers emerged as an integral part of the marketing campaigns of American businesses.

These four factors are closely intertwined; one might even argue that there is some interaction among them. Urbanization was a major manifestation of the new industrial society. The penny press of the 1830s and 1840s was distinctly an urban phenomenon. The decline of popular fascination with politics can been seen as a corollary to the urban-based growth of recreational activities (such as baseball and drama). Advertising reflected the rise of a consumer-based society. Each factor is important on its own, and the following discussion represents an attempt to show how each contributed to the change in journalism. The task is not to isolate the cause or to weight various factors; rather it is to examine the *configuration* of factors that led to change.

These four factors do not account for all changes in the American press during the middle decades of the nineteenth century, but they help to explain the transformation from a press enmeshed in politics (circa 1830) to a press that professed a disdain for politics (circa 1900).

Changes in American Politics

Although newspapers continued to remain an important part of the political process, they were no longer as central to politics as they had been in the age of Jackson.

Campaigning

Candidates began to campaign for themselves in the middle decades of the century, with little of the damage that self-promotion had caused earlier. In the 1820s and 1830s, self-promotion was deemed a badge of dishonor for any candidate. One Jacksonian stalwart expressed the common wisdom of the age when he noted that those with the "lust for office" deserved no respect.[9]

By midcentury, much of that disdain for self-promotion had lessened. What occurred to make such campaigning more acceptable isn't entirely clear. But candidates increasingly took to the stump in the 1850s and 1860s. The impetus for such campaigning may not have been philosophical; there's no evidence that Americans suddenly abandoned their distaste for political campaigns. Rather, the change may well have come for practical reasons: improvements in transportation (from roads to railroads) made it possible for candidates to campaign. Whatever the reason, they took to the stump as never before.

One of the best-publicized instances of candidate campaigning was in the 1858 Illinois senatorial contest between Stephen A. Douglas and Abraham Lincoln. Both candidates traveled extensively throughout Illinois, giving speeches and supporting local legislators who would vote for them when the legislature met to elect a U.S. senator. Aided by an extensive railroad network through the state, Douglas appeared in more than 60 Illinois communities, and he later claimed to have given about 120 speeches.[10] Douglas and Lincoln appeared together or on the same day seven times during that campaign.[11]

Douglas won reelection to the Senate and went on, in 1860, to campaign for the presidency as the nominee of the northern Democrats.[12] He lost in 1860, but he had demonstrated the power of campaigning, because he drew large audiences both north and south.

By the 1860s, most candidates, except for presidential nominees, took to the stump to draw voters' interest and support. While running for Congress in 1866, James A. Garfield gave 28 speeches during a seven-week period.[13] And even U.S. senators took to the stump in the 1880s and 1890s. Although they themselves did not face popular election, they depended on the goodwill and support of legislators, and so state legislative campaigns brought them before the public.[14]

The best-known noncampaigning candidate of the nineteenth century was William McKinley, who refused to take to the campaign trail when running for president in 1896. However, McKinley had campaigned vigorously in the early 1890s for congressional candidates, touring 16 states and giving more than 400 speeches just in one five-week campaign swing.[15] Some presidential nominees did campaign in the nineteenth century: Greeley in 1872, Blaine in 1884, and Bryan in 1896. All three lost, and Greeley's and Bryan's tours may well have marked desperate campaign tactics. Winners or not, they moved beyond the press advocacy that had been so central to campaigns in the Jacksonian era. Even William McKinley gave speeches to those who showed up at his home in Ohio.[16]

Speeches and campaign tours were just one of the new forums for candidates to take their views to the public. Some turned to magazines to air their views. Stephen A. Douglas wrote an article for *Harper's Magazine* in 1859 about political sovereignty. The appearance of the article created a stir, for it represented a major innovation in politicking as well as in magazines.[17] Magazines continued to play a role in party politics through the rest of the century. The Republicans, in particular, benefited from the attention and support of the *Nation*, *Harper's*, the *Independent*, and *Leslie's Weekly*.

Institutional Party Development

By midcentury, parties had begun to institutionalize the operations once performed almost ad hoc by party editors. In the 1820s and 1830s, editors such as Francis Preston Blair and Duff Green served as party organizers and ad hoc national campaign directors. They produced campaign newspaper extras and wrote letters to organize the party faithful in the states. On the state level, editors such as Thurlow Weed in New York played a similar role. By the 1860s, however, businessmen and other noneditors were increasingly involved in party affairs. August Belmont, a financier, headed the Democratic party in the late 1860s, and the chair of the Illinois State Republican party at the same time was Norman Judd, a Rock Island railroad attorney.[18]

As party organizations grew, no longer could they rely solely on the ad hoc efforts of various party editors (even if the editors had remained loyal party activists, which was not always the case). Spiraling campaign costs due to extensive propaganda efforts required reliance on the wealthy for campaign contributions. In the 1868 campaign, the Republican National Committee spent $50,000 in Indiana alone, and $40,000 in Pennsylvania.[19]

By the 1890s, campaign costs had risen further. In 1896, the Republican National Committee spent an unprecedented sum of $7.5 million.[20] Under the direction of businessman-turned-politician Mark Hanna, the committee distributed more than 15 million copies of campaign documents and organized a herd of campaign speakers. Wealthy businessmen financed this activity.[21]

Robert Johannsen notes that the organizational activities by Stephen A. Douglas in 1860 were "uncommon" compared with the preceding decade. The *New York Herald* in 1860 noted that few "have any just comprehension of the *expensive* and *complicated* machinery which prominent politicians of the present day invent and work to aid them in their ambitious schemes."[22]

Editors remained important in many campaigns in the late nineteenth century, but they did not have control of campaigns. Congressman Miles Taylor, from Louisiana, directed Stephen Douglas'

1860 presidential campaign. An editor, A. D. Banks, served on the campaign, but Douglas also relied extensively on the financiers and businessmen on his steering committee.[23]

In the large cities, the formation of political machines provided full-time jobs for many and created a large number of party workers to carry out the campaign tasks that once had been the province of newspaper editors. One observer at the turn of the century said that the *key* player in urban party machines was the "local lieutenant," who "devotes himself unremittingly to the people of his section of the ward." This party worker kept the party apparatus functioning, turning out voters on election day, doling out party favors, and serving as the invaluable link between party and populace.[24]

Decline of the Washington, D.C., Political Press

Changes in press-party relations paralleled the general decline of the political press itself, particularly in Washington, D.C., in the middle decades of the century. In the 1820s and 1830s, the Washington political press served politics on a national level, circulating political essays and propaganda throughout the land. In the 1840s, however, the vitality and reach of the Washington political press declined. This decline reflected the departure of powerful, activist political editors such as Francis Preston Blair (who sold his *Globe* in 1845). Blair's power within the Democratic party had so eroded by 1845 that the new Polk administration forced him out of his role as chief editor of the party. Thomas Ritchie, longtime editor of the *Richmond Enquirer* (Virginia), replaced him. But Ritchie's political skill and strength never matched Blair's.[25]

The decline of the Washington political press also stemmed from the controversy over political subsidies. The congressional printing contract system, operating since 1819, had assured party editors of lucrative contracts for doing the printing of each house (bills, laws, and debates). The profits from the contracts subsidized several key Washington political newspapers during the Jacksonian era, newspapers such as the *National Intelligencer*, the *Globe*, and the *U.S. Telegraph*.

Although the subsidies worked well in the view of editors (particularly those who received subsidies), the system broke down as it became politicized in the late 1830s. Editors who lost printing awards accused members of Congress of bad faith or argued that the editor who had won had cheated.[26]

Against the backdrop of such acrimony, the elections for the printer to each house of Congress became increasingly difficult. In 1837, the election for the printer of the House of Representatives required 12 ballots before Thomas Allen of the Washington, D.C., *Madisonian* won. Allen's election further underscored the discontent some in Congress felt with the printing contracts. Allen's original supporters, about 20 conservative Democrats, held the balance of power between mainstream Democrats, who supported Blair, and the Whigs, who supported Gales and Seaton of the *National Intelligencer*. The conservative Democrats refused to desert Allen. The Whigs, unable to elect Gales and Seaton, finally voted for Allen, defeating their longtime enemy, Blair. The contest left a bitter taste all around.[27]

Members of Congress began to play fast and loose with the general contract rules, too. According to the 1819 rules, each new Congress elected its own printer. In 1841, the lame duck Senate Democratic majority awarded the printing contracts for the *next* Congress to the Democratic editor, Blair. During the opening days of the new Congress, the Whigs, now controlling the Senate, removed Blair as printer in an acrimonious fight.[28]

Messy elections were not the only threat to the congressional patronage system. Some members of Congress complained that the official editors frequently erred in their reports, and thus urged that Congress hire its own reporters to guarantee accuracy.[29] Other members of Congress argued that the patronage contract system was too costly; they wanted contracts awarded on a low-bid system instead.[30] In 1846, Congress replaced the 1819 system with low-bid awards,[31] and editors no longer enjoyed the steady stream of political patronage.

Other governmental bodies set up their own printing offices, decreasing or ending partisan subsidies. In 1873, the New York legislature established the *City Record* to print all New York City corporation advertising at city expense. Brief notices would still appear in two morning and two evening newspapers, but the bulk of city advertising would no longer go to support the press.[32]

Competition for the District of Columbia Press

The departure of editors such as Blair, the end of partisan subsidies, and disputes with Congress all served to undermine the political role and power of the Washington press. The Washington political press also faced a challenge from papers around the country to report and interpret the proceedings of Congress. The resurgence of interest in national politics after the middle 1820s led to a greater desire to tap the news of the nation's capital. By the early 1830s, New York City newspapers, such as the *New York Journal of Commerce* and the *Courier and Enquirer,* began relying on expresses to speed the capital's news to New York.[33] In 1840, Congress began to allow out-of-town newspaper reporters to sit in its reporters' galleries.[34]

The telegraph also undermined the monopoly the Washington press held over national news and its interpretation. In the 1820s and for much of the 1830s, the key source of political news in the country was the Washington, D.C., political press. In Charleston, South Carolina, for example, news about Congress and the president came primarily from the Washington papers that arrived (about a week after publication) by postal rider or packet boat. By the late 1840s, the telegraph had preempted the dependence on the Washington newspapers.[35] No longer were the Washington newspapers central to the flow of political information and analysis in the nation.

The Inadequacy of Political Patronage

The decline of patronage marked a fundamental shift in party-press relationships. The disputes over patronage and the establishment of governmental printing offices explain much of that decline. But the importance of political patronage was diminishing anyway, because it could not provide enough money for the new newspapers of the middle and late nineteenth century. Editors and publishers had to look elsewhere for new sources of revenue to keep up with their soaring costs. Even if political patronage had continued at its 1830 rate, it could not have met the financial needs of most newspapers from the 1850s on. James Crouthamel writes that fixed costs for news gathering, labor, paper, and presses rose so markedly from 1830 to 1860 that newspapers required substantial capital.[36] The subsidies available from the political process in nineteenth-century America were more in keeping with the small newspapers for which almost *any* amount of money was substantial.

News-gathering costs grew in the middle and latter decades of the century. During the last three months of 1870, the New York *World* (edited by Manton Marble) spent $15,000 for special telegraphic dispatches and extra Associated Press reports dealing *only* with the Franco-Prussian War.[37] Throughout the 1860s and 1870s, the *Chicago Tribune* added new cylinder presses to meet growing demands in circulation and advertising. Such technological improvements demanded heavy capital investment.[38]

Definitions of news changed during the middle decades of the century and contributed to the spiraling costs of newspaper production. Antebellum political editors had been relatively passive in news gathering, producing political essays and extracting political news from exchange newspapers. The only genuine reporting of news, at least by twentieth-century definitions, was stenographers' reports of congressional or legislative proceedings.[39] By midcentury, reporting on news events was increasingly common, and the number of reporters on newspaper staffs rose.

By 1850, news staffs alone, in many metropolitan newspapers, had 10 employees or more,[40] and printing and distribution functions required additional workers. In 1845, the *New York Herald* had a staff of 13 editors and reporters in addition to 20 compositors and 16 press hands; *weekly* expenses ran about $1,400–$1,600. In 1850, the *New York Tribune* employed 130 persons, in addition to special correspondents.[41] And staffs continued to grow. By the middle 1870s, the *Boston Globe* (which was still precarious financially) had 14 or 15 workers in the newsroom and another 20 in the composing room. The *Globe*'s staff doubled by 1880.[42] Even the relatively staid New York *Evening Post*'s staff grew—from four in 1842 to nine by the late 1870s.[43] The general operating costs of the *New York Tribune* almost quadrupled over a 15-year period at midcentury, driven, in part, by the rise of news-gathering costs during the Civil War.[44]

Although spiraling costs were greatest in the metropolitan areas, editors of newspapers in small cities and towns were affected as well. In 1864, the Salem *Oregon Statesman* reported that the "costly transmission of news by telegraph, together with the largely enhanced price of paper and other material, render the expense of publication far greater than it formerly was."[45] William H. Simpson of the Belfast, Maine, *Republican Journal* complained in 1876 that "expenses of even a country paper have very greatly enhanced over former years."[46]

The Decline of Political Culture

The general fascination in politics that characterized the age of Jackson began to wane in the mid-nineteenth century.[47] As Michael Holt observed, many Americans of that era no longer saw a substantive difference between the Democratic and Whig parties. Consequently, he wrote, "malignant distrust of politicians as self-centered and corrupt wire pullers out of touch with the people spread like an epidemic during the 1850s. So, too, did dissatisfaction with political parties as unresponsive and beyond popular control."[48]

How widespread this disillusionment was within American society is not quite clear.[49] Ronald Formisano writes that antiparty sentiment had become a convenient cry for dissident political factions in the 1840s and 1850s.[50] Politicians from the 1840s on began to eschew partisanship.[51] Zachary Taylor, running for president in 1848, disavowed party considerations.[52] He ran with no platform, declined to take sides on most issues, vowed he had no opinions on political matters. Rather, he promised to serve the people.[53]

In the postwar era, suspicion of politicians and government continued; politicians appear to have done their best to destroy anyone's notion that government could be honest. Grant placed more than 40 of his relatives on the payroll, several of his aides were linked to a tax fraud scheme (the Whiskey Ring), and four cabinet members were involved in various kickback schemes.[54] The Credit Mobilier scandal touched many influential politicians. Stalemates between the two political parties produced bitter fights, both within and between parties. Legislative accomplishments were few.[55]

Corruption in the federal government was only the proverbial tip of the iceberg. Eric F. Goldman notes that corruption was "still more flagrant" in municipal and state politics. In New York, Boss Tweed turned both city and state government into "a vast and succulent barbecue," plundering tens of millions of dollars.[56] Americans demonstrated a disregard for politics and politicians in the 1870s. Seymour J. Mandelbaum writes that "politicians were derided as stupid demagogues, whose choice of a profession was almost certain evidence of venality."[57]

The decline of political culture did not erase all bonds between party and press, much less between the public at large and politics. Voter turnout remained fairly strong throughout the century, except for some drop-off in the late 1840s. Newspaper editors continued, as they had done in the age of Jackson, to advocate particular candidates and to be rewarded with some sort of patronage (e.g., appointment to office, ambassadorships, and the like) if their candidates won. Much remained as it had been, but much changed, too. Political culture no longer was as central to the lives of Americans, and no longer as central to their newspapers, as it had been in an earlier era. People did not cynically abandon or avoid the world of politics, but it no longer served such an important function within their lives as it once had done.[58]

Changes in the Press and News

New visions and practices in journalism transformed the American press in the nineteenth century. New definitions of news deemphasized politics and valued a more entrepreneurial vision of the newspaper. The measure of success in journalism was no longer political wisdom or advocacy but the ability to entertain, the acquisition of large circulations, and the generation of large revenues.

The new journalism of the nineteenth century first appeared in the so-called penny press of several major eastern cities—in New York, Philadelphia, and Baltimore. Certainly one can debate just how widespread this new journalism actually was and whether it was wholly apolitical. But it is clear that politics was not as central to the existence of the new journalism as it was to the mainstream political papers.

The best-known of the early penny papers was James Gordon Bennett's *New York Herald*, established in May 1835. The paper's debut was somewhat inauspicious. Bennett had scraped together $500 to start the paper. His office was primitive, and he was the paper's entire staff in its early months. Three months after the paper appeared, a fire destroyed the establishment; the paper resurfaced three weeks later. Because of its sprightliness and Bennett's inventiveness and hard work, the paper succeeded. By 1840, Bennett claimed a circulation of 51,000 (his daily, weekly, and extra editions)—14,000 more than the other daily newspapers of the city.[59]

Bennett's success was simply phenomenal, and it stemmed from his vision of what journalism could and should be. Four characteristics of this new kind of newspaper are particularly important: it was cheap, costing just a penny; it generally avoided politics; it gathered the news rather than providing political commentary and partisan advocacy; and it was bright and loud.[60]

Bennett's disdain for partisan newspapers came only after working more than a decade on Jacksonian political publications (the New York *Courier and Enquirer* and the Philadelphia *Pennsylvanian*). He became disillusioned with political journalism, particularly after the Democratic party refused to give him a $2,500 loan in the early 1830s.

"Van Buren has treated me in this matter as if I were a boy—a child—cold, heartless, careless and God knows what not," he told friends.[61] As the *New York Times* noted in 1872, when Bennett died, his disillusionment with politics led him to a new vision of journalism. "He had cut loose from party discipline and he resolved to cut loose from party altogether." His paper would "have no master but the public and should stand by public favor alone."[62] The first issue of the *New York Herald* promised: "We shall support no party—be the organ of no faction or COTERIE, and care nothing for any election or any candidate from president down to a constable."[63]

Bennett was a news gatherer. The first issue of the *New York Herald* carried Bennett's promise to "endeavor to record facts on every public and proper subject, stripped of verbiage and coloring, with comments when suitable, just, independent, fearless and good-tempered."[64] He covered the police courts, Wall Street, and the city at large. When prostitute Helen Jewett was murdered in 1836, Bennett demonstrated a "faithfulness to detail" that shocked some and surprised all.[65]

Newspaper obituaries in 1872 recalled Bennett's contributions to news gathering. Even his longtime competitors in New York City begrudgingly noted that he had set the tone for modern journalism with the *Herald*'s "spirit and enterprise" in gathering the news.[66] The *New York Tribune*, a longtime adversary of the *Herald*, wrote that Bennett "understood the value of news." The paper called him "the inventor of journalism in its latest and highest development as a means of disseminating all accessible contemporaneous intelligence."[67]

Style, entertainment, and excitement were all part of the *Herald*'s aim to entertain its readers. In 1872, the *New York Tribune* noted that the *Herald* had done so well because it had been "bright, sharp, insolent, personal, concise and novel" in its early days. "The paper immediately became disreputable and soon became popular. It offended all parties and all creeds."[68]

All these things were the foundations of the new journalism. All reflected a new vision about the role and purpose of journalism in America. The aim of Bennett's paper was not political advocacy but *success* as measured by news gathering and scoops, by ever-growing circulation, and by booming revenues. Public service was second to private gain. As the *New York Tribune* noted in 1872: "He had an unerring judgment of the pecuniary value of news. He knew how to pick out of the events of the day the subject which engrossed the interest of the greatest number of people and to give them about that subject all they could read."[69] More to the point, as the New York *Evening Post* noted when he died, he had not been a great journalist but he was "a great news vendor."[70]

The general view of news that Bennett espoused—nonpartisanship, a zest for news gathering, editorial audacity, and sensationalism—characterized other penny papers of that era. In 1838, A. S. Abell of the Baltimore *Sun* attributed his success to avoiding politics.[71] The early issues of the New York *Sun*, the first of the successful penny papers, carried no editorials because its editor wanted to avoid political affiliation.[72]

Not all newspapers, not even all metropolitan newspapers, endorsed all the new definitions of news pioneered by the penny papers. But even more staid newspapers copied some of the new journalism, distancing themselves from party, seeking revenues from sources other than political parties (from advertising in particular), and gathering *news.*

Newspapers, given the essentially business vision of the press that was emerging, also paid greater attention to advertisers. When the price of a newspaper dropped to a penny (instead of the six cents then commonly paid for a single issue of a partisan newspaper), the financial support of the press shifted from subscribers (and political patronage) to advertisers.

The Philadelphia *Public Ledger*, established in 1836, typified this new reliance on advertising. The paper promised: "We admit any advertisements of any thing or any opinion, from any persons who will pay the price, excepting what is forbidden by the laws of the land. . ."[73]

The penny press was not entirely apolitical. Bennett, for example, retained political opinions, supported Harrison in 1840 and Taylor in 1848. And when Horace Greeley established the *New York Tribune* in 1840, he did so as a spokesman for the Whigs.[74] Yet neither Bennett nor Greeley was a predictably loyal partisan in the mold of Francis Preston Blair; they themselves decided their political choices and did not consider themselves the agents of any particular party.

Urbanization

Although the changes in American journalism represent many things (including the decline of partisan subsidies to the press, a decline in American political culture, and the growth of an entrepreneurial vision of the press), much of what constituted the new dimensions in journalism was, at least at first, singularly urban. One historian attributes the Baltimore *Sun's* great success not only to its own efforts but also to its metropolitan setting. Baltimore was "vibrantly, brilliantly alive," and the spirit of the place spurred the newspaper.[75]

The metropolitan newspaper emerged as a force in American journalism during the middle of the nineteenth century, when cities came to constitute a larger share of the nation's population: in 1830, 8.8 percent of the population lived in "urban" areas (2,500 or more inhabitants); by 1850, 15.2 percent; by 1870, rising to 34.5 percent.[76] By the 1850s, virtually every family in New York City was buying a newspaper, and circulations soared. The *New York Herald* had an average circulation of 58,000; the *Sun,* 50,000; the *New York Times,* 42,000; the *New York Tribune,* 29,000; and the *Evening Post,* 12,000.[77] The greatest concentration of newspapers occurred in the larger American cities of the post–Civil War era. In 1880, daily newspapers in six cities—New York, Chicago, Philadelphia, Cleveland, Boston, and San Francisco—printed 51.1 percent of the country's daily sheets. New York City alone published 22.8 percent of the country's sheets.[78] The metropolis provided a huge and relatively easy-to-reach audience, and literacy rates there were higher than in rural America.[79] The metropolis, with all its diversity and anonymity, necessitated a newspaper that took a broad view of local events.

The face-to-face communication that had characterized so much of information at the local level during the antebellum period[80] was no longer possible in the growing cities of the nineteenth century. The prototypical partisan newspaper of the Jacksonian era had a small circulation (a few hundred), appeared weekly, and circulated within its own region. Its readers were the inhabitants of small villages and towns, and local farmers. Word of mouth supplied the everyday news of the village, from deaths to accidents or other depredations of nature and hostile neighbors. The weekly newspaper could not be the *original* source of such news. This was true even in the small cities of the antebellum era. Samuel Hays writes that, prior to industrialization, cities had been relatively small, compact, and integrated pedestrian communities where people could walk between their homes, jobs, church and school, store and recreation facilities. In these "face-to-face" communities, personal contact was the basis of human relationships and, thus, of communication.[81]

In *City People,* Gunther Barth notes that the physical growth of the city—more people spread out over an ever-increasing area—meant that gossip and first-hand knowledge were no longer sufficient as sources of information about one's community.[82] But the city was not just home to more people. It was also the center of new types of activities. Rather simply put, more was going on in the city than elsewhere. Not all of it was wonderful or exciting; the prevalence of crime and disease, for instance, added no luster to urban life.[83] But it was, in a sense, a place where things happened. The very complexities of organizing and maintaining large numbers of people in one place demanded activities or efforts unheard of in smaller villages and towns: traffic facilities (pavement, wagons, and the general transit systems), housing (for both inhabitants and visitors), communication networks (telephones and telegraph), and the problems inherent in any such setting (sanitation, fire and police protection).

Personal experience and interpersonal communication were no longer enough to make sense of the city, but the newspaper could take on that task. As Klein and Kantor write, "Only the newspaper, whose circulation skyrocketed in the industrial city, could cover every area of urban life."[84]

Through its general coverage, the newspaper could signal to its readers the key local concerns, such as smallpox or unsanitary living conditions. The newspaper helped readers keep abreast of general events in their city—those that had already occurred as well as those that were soon to happen.

The city was also the home of new types of leisure activities in the late nineteenth century, and newspaper content reflected these activities. Urban newspapers devoted a fifth or more of their content to leisure-time activities, such as sports, theater, reading, hobbies, and music.[85]

Sports

Sports, both participatory and spectator, were important urban activities in the middle and latter decades of the century. Baseball, cycling, croquet, football, cricket, golf, tennis, sledding, skating, rowing, yachting, and dozens of children's games, all experienced a surge of popularity in the latter decades of the century, particularly in the city.[86]

Baseball, in its inception before the Civil War, was distinctly an urban phenomenon. The first baseball club in New York City appeared in 1845, and its popularity had spread widely by the 1850s. In 1869, Cincinnati fielded the nation's first professional team (the Red

Stockings). The club traveled more than 11,000 miles, winning 56 games (losing none, tying 1).[87] And baseball was a spectator sport. In 1888, the *New York Times* reported that 40,000 people attended a Sunday baseball game in Philadelphia; 20,000 more had tried to get into the new ball park but failed.[88]

The press took note of these new activities and new interests of its readers. One author noted that sports news, "next to crime, made the most exciting news of the late seventies and early eighties." The variety of sporting news was amazing, he noted, and popular interest was high, too.[89] The *Boston Globe* found that reports on walking matches could boost circulation by 30,000 newspapers.[90]

In 1867, the *Chicago Tribune* devoted two and a half columns to an inning-by-inning account of a game between Chicago's baseball team, the Excelsiors, and the Washington, D.C., Nationals.[91] Even more staid newspapers took note of the world of sports; the New York *Evening Post* added a sports editor in 1886.[92]

Theater and Other Entertainment

Metropolitan newspapers reported on many leisure-time activities. The rich cultural life of the cities provided an environment in which the arts received a great deal of attention. Going to the theater, particularly in the city, was a pastime in the late nineteenth century. Improvements in the theaters themselves added to their attraction. By late in the century, many had added electric lights. They also had designated sections of cheaper seating now, which increased access.[93]

Theaters did not provide the only leisure-time activity in the metropolis. There also were libraries, art museums, and lectures. On Sunday, October 24, 1897, the *Boston Globe* provided a synopsis of 12 plays running in the following week, and announced a lecture by an Arctic explorer and vaudeville productions at area theaters. That issue of the *Globe,* under the heading "Novelties at the Zoo," also reported that polar bears were on display there and a lion tamer would be at work the following week.

The newspaper was not just a chronicler of leisure-time activities, it was a leisure-time activity itself. The *Boston Globe,* for example, provided daily installments of a novel in 1897. And the weekday issues of the *Globe* provided jokes for readers, while the Sunday newspaper contained comics to amuse and entertain readers. The growing size of the newspaper (12-page dailies were common in many cities on weekdays by the latter years of the century, with Sunday papers running to 36 pages or more) and entertaining content meant that the newspaper was a part of the leisure-time activities of many.

The city provided a focal point for changes within American journalism. The sheer size of the growing cities of nineteenth-century America and the amount of activity within them necessitated new functions for the press: the observation and description of events and activities that were increasingly part of newspaper content.

The Rise of Advertising

Industrialization also facilitated changes in American life and journalism. Industrialization changed the way in which commerce was conducted and made advertisers a major constituency of the American press.

The Industrial Revolution

Before the Civil War, the organization of economic life in the United States had been fairly simple; businessmen operated within small, localized markets.[94] Early manufacturing plants were small in capitalization and output. Barriers to cheap transportation of goods reinforced the local nature of markets, and businessmen offered their wares to their community—a community generally limited to the distance a horse could travel in a day.[95]

But by the 1880s and 1890s, the main attributes of an industrialized economy were in place: large-scale factory production, an urban work force, strategic centers of investment capital, and extensive marketing of standardized products.[96] As one historian has noted, the American industrial revolution "transformed the United States from a country of small and isolated communities scattered across 3 million miles of continental territory into a compact economic and industrial unit."[97] That transformation in American life was simply astounding. Agriculture had been the way of life—part of the Jeffersonian vision of the republic—and until the 1880s it was the foundation of national wealth. But the 1890 census recorded agriculture's eclipse by manufacturing. By 1900, the value of manufactured products was more than double that of agricultural products.[98] This new age was characterized not by tilling the land but by mass production, with a high degree of mechanization, accurate machine tools, uniform quality of materials, and high capital investment.[99]

The Need for Marketing

The tremendous increases in production, delivered via a far-flung distribution network, would have amounted to little if consumers had not known about the vast new supply of goods available. Indeed, marketing was an essential complement to mass production and mass distribution.

When production output was small and distribution limited to a fairly narrow region, marketing was less a concern than it became later in the century. Early in the century, a small advertisement in the local newspaper could alert most in the county about goods made by a local cobbler, for instance. Many considered a sign outside the shop to be adequate advertising, and word of mouth usually could maintain a business in a local area.

By the latter decades of the century, however, businesses could not survive if they were inattentive to marketing. With mass production, the financial stakes were much higher. The village cobbler in 1820 or 1830 had but 8–10 pairs of shoes to sell at any one time, but the shoe manufacturer in late-century New England could easily produce hundreds of pairs of shoes a week. Such stock represented a major investment in raw materials, not to mention the capital investment in the machinery used in such mass production. The financial stakes were now so high that manufacturers and distributors were forced to exert themselves more than ever before to induce consumers to buy their goods.

National distribution of goods naturally precluded selling only to those who walked by a shop and saw its sign outside or to those who knew a cobbler (or some other producer of goods) personally or by reputation. The New England shoe producer who sought to sell goods in Oregon could not rely on word of mouth; national markets required national marketing.

By the late nineteenth century, American manufacturers had come to rely on many forms of marketing to reach the consumer: salesmen, billboards, free samples, calendars, blotters, and signs on barns. Many businesses relied on advertisements in the leading mass media of the day—newspapers and magazines. Most businessmen relied on a variety of marketing techniques, although some clearly had preferences. Life insurance advertising generally appeared in magazines. Quaker Oats relied on calendars (with the friendly Quaker beaming at all), cookbooks (which not so surprisingly stressed the use of oats), and door-to-door giveaway of free samples.[100]

Marketing became a major concern because hundreds of consumer goods were sold nationally by the 1880s and 1890s: beer, home remedies and patent medicines, soaps, baking powder, cocoa, pianos, seeds, typewriters, bicycles, and mail-order dry goods. Other than patent medicines, most of these items had never had national distribution before the 1880s.[101]

American newspapers advertised many of these goods. In 1898, the Milwaukee *Evening Wisconsin* had national advertising contracts with 80 different companies,[102] selling such diverse products as patent medicines, books, soaps, food, and food-related products. Even small rural papers had national advertising patronage. The Pendleton, Oregon, *East Oregonian* had accounts with five patent medicine companies in the 1880s.[103]

The Value of Advertising

Many manufacturers came to believe that advertising was fundamentally vital to success in business. At the very least, it served an economic function of linking producers and consumers. But some dared to believe that advertising might create demand. In either case, advertising was an essential part of the nation's new economic order.[104]

The manager of a leading New York City department store in the late 1890s claimed that advertising was "the fundamental thing—the cornerstone; therefore it demands the attention of the head of the business."[105] The head of the Angier Chemical Company, a patent medicine firm in Boston, said that advertising was crucial to good business.[106] In 1915, R. J. Reynolds recalled that he had spent $4,000 for advertising in 1894 and had seen his business increase dramatically. Encouraged, he spent $20,000 on advertising in 1895 and his business doubled.[107] He believed that advertising was a necessary part of doing business, and he claimed he spent between 2 and 3 percent of annual sales on advertising.[108] James B. Duke, the leading figure in the cigarette industry, built his firm's fortune in the 1880s and 1890s through business acumen and aggressive marketing; he spent $800,000 on advertising in 1889 alone.[109] A. T. Stewart, an early department store magnate, said, "He who invests one dollar in business should invest one dollar in advertising that business."[110] W. G. Thomas, manager of the H. O'Neill Dry Goods Company in New York City, said that every dollar spent on advertising produced two dollars in return.[111]

Reliance on Newspaper Advertising

For many businesses, newspapers were the most effective vehicle for advertising. Growth in newspaper circulation throughout the country provided advertisers with broad and relatively cheap access to most American consumers. The frequent publication schedule of newspapers (daily in all urban areas and daily even in many smaller towns) was best for high-volume businesses. Businesses had advertised in the press since colonial days, and advertising had grown throughout the century, paralleling the emergence of new and wider markets. But in the late nineteenth century, as never before, a wide variety of businesses—carriage makers, bicycle manufacturers, railroad agents, hoteliers, department (dry goods) store owners, food processors, and others—turned to the American newspaper as the major vehicle for their marketing.

E. H. Morse, principal of a business college in Hartford, Connecticut, told his colleagues at a business-college teachers convention in 1898 that newspaper advertising was the best forum for marketing: "Of all the methods of practical publicity that I have tried, and I have tried a good many, I find repeatedly that the newspaper is the foundation. It leads both in reaching the people and producing the results. People read the daily newspapers for the sake of getting the news. This means the news of business as well as the news of politics and war. An advertisement is business news."

Morse believed that people saw "the daily paper as the up-to-date medium by which the newest knowledge is disseminated," and, thus, approached it with a good deal of trust.[112] Across the business world, owners and managers testified that *newspaper* advertising was the path to commercial success. A manufacturer of carriages and agricultural implements attributed his firm's "phenomenal" success in carriage sales to newspaper advertising. The firm advertised *only* in newspapers and had no other marketing schemes (such as circulars or traveling salesmen) for its products.[113] E. S. Burnham, founder and manager of a company specializing in food products and beverages, believed advertising was absolutely essential to his business. He relied on newspapers and magazines for his marketing campaigns, but he said that newspapers were the cheapest and most effective means for reaching the public.[114] Dr. R. V. Pierce, a patent medicine manufacturer, said that newspapers were a leading advertising medium because they were relatively cheap and because they circulated widely in the country.[115]

The popularity of newspapers as an advertising medium was widespread. Boston theaters relied almost exclusively on newspapers for advertising. The Park Theater in Boston had an annual advertising budget of about $20,000 in the early 1890s; $18,000 went to newspapers ($8,000 to dailies; $1,000 to small weeklies, and $9,000 to Sunday papers).[116] George H. Daniels, general passenger agent of the New York Central Railroad, said that daily newspapers were the best medium for his advertising. "Their frequency of issue makes them very desirable mediums for our advertising, and their character makes our reading notices particularly appropriate for their columns."[117]

Many kinds of businesses thus came to rely on the American newspaper as a vital link to the consumer. The economic necessity of such reliance is probably best illustrated by the example of the department store, the great palace of consumption that came to dominate much of retail trade in the late nineteenth century.

The Department Store

The department store was a product of an industrialized, urban-based society. Urban growth — 22 percent of the population in 1880 lived in cities, rising to 33 percent in 1900 — created a sizable market for dry goods merchants.[118]

The trend toward department stores dated from midcentury, but large-scale retailing was not common until about 1880.[119] Some of the best-known stores (Macy's, Bloomingdales, Lord and Taylor, B. Altman) were in New York City. However, department stores drew consumers not just there but also throughout the country — in Columbus (Lazarus), Cincinnati (Shillito), Chicago (Marshall Field and Carson-Pirie-Scott), Philadelphia (Wanamaker), Boston (Jordan Marsh, R. H. White), and San Francisco (Emporium). Gimbels began in Vincennes, Indiana, and expanded to Milwaukee and Philadelphia by century's end.[120]

Department stores were particularly dependent upon newspaper advertising because of the economic structure of the retailing business. The primary test of a department store's performance was *stock-turn,* that is, the number of times stock on hand was sold and replaced each year.[121] This high volume allowed lower profit margins and lower prices relative to the smaller neighborhood stores. But this emphasis on volume sales required a steady stream of customers. The emphasis on volume also dictated price reductions (sales!) on slow-moving lines of goods. All this—volume, steady clientele, and sales—dictated newspaper advertising and, in most cases, daily advertising. Before radio and television, only newspapers could reach a sizable segment of the population on a daily basis.[122]

Advertising was not a complete guarantee of financial success; a store still needed good merchandise and good sales people. But department store managers and the leading department store trade publications recognized that advertising provided the necessary linkage between consumer and supplier. A writer in the trade journal *Dry Goods Economist* stressed the need for advertising: "Might as well try to successfully run a soda fountain under the Pyramids of Egypt as to try to run a modern dry goods store without a reasonable use of printer's ink, unless you want to run it into the ground."[123]

Macy's, one of the largest and most successful department stores of the era, relied extensively on newspaper advertising. Between 1888 and 1902, Macy's spent an average of 1.58 percent of total net sales on advertising.[124] The percentage essentially doubled during that period, rising from 1.16 percent in 1888 to 2.11 percent in 1902. The percentage increase is more impressive when one notes that net sales grew by nearly 400 percent during the same period. The advertising budget for 1888 was just under $60,000; it rose to $113,531 in 1896 and to $227,142 by 1902. In the late 1890s, Macy's had a five- or six-column ad in Sunday newspapers and a single column weekdays. One historian notes that New York City newspaper readers could "hardly escape" seeing a Macy's ad daily.[125]

By the 1890s, the leading newspaper advertisers in New York City and Boston were all department stores.[126] One advertising trade journal writer estimated in the late 1890s that a single large New York City department store would spend $100,000 a year on advertising.[127] John Wanamaker, the department store magnate in Philadelphia, believed that newspapers were the best marketing device for his stores. "I owe my success to newspapers," he said.[128] Wanamaker reportedly believed that he could not go a single day without newspaper advertising.[129] Wanamaker estimated that he spent as much as $400,000 a year on advertising in Philadelphia in the late 1890s.[130]

Conclusions

American society and journalism changed dramatically during the nineteenth century. The partisan press declined as the vibrant (and disputatious) mainstream of American journalism. New definitions of news arose, nurtured not by political parties but by business interests.

Partisan journalism declined as politics itself declined in popularity. Moreover, party patronage could not keep pace with the expanding financial needs of the American newspaper. Party patronage had been most useful for the small-scale low-cost newspapers of the 1820s and 1830s. The metropolitan newspapers of the late nineteenth century needed additional funds to survive.

This decline in the presence of politics and patronage is highly significant, for it marks the weakening of political parties as the key constituency of the press. It also marks the decline of a press, and of news, that revolved around politics.

Parallel to this partisan decline was the rise of a business view of the press: newspapers should be unaffiliated with party, dedicated to presenting interesting news to ever-expanding markets of readers. The new journalism was born and bred in the city. The city was an arena in which the press *could* grow (large populations meant larger reading audiences), but the city also created new roles or functions for the press that newspapers in small cities and towns soon copied. Just as urbanization helped to create a new vision of the press, so, too, did the broader developments of industrialization help shape the American newspaper, both in metropolitan areas and in small cities and towns across the land. Just as politicians had once seen the press as the key to electoral success, so now business people came to see the press as the key to financial success. This rise of a new constituency is highly significant, for it brought with it a new set of expectations and demands for the press.

All this provides the foundation for the commercialization of news. The decline of politics and party patronage cut the press adrift from its partisan moorings. The rise of a business vision of the press pushed it toward a market-driven environment. With industrialization, advertisers—who valued the marketing potential of the press— emerged as the key constituency of the press. By century's end, editors defined news in an environment far different from that of the age of Jackson.

Chapter Three

Advertising and the Press

The questions always to be asked are: What class of persons does this publication reach and are they likely to be purchasers of my goods?

          —Advertising Experience, *June 1899*

In 1894, a writer for the advertising trade journal *Fame* observed that it was a well-known fact that only about a half dozen U.S. newspapers (out of nearly 16,000)[1] could survive without advertising. Advertising accounted for the majority of a newspaper's revenues, he argued, noting that subscriptions at best "barely pay for the cost of the white paper" on which the news is printed. He added that publishers and editors needed to consider carefully the needs and interests of advertisers.[2]

Advertising's presence in the American press grew dramatically in the late nineteenth century. Advertising was virtually nonexistent at the time of the Civil War; by World War I, advertising expenditures had passed a billion dollars annually.[3] In 1905, two leading advertising specialists wrote that ". . . advertising, as we understand it, is a development of the past half century."[4]

Advertising's importance to the press grew by two key measures: the total revenue it produced and the proportion of overall income it represented. Alfred McClung Lee estimates that advertising brought in $39 million for newspapers and magazines in 1879, rising to $71 million in 1889 and $96 million by 1899.[5] More significant is the *percentage* of income newspapers and periodicals derived from advertising. Alfred McClung Lee estimated that in 1879, newspapers received 56 percent of their revenues from subscriptions and 44 percent from advertising. Twenty years later, those percentages were nearly reversed— 54.5 percent from advertising and 45.5 percent from subscriptions.[6]

Whatever the exact proportion, advertisers clearly had arrived as the key constituent of the American press. Their vision of the press was fundamentally commercial in nature. They cared little about the news function of the press and sought, instead, to assure that newspapers

served their own marketing needs. They provided much of the newspapers' revenues and profits, and, in turn, expected a grateful press
to help them when possible. Early in the century, politicians had
certain expectations of the newspapers they subsidized. They demanded partisan advocacy for themselves and their parties and loyal
support for their political ventures. By century's end, as political patronage waned and advertising grew, advertisers who patronized the
newspaper came to expect advocacy on *their* behalf. They frequently
demanded that newspapers be loyal supporters of their business ventures. In short, advertisers propelled the commercialization of news.

The Growth of Advertising

The Rise of the Advertising Agency

The focal point for advertising's growth and importance in the late
nineteenth century was the advertising agency. The agency served as
the major link between businesses and the press. One Ohio editor
estimated in the 1890s that at least 80 percent of American advertisers
placed their ads in newspapers through agencies.[7] Although the
foundations of the advertising agency were laid in the middle of the
century, their major growth came in the last two decades of the century. In 1888, one publishers' group listed 228 advertising agencies in
cities large and small.[8]

Businesses increasingly relied upon advertising agencies to help
them place ads and run advertising campaigns. That reliance made
sense. Most business people would have had difficulty choosing the
appropriate medium for their advertising, given the 20,000 newspapers and periodicals in the country at the time, with overlapping circulations and varying reading audiences and publication schedules.

For newspaper publishers, advertising agents virtually spun gold.
One Ohio publisher in the 1890s noted that advertising agents "add
to the publishers' prosperity unmistakably," guaranteeing the newspapers' livelihood and financial success.[9]

Organizing Advertising

Advertising agents succeeded because of their promotional acumen
and their ability to coordinate marketing campaigns. For businesses,

they designed advertising campaigns and slogans, placed ads, and attempted, in a limited way, to measure advertising efficacy. For newspaper publishers, advertising agents became reliable middlemen who understood the newspaper business and who often guaranteed payment for ads. Also, it was better and easier to deal with 10 agents than 200–300 individual businesses.

Beyond their day-to-day work in advertising sales and copy, agents contributed to the organization of advertising through their trade publications and newspaper directories.

Advertising Trade Journals

Published monthly or quarterly, advertising trade journals circulated among clients, would-be clients, advertising aficionados, and others interested in the newspaper or magazine industries. Approximately two dozen advertising magazines appeared in the late nineteenth century, including Pettingill's *Advertisers' Magazine*, Charles Austin Bates's *Criticisms* (New York), *Kings' Jester* (New York), Procter and Collier's *Advertising* (Cincinnati), Rowell's *Printers' Ink* (New York), and Artemas Ward's *Fame* (New York). New York led in the largest number of advertising-related magazines, but publications also appeared in Boston, Chicago, Kansas City, and Columbus, Ohio.[10] These publications extolled the virtue of advertising, gave advice to businesses about advertising, provided critiques of ads, and discussed leading advertising issues (circulation, demographics, deceptive advertising).

Newspaper Directories

All U.S. newspapers were surveyed for key information about circulation and readership; the surveys were then compiled in newspaper directories. George P. Rowell issued the first of these directories in 1869. By the middle 1890s, about a dozen directories appeared annually; others, every other year. Among the directories published in the 1890s were: *Rowell's American Newspaper Directory; N. W. Ayer and Son's Newspaper Annual; R. L. Watkins* (Prospect, Ohio) *Annual Advertisers' Gazette;* Charles H. Fuller (Chicago) *Advertisers' Directory;* J. W. Thompson's *Red Book;* Edwin Alden and Brothers (Cincinnati) *Newspaper Directory;* Dauchy and Company (New York City) *Newspaper Directory;* Bates and Morse (New York City) *Advertiser's Handy Guide;* and Pettingill's *Newspaper Directory* (Philadelphia, New York, and Boston).

Following Rowell's example, the directories provided businesses with crucial information about newspapers: circulation, time of publication, political affiliation, and subscription cost. Some directories also provided information about the economic environment of each town (industries, banks, and universities) that would be valuable to businesses that wanted to advertise efficiently.

Through all this, advertising agents sought to fashion successful marketing campaigns and assure that the American press would serve advertisers' interests. Significantly, advertising agents worked to graft their own definition of what constituted good newspapers onto American journalism by focusing on characteristics of newspapers (such as circulation and demographics of the reading audience) that best suited their business goals.

Where to Advertise?

Circulation had always been a badge of pride for American newspapers. In the 1830s, Francis Preston Blair had cited the growing circulation of the Washington, D.C., *Globe* as proof of the strength of the Jacksonian Democrats and the popularity of Andrew Jackson and his policies. Circulation was still important in the late nineteenth century, but for a different reason. For advertisers and publishers alike, circulation had business value.

The first step in successful marketing was in choosing the proper newspaper (or magazine) for an ad, and the first step in choosing that medium was to look at its circulation. Because advertising agents wanted to assemble the largest possible audience for their ads, they naturally valued high circulation. In its 1877 newspaper directory, the S. M. Pettingill and Company Advertising Agency pointed out that knowledge of newspaper circulation was essential to good business.[11]

But ascertaining the actual size of a newspaper's circulation was not easy. Publishers were not required by law in most states to give a truthful accounting of their circulation. Moreover, given that higher circulation generally meant higher advertising rates, publishers had a financial incentive to inflate their circulation claims.

Such mendacity was no surprise. Dr. R. V. Pierce, a leading patent medicine manufacturer (and, one assumes, no amateur in distortion), complained in 1896 that "circulations are so greatly exaggerated in many cases that what one is getting for his money is an unknown quantity." Pierce argued that newspaper publishers were adept at juggling their books and even falsifying post office receipts (of issues mailed), to create "verification" of inflated circulation claims.[12] Various advertising trade journals repeatedly warned that publishers lied about circulation.[13]

Because advertisers and their agents depended upon newspapers as marketing tools, they needed accurate circulation figures. *Advertising Experience* in Chicago claimed, "The advertiser has a right to every bit of information which the publisher can give him that will aid him in determining just what he is getting for his money."[14] Scarcely an issue of an advertising trade journal appeared without some discussion of circulation.

The proper definition of circulation also provoked debate. Some publishers counted the number of newspapers printed, while more conscientious publishers counted those actually sent to news dealers and delivery boys. Some advertising agents and advertisers argued that the latter figure was too high because it did not account for unsold copies, that circulation meant only papers readers actually received.[15]

Advertising industry leaders were confident that their efforts to provide reasonable circulation estimates and to force publishers to tell the truth were successful. Artemas Ward, who edited the advertising magazine *Fame*, wrote in 1892: "Every year brings us nearer to the truth in the statements made by publishers, if taken on average. Colossal liars will always exist, but year by year advertisers become better informed."[16]

Demographic Concerns

Most advertisers sought a particular market for their goods, and it behooved them to advertise in newspapers that reached those consumers. Some products were clearly appropriate only in certain areas. As the Pettingill agency noted in its 1877 newspaper directory:

What use would it be to advertise a fever and ague cure in a locality where there never had been and in all probability never would be a single case of fever and ague? Such advertising would be as absurd as for a dealer in ardent spirits to rent a corner for a bar-room in a hall devoted to the exclusive use of the Sons of Temperance. And this same fact or principle runs more or less through all manner of advertising.[17]

Such logic dictated that advertisers view readers not as a monolithic mass but as differentiated by class, location, purchasing power, religion, or even race.

Advertising agencies dealt extensively with the composition and quality of newspaper circulation, bringing a businesslike approach to the selection of media. *Advertising Experience* advised that a particular medium should not be chosen because a potential advertiser likes its looks or editorial stand or because other advertisers use it. "The questions always to be asked are: What class of persons does this publication reach, and are they likely to be purchasers of my goods?"[18] A writer in the advertising trade publication *Kings' Jester* advised that advertising agents should consider "the character of a publication when making contracts," including its class of subscribers, territory, and "the pecuniary condition of the people whom it reaches."[19] One writer in the trade journal *Advertising Experience* warned that a medium's appropriateness for a product must be judged carefully. It wouldn't pay, he contended, to advertise Van Camp Pork and Beans in a Jewish newspaper.[20]

Advertising agents promised to provide help in choosing among the thousands of publications with their thousands of different audiences.[21] In particular, advertising agents claimed to provide the demographic information that could guarantee careful and systematic advertising campaigns. Lack of care could doom an advertising campaign, regardless of how much money a businessman was willing to spend. The Pettingill agency correctly noted that most advertisers "had no competent knowledge of the newspaper and periodical press; no accurate information with regard to the special wants of special localities; no mastery of the best modes of reaching the minds of the people in that persuasive manner which sets money in circulation through the channels of trade." Only the advertiser who depended on the expertise of advertising agents could expect to survive.[22]

Charles Austin Bates, in New York City, advised advertisers to consider the class structure of various newspaper audiences. As an example, he cited the shrewdness of a St. Paul, Minnesota, department store advertising manager who tailored his ads to his audience, relying on the *St. Paul Dispatch* to reach "the great masses" while choosing the *St. Paul Pioneer Press* to reach upper-class patrons.[23] Artemas Ward, in *Fame*, warned businesses that some cheap newspapers with high circulations were read quite quickly ("to kill ten or fifteen minutes of time spent in a street car") and thus not a good investment despite the relatively low cost of advertising.[24] And an article in *Printers' Ink* urged businesses to advertise in newspapers that reached women. The advertising expert Nathaniel C. Fowler wrote:

Much as men read advertisements, women read them more. The advertisements in a popular daily, the people's paper in every sense, are read by women as much as the news itself. The advertisers in a decent paper give to the women of home as important information as any other part of the newspaper, and they are read just as carefully, sometimes more so. *A woman who does not read advertisements would not be a woman, consequently all women read advertisements.* Women are the buyers of everything everywhere. Women are the active partners of home and the silent partners of the office . . . Woman is the pivot which turns trade.[25]

Advertisers, it was clear, admired a newspaper more for its potential as a marketing tool than as a civic institution.

Advertising's General Influence on Content

In addition to circulation and demographics, advertisers and their agents also were concerned in every way with the treatments newspapers used to showcase their ads. They were concerned with where the ads appeared, what the ads looked like, and what the news content around the ads conveyed.

Placement of Ads

Advertisers and their agents in the late nineteenth century often stipulated that a particular advertisement must be placed in a specific position (e.g., page 2, top of column 2) and in particular relation to other content (e.g., next to regular newspaper articles [called reading matter] and *not* next to other ads). Naturally, advertisers also often insisted that their ads never appear near an ad from a direct competitor.[26]

Between 1889 and 1893, R. H. Macy and Company, a New York department store, sought to avoid pages on which competitors' ads were concentrated. Macy copy appeared regularly as the only advertisement on a page otherwise devoted to reading matter and usually appeared alongside articles of special interest to women.[27]

Placement had become a standard part of advertising contracts by the latter years of the century; few ads were allowed "the run of the paper." The manufacturers of Peruna, a popular patent medicine, were emphatic on placement. One ad contract in 1884 stipulated: "Said advertisement is to appear at the foot of a column alongside of reading matter in its entirety, or immediately following reading matter, on any page with not less than two columns reading matter . . ., reading matter published as advertisements not to be regarded as purely reading matter . . . Under no circumstances do we pay for insertions not made EXACTLY as per agreement."[28] Dauchy and Company, a New York advertising agency, stipulated that ads for Dr. Mettaur's Headache Pills "not be placed in the same column with, or adjoining any other Medical Advertisement."[29] And N. W. Ayer and Son made a similar demand in the 1880s for another patent medicine, Mishler's Iron Bitters.[30]

Given their importance to a newspaper, advertising agents could be adamant about placement. When one Ohio editor tried to negotiate with N. W. Ayer over placement of an advertisement, the agency refused, noting: "You are greatly mistaken if you think at any time we stated we would accept less than top of column and next to reading on Iron Bitters, or first advertisement following a broken column of reading [matter]." Ayer, noting that the editor wanted to place the ad among other ads, said, "We could not think of that."[31]

When the same Ohio editor would not provide the placement required by the firm Edwin Alden and Brothers, that agency withdrew the advertising order.[32] One advertiser left the *Chicago Daily News* altogether because the paper accepted an ad from his chief competitor.[33] The editor of a small daily in Ohio said that placement issues were the bane of his existence.[34]

Reading Notices

Some advertising agents also sought to present their commercial messages as news. In the late nineteenth century, "reading notices"— essentially, advertisements designed to appear as news articles— were popular with advertisers and advertising agents. They believed that such ads would draw more readers because they appeared to be news. Consequently, readers would tend to be more receptive to a product promoted by a supposedly independent source [viz., the newspaper] than to an advertiser's pitch. The *Pittsburgh Leader* in 1897 ran one story headlined:

COASTED DOWN THE CAPITOL STEPS
A Bicyclist at Washington, D.C., Successfully Performs
A Remarkable Feat

The article included a line-drawing of a bicyclist riding down the capitol steps, and the article began by noting that his actions, done as part of a wager, took a good deal of nerve. The third paragraph digressed to nerves in general, the fourth to ill health and its symptoms, and by the sixth, the reader got the real pitch: Dr. Pierce's Golden Medical Discovery. "It makes rich, red, pure blood and sends it to every part of the body, renewing and rejuvenating every tissue and fiber . . . it gives new life."[35] A reading notice in the *Cincinnati Tribune* in 1894 said:

FRIENDS OF THE PUBLIC
Men of Mark Who Gather
And Transmit the News
AND HOW THEY EXHAUST
Some Personal Sketches and Incidents
Of Brain Workers in the Highest
Walks of Life

The story at first appeared to be a profile of the Washington, D.C., press corps. The first two paragraphs detailed the hard work of these correspondents. The third paragraph repeated that Warners' Safe Cure was a sure way to avoid the illness that came from too much "brain work."[36]

Reading notices were common in papers, from small-town weeklies to metropolitan dailies. Some advertisers claimed that they relied solely on reading notices. Major American newspapers, such as the New York *World*, had standardized rates for these notices. The front page cost far more than inner pages. The *Chicago Herald* in the early 1880s interspersed reading notices among its regular news articles.[37] The *Chicago Record*, in the 1890s, carried a warning in the article "A Dangerous Diet: How Meat May Cause Disease and Even Death"; these fates could be avoided (one discovered, in the fourth paragraph) by using Warners' Safe Cure.[38]

Some papers in smaller towns, such as the *McMinnville Telephone Register* (Oregon), carried a variety of reading notices, including ones that touted the healing power of Dr. Williams' Pink Pills for Pale People.[39] Even partisan papers could not resist. One 1886 campaign daily in McMinnville, Oregon, published reading notices for consumer products.[40]

Perhaps only the naive could read for long without realizing the commercial nature of the article, and there were complaints that the reading notices debased the newspaper. One editor warned that a reader might admire the "nerve and ingenuity" of advertisers who cleverly cloaked their sales pitch in news-story style, "but he will bear an indefinable grudge against the paper."[41]

Some publishers, however, were either unaware of or chose to ignore the potential for backlash. The *St. Paul Globe* endorsed the reading notice, arguing that often it was read by "persons that do not intentionally peruse advertising . . . It is insidious, attractive and interesting. Appearing as it does in a semi-news way, it will be read and thoroughly considered, because it carries the endorsement of the medium in which it is published."[42]

Advertising agencies insisted on making these ads look like news. Pettingill's placed one ad as a reading notice in 1870 with instructions to publishers that it was to appear "as a selected article . . . with nothing to indicate it as an advertisement."[43]

In some instances, though, advertising agents found they did not need to insist. Many publishers welcomed the ads disguised as news because they wanted the revenue.[44] In fact, many newspapers readily printed reading notices, charging top prices for doing so. In the 1890s, most Boston newspapers, for example, allowed reading notices. Only the *Boston Herald* changed the type face for the reading notices while other papers produced the reading notices in the same type face as their other articles. The *Boston Herald* charged two dollars a line for page 1 with a minimum of 50 lines.[45] The business manager of Joseph Pulitzer's New York *World* was happy to have the revenue from reading-notice advertisements.[46]

Reading notices also appeared because they were often a condition of general advertising contracts. In 1885, for instance, N. W. Ayer and Son placed an ad for a patent medicine called Athlophoros (touted for rheumatism and neuralgia). Part of the contract stipulated that the newspaper publish a reading notice. "It must be set in the type used by you for reading or news matter; and must be the first notice following pure reading matter."[47]

Dauchy and Company, the New York advertising agency, stipulated in its contract with a small Ohio weekly that the newspaper endorse one of the products (Professor Loisette's Memory Discovery and Training Method) of the agency's client in order to obtain the contract for the advertisements. The agency even provided the endorsement: "Prof. Loisette's Memory System is creating greater interest than ever in all parts of the country and persons wishing to improve their memory should send for his prospectus free as advertised in another column."[48]

Edwin Alden and Brothers Newspaper Advertising Agency placed ads for one product and asked each newspaper taking the ads to run, without charge, a short endorsement of the product: "We would call the attention of our readers to the advertisement of McMonagle and Rogers' 'Fruit Flavors' in this issue. The goods are meritorious and are all that is claimed for them. Be sure and see advertisement in this issue."[49]

At least one nineteenth-century publisher resisted demands for reading notices. John Hopley, of the *Bucyrus Journal* (Ohio), had constant battles with several agencies, including N. W. Ayer and Son, Dauchy and Company, and Edwin Alden and Brothers, over reading notices. Hopley refused to run reading notices. The whole scheme, he said, didn't mesh with his idea about news and newspapers. He told the Alden agency that he would not sandwich among "bona fide reading matter" that which was disguised "either in setting or in composition or in both, as reading matter."[50] Hopley noted that reading notices were not the style of his paper and that he had consistently refused to print them. Even though many "papers may have fallen into this custom," Hopley said that "many filthy beasts and a very few who are a trifle better than filthy beasts" chewed tobacco, yet *he* would not do so.[51] Hopley blamed the subversion of the newspaper on advertising agencies.[52]

Whether this fight characterized advertising agency–newspaper relationships elsewhere is not clear. Edwin Alden and Brothers, a Cincinnati advertising agency, insisted that the insertion of reading notices was a practice "followed by thousands [of newspapers] all over the country."[53] Dauchy and Company, a New York advertising agency, told Hopley that he must supply reading notices to keep his contracts. Dauchy continued: "Of course, if you have a rule . . . which prevents you from inserting reading notices, *then we shall have to give up the idea of trading with you this time*, which would be a pity, as we do not know whom we had rather do the business with than you . . . The reading notices must go in if anything else does."[54] Although some agents would not dump a publisher for such a refusal, this agent conceded that most publishers would expect to lose the contract, and so would comply with demands to print ads disguised as news.[55]

Many nineteenth-century advertisers did not share Hopley's notions that news and advertising were not to be mixed. Rather, they saw the newspaper as central to their marketing campaigns, and wanted to make the best use of the newspaper in that marketing process. What better way than to use the guise of a news story?

Newspaper Puffs

Some advertisers expected free publicity and promotion from newspapers in the form of "puffs." Puffs were often quite subtle: a review of a concert might note, in passing, that the music came from a Steinway piano, or the gun used to catch a dangerous criminal was a Smith and Wesson.

Some advertising agents emphasized that puffs were the price for more advertising. A writer in the trade journal *Advertising World* contended that puffs were advertisers' "due." A newspaper, he wrote, "should mention its advertisers whenever possible, in a newsy way. In fact it should do everything within its power to bring results to those who are using its columns."[56]

Publishers said that the pressure for puffs from advertisers was constant and intense. H. E. Hoard, publisher of the *Montevideo Leader* (Minnesota), complained that advertisers saw the news columns as their own province and constantly were trying to get puffs within news stories.[57] At their annual meeting in 1877, the members of the New York Press Association noted the pressure on them to give puffs to advertisers.[58] Even *advertising* publications admitted that the pressure for puffs was great.[59]

This surreptitious form of advertising was so common that one agency, the Ferguson Telegraphic News Service, specialized in reading notices and newspaper puffs. In its ads, the firm promised to concoct news stories that would promote products and claimed to have helped several clients (including Unexcelled Fireworks Company, Starin's Transportation Company, Brighton Beach Racing Association, and Traveler's Insurance Company).[60] Ferguson said such ads ran in newspapers like the *St. Louis Republic* and the *St. Louis Globe-Democrat*, the *Boston Globe*, *Boston Post*, and *Boston Traveller*, the *Denver Republican*, the *Omaha Bee*, the *Chicago Times* and *Inter-Ocean*, the *Cincinnati Enquirer* and *Cincinnati Commercial*. Ferguson's proposals won the praise of the advertising trade journal *Printers' Ink*, which noted that this was a "common enough practice" and highly beneficial for advertisers.[61]

The schemes for obtaining free publicity were many. One writer offered to promote products in a serialized story. The story would concern the adventures of some young boys; as a subplot, they would go door to door selling a particular product, which would be mentioned by name.[62] *Printers' Ink* advised businesses that they could earn publicity by sponsoring good deeds. A department store, for example, could refurbish a house that had just burned; the value of such publicity would be worth far more than the cost involved.[63] Advertisers also discovered that they could attract newspapers' attention by sponsoring product-related events. The E. C. Stearns bicycle company organized a transcontinental bicycle race in 1896 in conjunction with Hearst papers in San Francisco and New York. More than 400 riders participated, all using Stearns bicycles. *Printers' Ink* praised the event as "one of the greatest advertising feats ever attempted."[64]

The Blurring of News and Advertising

Exactly where advertising agents' pressure ended and a newspaper owner's participation began is hard to determine and perhaps not crucial, for both were willing participants in the commercialization of newspaper content. The line between reading notices or puffs and legitimate stories about business enterprises, for instance, was sometimes narrow.

Businesses received much laudatory coverage in the late nineteenth century. One small-town weekly, the *Oakland Observer* (Oregon), printed in its *news* columns a variety of promotions for local businesses:

C. H. Medley, the model grocery man, is up with the times. He keeps a full line of everything to be found in the first class grocery. Specialties are scarce at this season of the year, but an assurance is given that Medley has a full line, if any can be found.

One of the best ways of saving money is to exercise care in spending it. It is extremely improvident to spend your money for inferior articles. Money is hard to get and it should be expended carefully. When you buy of E. G. Young & Co., you have the assurance that you are not expending money foolishly for you know by actual experience that they sell only the best goods at the lowest prices.[65]

Another small-town weekly, the *Woodburn Independent* (Oregon), routinely carried a "Local Jottings" column with news on society, local churches, farms and crops, crimes, and other local events. Interspersed among the items were promotions for local businesses:

Read Matsons new ad. in this issue.

Spectacles and eye glasses at Cornwall's.

Oregon Oak Axe handles 25¢ at the Bargain Store.

One dollar a pair for kid gloves. They are hummers! At Goodman's.

LADIES IN UNIFORM. That's the way they look, unless they buy their dresses and jackets at Goodman's; where there are no two alike. New styles, pretty cheap.[66]

Other small-town and small-city newspapers frequently carried similar promotions for businesses in their news columns.[67]

In metropolitan areas, department stores received a lot of news coverage. Some stories were legitimate news, for the opening of a department store in the late nineteenth century was a major event in most American cities. In Cincinnati, in 1894, a large crowd gathered to watch the electric lights (yet another bit of excitement) go on in a new department store, illuminating the building room by room. When the entire building was lighted, the crowd cheered.[68] In the same year, the *Chicago Herald* was not exaggerating when it hailed the opening of a new department store as a public event.[69]

But department stores also represented the single largest source of advertising revenues for newspapers. Within that context, some articles seemed closer to puffery than to real news. Perhaps they were reading notices, perhaps puffs, perhaps news. The point is, whatever the source of the story, it looked to be a news story but was essentially a form of advocacy for an advertiser. The *Boston Globe* covered a large sale at one department store, calling it a brilliant success that would continue next week with even better bargains. That day, the *Globe* also carried display ads for the store.[70] Such stories were common.[71] The *Cincinnati Tribune* heralded the opening of one store, noting:

KNOPF'S & CO'S OPENING
IF YOU MISSED IT YOU WILL BE VERY SORRY
As It Was One of the Greatest Events of the Kind That Ever
Happened Here[72]

Some editors and publishers were, at least from the advertising agent's point of view, inexplicably narrow-minded in defining news. The *Boston Globe* began to segregate advertising and news in the late 1880s. But agents rose to the challenge and sought ways to circumvent vigilant editors who wanted to fill their columns only with genuine news. The goal of agents remained that of obtaining "advertising free of cost."[73]

One way to circumvent purist notions of news was bribery. Advertisers and their agents paid reporters to write flattering news stories. In 1894, *Printers' Ink* carried the article "How to Get Free Advertising Legitimately," which advocated modest retainers for reporters to ensure puffs. "Any concern of average size and importance would do well to pay a good newspaper man a few dollars a week to look after their interests in this respect."[74] Another *Printers' Ink* article noted: "A five dollar bill in the hands of a reporter or editor will often secure what fifty dollars would not buy at the counting room."[75] A third *Printers' Ink* article advised hotel managers to pay reporters a few dollars a week to kill stories that might make the hotel look bad, such as a suicide, and to assure coverage of other, more favorable items (for example, the presence of a celebrity at the hotel).[76]

Printers' Ink was not alone in urging advertisers to curry favor with reporters. The Boston trade journal *Profitable Advertiser* also counseled that cultivating reporters would pay great dividends. Hotels should give their best low rates to newspaper reporters because "the advertising that will result will be of incalculable value," the journal said. It advised railroads to give free passes to reporters. "Nothing will ever be said about a railroad by a reporter that will injure it, if the railroad has made the reporter its friend. The friendship of newspapermen never hurt anything, not even a great corporation, and it is apt to do an inestimable amount of good."[77]

Befriending or even bribing reporters was not always enough, however. As *Printers' Ink* noted, suspicious editors could easily delete promotional items in regular news stories or completely kill stories created to promote some business. In that case, the advertiser was advised to try to influence the news through the newspaper's business office. *Printers' Ink* said, "Free advertising for advertisers should generally be secured through the business end of the paper."[78]

Not all advertising agents advised trying to subvert the newspaper through the counting room. Artemas Ward of *Fame* argued that "the space of a newspaper belongs to itself. The honest way to use it is to leave the news departments absolutely free from business office interference or control, and then sell the advertising space for what it will bring."[79]

Whether *Printers' Ink,* with its exhortations to bribe and payoff, or Ward, with his respect for the integrity of the *news*paper, represented the majority within the advertising industry is not clear. But it is clear, at least from various complaints within the newspaper industry, that editors faced pressure from advertisers through the newspaper's business office.

Editorial Support for Advertisers

Advertisers also expected newspapers to become their advocates before the public. In particular, advertisers wanted newspapers to support brand-name products and to oppose licensing and regulation of the patent medicine industry.

The battle over brand-name products was a major one in the emerging consumption society. Advertisers invested large sums to market a particular brand-name product (often over-the-counter drugs), only to find competitors offering cheaper generic versions of that product. This substitution of generic for brand-name products drew the wrath of brand-name producers, for they found competitors trying to serve the demand created by the brand-name advertising. The targets in the "war on substitution" were merchants (primarily pharmacists or grocers) who offered something "just as good" as the brand-name article requested by the customer. For instance, a merchant might try to convince a customer that his own locally prepared remedy was comparable to (and often cheaper than) a heavily advertised national patent medicine.

In the war on substitution, advertisers enlisted the help of American publishers. Mott Pierce, president of a patent medicine group, urged publishers to fight substitution "to expose fraud. Your responsibility is great."[80] Advertisers asked newspapers to editorialize against the practice. Advertising agents in New York circulated short editorial squibs to American newspapers to include in their columns; for example:

Say No and stick to it when you are urged to buy something "just as good" as the article you asked for. Please notify this office if any store keeper or clerks in town try to palm off a substitute on you . . . The publishers of this newspaper will be glad to learn of any case where an attempt is made to give a customer a substitute for some proprietary article of established reputation.[81]

Some publishers complied. S. G. McClure, editor of the Columbus *Ohio State Journal,* said in 1901 that it was the duty of newspapers to expose the fraud of substitution. But McClure did not discuss exposing such fraud as a public service; rather he said it was a "business courtesy . . . which every newspaper . . . can afford to extend."[82]

Advertisers also wanted newspaper support in preventing licensing or regulation of patent medicines. Many legislatures proposed labeling laws that would have required patent medicine manufacturers to disclose product contents. Such disclosure would have hurt sales, in part because many consumers—some of them temperance people—were unaware of the amount of alcohol in many elixirs. Consequently, patent medicine manufacturers battled the labeling laws as strongly as they could, and they enlisted newspapers' help.[83] In 1897, the *Cincinnati Post* condemned a proposed Ohio labeling law as an attempt "to drive proprietary medicines out of the state . . ."[84] And some companies insisted that such editorial support be guaranteed in advertising contracts. J. H. Zeilin and Company inserted the following clause in its advertising contracts with newspapers in the 1880s: ". . . nothing shall be published which may be calculated to injure the business of J. H. Zeilin & Co., or by mentioning the same in censure; but will exert ourselves to protect and promote their interest."[85]

Pressure on the News

Attempts at Censorship

Given their view of the American newspaper as an integral part of their own marketing campaigns, some advertisers and their agents were not shy about offering editors and publishers advice on what made a good newspaper. In particular, advertisers and their agents wanted newspapers to be bright and entertaining, compliant to advertisers' political and social interests, and to suppress news that might hurt an advertiser. Advertisers opposed anything that did not further that effort.

One advertising trade journal writer said that newspapers shouldn't attack one another because it detracts from their dignity, rendering them less useful for advertising.[86] An article in the advertising journal *Fame* assailed the *New York Tribune* because it printed the obituary for James G. Blaine near two ads, one for soap and one for patent medicine. The *Fame* writer argued that this was "truly a horrible setting for the last tribute to a dead statesman."[87] Yet *Fame* long had insisted that ads should be next to news, so what was the difference here? The article argued that the obituary's placement was "one of *questionable value to the parties whose advertisements figured in it.*" The obituary should appear in a special supplement (without ads) so as "not to shock the proprieties of its readers."[88] Or, one should add, so as not to hinder the pitch of the salesman.

Advertisers and their agents also sought, at times, to sanitize the news by suppressing articles that might harm their business image. *Ad Sense*, a Chicago trade journal, attacked newspaper coverage of a fire at a New York cigar plant. Newspapers had printed the name of the firm; inspectors said the fire was due to "a poor grade of tobacco." *Ad Sense* argued that the name of the firm should not have been printed. "As the firm's name was used, there is every reason to believe that it must have counteracted many thousands of dollars' worth of paid publicity."[89] The double standard here is obvious: names should be included when they could help a business (in puffs) but deleted when they might cause harm. The expectation was that the newspaper be an active partner in both promoting and shielding businesses and their products.

In New York City, a dry goods store on Sixth Avenue tried to suppress news that it faced a lawsuit. Store workers had falsely accused a young woman of shoplifting and had roughed her up before police arrived. She had stolen nothing and decided to sue. A representative of the store visited the major New York City dailies, urging that the business be identified only as a dry goods store. Five of the six newspapers approached complied; the New York *Sun* alone printed the name of the store and recounted the visit from the store's representative.[90]

Some advertisers and their agents tried to dictate to newspapers on issues far removed from their own ads. In the 1896 presidential campaign, some advertisers and their agents made clear that newspapers should not endorse the Democratic nominee, William Jennings Bryan, whom they saw as antibusiness. The advertising trade journal the *Newspaper Maker* warned publishers that they would lose advertising contracts if they endorsed Bryan.[91] William Randolph Hearst's *New York Journal*, a prominent Bryan supporter, experienced a major drop in advertising in the second half of 1896, with many advertisers boycotting the paper until Christmas.[92]

Advertisers didn't intrude just on presidential endorsements. Department stores in New York City also boycotted the New York *Evening Post* in the late 1890s over its editorial policies on a protective tariff. The background to the boycott is worth noting, for it illustrates how advertisers sought to influence the coverage of news that somehow affected them, even tangentially.

The New York *Evening Post* long had endorsed free trade and, in the 1890s, assailed high protective tariffs. The paper criticized the New York customs in early 1899 because customs officials, reacting to pressure from New York City merchants, were strictly enforcing a $100 limit on foreign goods brought into the country. Americans who had been abroad found their baggage carefully searched upon return.[93]

The *Evening Post* attacked this "baggage abuse" and argued that the money the government might recover from strict enforcement of the $100 limit was hardly worth the trouble. The *Post* also assailed local merchants who had lobbied for the crack down. In particular, it attacked Christopher C. Shayne, president of the merchants' association.[94]

The merchants disliked the *Evening Post's* crusade, and they most objected to a *Post* article on March 8, 1899, based on an interview with a woman who had been searched at the customs house. She asserted that the $100 limit was unreasonable because clothes made abroad (particularly in London and Paris) were better than those made in New York:

WOMEN'S CLOTHES ABROAD
TO BE HAD BETTER AND CHEAPER
THERE THAN HERE
Gowns from Paris—Workmanship and
Design—Prices of London Coats—Ex-
periences at Home—Dresses Soiled
on the Pier

The article cited prices paid for clothes abroad and reported that the same articles cost more in New York City.

Within a few days, most dry goods merchants had withdrawn advertising from the *Post*. The paper noted that absence, saying that the merchants had asked the paper to cease its discussions of "baggage abuse." The *Post* argued that the issue centered on the principle of editorial independence; the paper supported free trade and vowed that advertisers would not succeed in censoring it.[95]

The boycott created sympathy for the newspaper. The paper ran supportive letters to the editor in late March and throughout much of April 1899. One letter writer attacked the boycott as a "press gag." And a minister, C. C. Parkhurst, said he did not believe one department store owner's denial of pressure on the *Evening Post*. "I do not find my own mind greatly affected by his denial, and seemingly, other minds have been just as little affected."[96] Even other newspapers sided with the *Post*, which excerpted supportive editorials. The Chicago *Times-Herald* condemned the merchants for a conspiracy to boycott the *Post*. The Chicago newspaper noted that such advertising pressure was common, claiming that on more than one occasion Chicago merchants had threatened the *Times-Herald*, but its resolve had usually prevented boycotts.[97]

One advertising trade journal decried the department store action but indicated that the newspaper had probably invited such retribution. According to *Profitable Advertiser*, the *Evening Post* had "an inalienable right to express its opinions," but it had no right to expect the New York merchants to tolerate such views. In such situations, "it would appear that a newspaper should exercise a little discrimination in such matters . . . especially when such articles are not of vital importance anyway."[98]

Promoting the "Bright Side of Life"

Many advertisers and their agents attempted to impress upon editors and publishers their own broad definition of news and then leave it to those editors and publishers to deliver a product compatible with advertising. The general guidelines were fairly clear.

First, newspapers should avoid politics. In particular, they should avoid criticism of public officials, because it might alienate readers and diminish the appeal of advertisements.[99]

Second, newspapers should be optimistic and happy about the world. One advertising trade journal writer noted that advertisers wanted newspapers to "present more of the bright side of life." Discouraging, gloomy news depressed the public, and depressed readers were not good consumers.[100] One writer argued that circulation and advertising could be maintained only when news columns became "brighter, better, newsier, completer than before." The successful newspaper, he wrote, "must be vivid, bright, pyrotechnic enough in its features to force itself into popular attention at every turn."[101] One advertising trade journal writer defined the ideal newspaper as having short paragraphs "about fine things and fine people," and many interesting small items. Also it should not take politics too seriously, "for that is the humor of the crowd."[102]

Third, newspapers should contain something of interest to everyone in the potential reading audience, but particularly to women. Nathaniel C. Fowler, one of the most prolific promoters of advertising in the late nineteenth century, argued that the successful newspaper prints something for everyone:

The great daily, filled with the bright news of the day to whet the appetite of the readers with its children's columns, its women's column, its column of style, its miscellany, is the paper which has the great circulation and the one which pays the advertiser more to the square inch than any other paper can pay to the square foot. There is not a single case on record of any daily paper succeeding in this or any other country which does not arrange its matter, from editorials to its news, so as to be pleasantly absorbed by the women of the day.[103]

Conclusions

Advertisers operated with a vision of the press that valued the newspaper's ability to help them make money. Given advertisers' importance to the press in the late nineteenth century, that vision propelled the commercialization of news.

Early in the century, politicians had seen the newspaper as the tool for reaching voters. As such, they subsidized newspapers, provided advice, and expected political support and advocacy in return. Advertisers, late in the century, viewed the newspaper as a tool for reaching consumers. They subsidized the newspaper through their advertising, provided advice, and expected support and advocacy for their interests in return.

Advertisers saw newspapers as integral to their marketing campaigns and evaluated newspapers on how they could aid in such efforts. From the advertisers' point of view, the quality of a newspaper was based not on its ability to produce news but on such things as the size of its circulation, the demographic profile of its readers, and its willingness to accommodate advertising interests (through placement, reading notices, puffs).

Advertisers' marketing vision of the press went beyond their own ads. Advertisers defined "news" as whatever would best support their advertisements rather than as information the public needed. They worked hard to force their self-serving definition of news on publishers and editors. They appropriated the form of a news story to hide their ads as news reports (e.g., reading notices). They demanded that newspapers endorse their products as a condition of receiving advertising contracts. They demanded (and often received) puffs in newspaper columns. When stymied by recalcitrant editors or publishers, they bribed reporters or newspaper business-office personnel to obtain favorable "news" coverage. They demanded that newspapers support their battles against substitution and patent medicine labeling. As they saw it, the entire newspaper was their province. Some advertisers went so far as to blacklist newspapers that endorsed the 1896 Democratic presidential nominee. And advertisers clearly preferred news free from unpleasantness.

Many editors gave in to the pressure from their major patrons and commercialized the news. Reading notices and puffs were common. Some editors gave great prominence to articles featuring—and praising—advertisers.

But not all editors buckled under. Some resisted the pressure for free advertising, some refused to disguise ads as news, some refused to change their political views to satisfy advertisers. But the pressure to do so was ubiquitous, constant, and at times successful.

In the advertisers' view, this definition of the newspaper made sense. In looking out for their own interests, advertisers naturally wanted the newspaper to be an efficient marketing vehicle for their products. But the interests of advertisers were not the only ones that mattered, and therein lay the problem. Advertisers did not see the inherent public value of news; rather they saw newspapers as merely the setting or format for what really mattered to them—their own private interest in selling goods. The power and influence of advertisers within the newspaper industry were great, and they used that power and influence to promote the commercialization of news.

Chapter Four

Newspapers as Businesses

When a Missouri editor complained in the 1890s that "people seem to forget that a newspaper is primarily published as a business enterprise," he was simply pointing out one key aspect of journalism of that era: the newspaper was a business, and news was valued and defined within that context.[1]

As businessmen of the late nineteenth century, American publishers were involved in the mass production of a commodity that demanded attention to organizational and financial concerns that would have been quite foreign to the crusading political editors earlier in the century. Publishers coordinated production, sales, profits, and journalism in what many times were huge, diverse operations. In this light, content often was valued for its contribution to the overall business rather than for its inherent ability to inform.

Moreover, the newspaper in the vision of *those who produced it* had changed since the early nineteenth century. Although some newspapers still had close ties to politics, many publishers and editors had a much more myopic view of their role in society. Many thought of the newspaper as *nothing more* than a business. As one trade journal writer noted in 1898, "The difference between a haberdasher and a newspaper is that the former sells furnishing goods and the latter sells advertising space and news."[2] Thomas Downey, circulation manager of the *Boston Globe*, said in 1901 that "in printing a newspaper, the primary object is to make money."[3] C. F. Chapin of the *Waterbury American* (Connecticut) said that "the newspaper, then, reduced to its lowest terms, is a business enterprise . . . It has owners like a shop or factory, who like it best for the dividend it pays. It has employees who earn a living by giving to it the labor of their hands and brains. It has customers, as the term is used, subscribers and advertisers, to whose tastes both editor and publisher must cater if their patronage is to be kept."[4]

Economic considerations fueled this business mentality. Managers came to organize, oversee, and then to dominate the press of the era. Spiraling start-up and operating costs forced papers to develop business strategies to survive. Such strategies brought order and organization to the press, but they also influenced the news process and thus contributed to the commercialization of news.

The Growth of a Managerial System

As business historian Alfred Chandler, Jr., has noted, a key characteristic of changes in American business in the nineteenth century was the emergence of a managerial class to organize and coordinate the diverse operations in production, distribution, and marketing of goods. The rapid growth in the mid-1800s within the American newspaper produced differentiated units, each with specialized functions. In American newspapers, such units generally were (1) news gathering and editing, (2) production (typesetting, printing, folding, etc.), (3) distribution and circulation, (4) advertising, and (5) business (e.g., accounting).[5]

Each unit had its own manager and responsibilities. The advertising department sold space and dealt with advertising agencies.[6] The circulation department dealt with distribution and delivery. The production department dealt with typesetting and the other aspects of physical production of the paper. Only one department had news as its major concern.

The varying perspectives on news and newspapers *within* the newspaper can be seen in the discussions of the National Association of Managers of Newspaper Circulation, established in 1899. Circulation managers defined a successful newspaper as one with high circulation and prompt delivery, and they saw the editor as a major obstacle to these goals. As one circulation manager argued, editors were too far removed from the reality of life to understand what news should be included in a paper. The obvious lesson was, the circulation managers knew best:

While he [the editor] may write editorials that will stir the community to its depth and move nations and empires with their force and logic; yet his ideas of what is news may be all wrong. What does he know of the "kind" of news demanded by his readers? That, it appears to me, is the paramount question at issue. Do they want a paper whose columns are filled with the stuff commonly called "yellow"? Do they want sensational stuff or orthodox sermons? Do they want suicides, murders, etc., dished up daily, or reports on church conferences and the more commonplace happenings of every day life? . . . The circulation manager is in the best position to understand the tastes of the reading public.[7]

Circulation managers complained bitterly about editors who delayed publication because of some late-breaking event. G. R. Mundy of the *Philadelphia Inquirer* said, "I think one thing would be to get your papers to understand that the circulation department of today must run the newspaper and not the editorial department."[8] Circulation managers felt compelled to advise editors about news stories and to suggest articles that would bolster circulation.[9]

Supervising the various departments of the newspaper was the publisher. The emergence of the publisher signals a substantive and far-reaching change within the internal organization of the American newspapers. Early in the nineteenth century, newspapers were frequently the product of a single person who produced the content, set the type, ran the press, managed the business affairs, and often delivered the paper. Some larger papers had more elaborate organization; in the 1830s, the *Boston Daily Advertiser* had an editor, a chief political writer, and several correspondents. But most staffs were small. That changed by the end of the century. The differentiation and specialization that arose led to the advent of a business manager (the publisher), who eventually headed the entire operation. Accompanying this change was a new attitude about the roles of publishers and editors. A common refrain was that the Age of the Editor—exemplified by men like Horace Greeley or Samuel Bowles or Henry Raymond—was gone. Some industry commentators clearly didn't lament the loss of the old days. One trade journal writer noted that editors suffered from a myopic concentration on news. Only the publisher kept an eye on the *entire* newspaper, providing the financial security that healthy advertising and circulation could bring to news gathering. "The publisher is a man of business, business over all. He conducts the paper that it shall yield profit. He does not begrudge money for news or for anything else that will make his paper more attractive, but he withholds consent to expenditures beyond income."[10]

Many publishers, who often were hired for their managerial ability, were not attuned to journalism. Lucien Swift became the managing editor of the *Minneapolis Journal* after seven years in the company's business office. The new editor of the *Chicago Mail* in 1895 had been a railroad passenger agent with a reputation as a good advertising writer.[11]

Newspapers might be just one of several businesses owned by the same person. In 1888, the *Boston Herald* was sold to John Stetson, who also owned the *Police News,* a theater, a bar, a pool room, and a loan office.[12] H. H. Kohlsaat bought the Chicago *Times-Herald* in the 1890s after making his fortune in the restaurant and bakery businesses.[13] Merchants established the *Cincinnati Tribune* in 1893.[14] Walter Edge, who owned the largest hotel advertising agency in the United States, started a daily newspaper in Atlantic City in the mid-1890s.[15] A street railway magnate, Charles T. Yerkes, headed the syndicate that bought the Chicago *Inter-Ocean* in 1897.[16]

So the vision of the newspaper as a business should not come as a surprise, given the background and concerns of many publishers. One publisher noted that the newspaper was not a missionary or a charitable institution but a business that published "news which the people want and are willing to buy." Sales were the criterion of success. "If the people will not buy and read your paper, you may as well leave the business."[17] When William D. Sohier took control of the *Boston Journal* in the 1890s, he sought to dispel any doubts about his goals for the paper: "This property has been bought for business purposes . . . You cannot put that too strongly."[18]

Profit and loss naturally were concerns of editors throughout the century; even crusading antebellum editors wanted to eat! But the overriding vision of the newspaper as a profitable business was a jarring change from early in the century.

This business mentality made sense. Newspapers had evolved into costly news-gathering and news-processing institutions by the late nineteenth century. The capital needed to run a daily newspaper dictated close scrutiny of costs. When the *New York Recorder* was established in 1891, an industry observer wrote that it began with "practically unlimited capital behind it" from men who were aware of the huge investment needed to start a daily newspaper.[19] A well-established metropolitan daily newspaper could sell for hundreds of thousands of dollars in the 1890s. The New York *Mercury* sold for $300,000 in 1894 and the San Francisco *Morning Call* for $360,000.[20]

The daily newspaper (particularly in metropolitan areas), like other American businesses involved in mass production, was capital intensive. Property and buildings were expensive, as was the machinery for producing papers. Around 1890, James Gordon Bennett bought a block of land for $300,000 and spent $600,000 building a new home for his *New York Herald.*[21] The new office of the *Chicago Tribune* in the 1890s cost $750,000 — $500,000 for the building and the balance for new machinery.[22] Industry observers valued the *St. Paul Dispatch* at $500,000 in 1895, with a new four-story plant and 12 new Mergenthaler electric Linotypes. The *Dispatch* was hardly one of the country's largest-circulation dailies. Its evening edition in the middle 1890s reached about 31,000 customers and its Sunday edition about 35,000.[23]

Business Costs

The cost of doing business naturally rose during the century. Costs were greatest for metropolitan newspapers. *Printers' Ink*, the advertising trade journal, estimated in 1890 that most newspapers in large cities (e.g., New York, Chicago, Boston, San Francisco, St. Louis, Cincinnati, Philadelphia, Baltimore) each spent between $5,000 and $12,000 annually on special dispatches, more than $100,000 on local news, about $100,000 a year on composition, and more than $200,000 a year on paper.[24]

The nation's largest newspapers, in New York City, naturally had the highest expenses. *Printers' Ink* estimated that the New York *World* spent more than $1.3 million a year on special dispatches, local news, composition, and paper. Other urban papers also required large amounts of money. *Printers' Ink* estimated that the *Cincinnati Enquirer* spent $252,000 a year for paper. The *Chicago Herald* used 60–70 tons of paper for every Sunday edition, costing about $265,000 a year.[25] In 1896, the *St. Louis Globe-Democrat* reported that its average annual expenditure on telegraphic services was $140,000.[26] Four New York newspapers (the *Times, Tribune, Herald,* and *World*) usually replaced their type once a year, at an average cost of $13,000.[27] E. W. Stephens, a journalist, noted that the *New York Tribune*'s expenses in the 1880s ran about $900,000 a year.[28]

The size of newspaper organizations grew, too. In 1860 the *New York Herald*'s corps of editors and reporters numbered only seven, and two or three others contributed regularly to the newspaper. By 1890, the corps numbered over 100, not counting special correspondents in American news centers and Europe.[29]

Machinery also increased costs. A major characteristic of American business in the late nineteenth century was the shift from labor-intensive organization (many workers doing one task, such as scores of people setting type by hand) to capital-intensive organization (work primarily done by machines that required relatively large amounts of capital to acquire). To a great extent, American newspapers followed that pattern.

As some business historians have noted, mass production refers not so much to the size of production as to its speed. Hence, many American businesses, including newspapers, adopted relatively expensive high-velocity machines that replaced human workers.[30] In 1893 at the Chicago World's Fair, R. Hoe and Company exhibited a new press—the Quadruple Stereotype Perfecting Printing Machine—that could print and fold 48,000 four-, six-, or eight-page papers an hour. Hoe had also produced the Sextuple Stereotype Perfecting Press, which the *Chicago Herald* called "a monster machine of double the capacity of the quadruple . . . The full sized press costs a fortune."[31] The San Francisco *Call* had two quadruple Hoe presses in 1895, giving it a capacity of 96,000 eight-page papers an hour.[32]

In 1892, one journalist marveled at the speed in production. He recalled that the press at his first newspaper could print 1,000 impressions an hour. That was in 1840. By 1890, on his last newspaper job, the paper was printed from stereotype plates on six perfecting presses with an aggregate capacity of 72,000 complete quarto pages an hour. He added, "These rapid improvements have involved the sinking of considerable capital."[33] An Ohio publisher recalled that "printing on the old hand press was a slow process, about 300 an hour being the outside limit."[34]

Changes in production at the *Chicago Herald* in the 1880s demonstrate the use of high-velocity machinery. The *Herald*'s early edition had to be produced fairly quickly to make the first mail trains, which carried them to suburban subscribers. In the early 1880s, the *Herald* had only two relatively small presses, each producing an eight-page newspaper. To produce a 16-page paper, the *Herald* ran half on each press, employed workers to put the two parts together, and hired extra mailing clerks to compensate for the time lost to collation. By the 1890s, however, the *Herald* had a double-decker press that could print the entire 16-page newspaper, ending the need for the collating crew and the extra mailing clerks. The paper could be shipped out of the office within 20 minutes of the time it came off the presses.[35]

The business mentality of late nineteenth-century journalism was clearest in metropolitan newspapers, where publishers faced the most intense competition for news and advertising and where costs were the greatest. But publishers and editors of smaller papers had similar concerns. The editor of a small Ohio daily in the 1890s noted that newspapers had once been the province of "the men who loved their calling not for the money it made but for the opportunities it afforded for self growth and for exerting an influence in the world.

They loved journalism for its own sake; it had other charms for them than money." Now all that had changed. He went on to say that the tremendous success of the newspaper in the late nineteenth century had attracted "the sensitive attention of capital."[36] J. A. Woodson of the *Sacramento Record Union* (California) said in 1892 that metropolitan newspapers were not alone in their attention to business concerns; country newspapers had "a tendency to ape city airs."[37] John Hicks of the Oshkosh *Northwestern* noted in 1886 that all newspapers were essentially businesses: "Publishing a newspaper is a species of manufacturing. The printing office is a factory" and should be run in a businesslike manner.[38] W. S. Cappeller, editor of the *Mansfield News* (Ohio), said in 1892, "The old idea that the press is a public charity is fast passing away."[39] And A. H. Lowrie of the Elgin, Illinois, *News*, said in 1885, "Primarily the paper is made to sell."[40] The president of the Nebraska Press Association said in 1896, "We should . . . conduct our business upon business principles."[41]

Some big-city business practices had not reached the smaller dailies or country weeklies of the late nineteenth century. Operating costs were much lower outside large metropolitan areas. In 1892, one writer in *Newspaperdom* estimated that only about $6,000 capital was needed to start a small country daily.[42] In 1891, Adolph Ochs, in Chattanooga, Tennessee, said a small daily newspaper, with a circulation of 750, could be run for about $10,000 a year, with advertising accounting for 60 percent of revenues.[43] One writer estimated in 1889 that small local weeklies could be started with $1,000.[44]

Though various newspaper industry writers recognized that costs were lower outside metropolitan areas, they noted that costs were rising even in the hinterlands, and that revenues were substantially lower there. That meant editors and publishers needed to pay close attention to costs.[45] At meetings of publishers and editors from small dailies and country weeklies in the middle 1890s, business concerns were high on the agenda. In the early 1890s, discussions at the National Editorial Association annual meetings included newspaper business departments, circulation growth, contests and premiums (to lure subscribers), profits (how to get them, how to increase them), and advertising revenues.[46]

Editors and publishers of small dailies or country weeklies were involved in businesses other than journalism. In his study of Washington Territory newspapers in the late 1880s, Myron K. Jordan found that 58 percent of the territory's 30 editors also were engaged in other businesses.[47] J. J. Browne, a banker and real estate developer in Spokane

Washington, owned the *Spokane Chronicle*.[48] Some editors served as
the local agents for various patent medicine businesses.[49] J. E. Day,
editor of the weekly *Woodburn Independent* (Oregon), was a business
agent for the Mutual Benefit Life Insurance Company of Newark,
New Jersey.[50]

Business Strategies Guiding Newspaper Operations

Four major imperatives guided newspaper owners in the late nineteenth century: they sought to keep operating expenses low; they
tried to produce a fairly predictable product; they marketed their
product to the public; and they banded together to establish mutual-
aid groups (trade associations) to promote their business interests.

Keeping Operating Expenses Low

Given the large amount of money needed to start or maintain an
urban daily newspaper, publishers naturally sought to keep operating
expenses low. Wages constituted a major operating expense. Publishers, like many other businessmen of that era, wanted to get the most
work from their employees for the least money possible. Publishers
complained about labor costs, sought to prevent or destroy collective
bargaining, worked to reduce wages, and avoided overtime.

Part of the fascination that technological advances, such as typesetting machines, held for publishers stemmed from the belief that
such machines would cut costs and minimize worker power. John
Mack, publisher of the *Sandusky Register* and president of the Associated Ohio Dailies, told his fellow Ohio publishers that the typesetting machine "is destined to solve the most difficult problem of the
present in the business management of the daily paper; a problem of
the control of organized labor."[51] One industry writer in *Inland Printer*
estimated that Linotypes cut composition costs about 75 percent for
most newspapers.[52]

Publishers were equally tight with reporters. They commonly used
two systems of compensation—a fixed weekly salary or payment by
space (by the amount of copy actually printed).[53] One Boston publisher noted that in the 1890s he frequently shifted reporters between
a fixed salary and space. He told his fellow publishers that such a

system produced the most news for the least amount of money.[54]

In general, pay was low.[55] Bonuses or pay raises were awarded only for stories of unusual interest or excitement. One reporter, dispatched to cover a drowning, discovered that the putative victim had really survived. He cursed his fate. If she had drowned, he would have received six dollars for the story instead of two. Moreover, he had "lost the chance of another profitable" assignment.[56] Even reporters had incentives to commercialize news. Pay was not only low, it was also frequently reduced unilaterally by management. Some papers consistently cut wages earned by space writers[57] while demanding high productivity. Reporters often were expected to produce a dozen or more articles a day.[58]

Given these conditions, few stayed in journalism for long. Reporting became the province of the young and inexperienced. In New York City, for instance, most reporters around the turn of the century received from $3 to $10 a week on space. One trade journal writer pointed out that only young reporters—without families or other responsibilities—could live on such a salary.[59]

Long hours and low wages drove out older men: "Gray hairs and men in their prime are at a discount," wrote one observer in 1896, "and only the sprinter and champion or prize winners are tolerated."[60] Gray hair was "a scarlet letter" in a business that preferred young workers.[61]

The long hours and the hard work harmed reporters' health. When E. O. Chamberlin of the New York *World* died in 1898, one writer remarked that he "fittingly died almost in harness" as a "comparatively young man" at age 38. "His death illustrates to a high degree that the newspaper profession exacts from its devotees an expenditure of nervous and mental force not paralleled in any other business."[62] When journalists proposed building a home for retired newspapermen, one writer noted that such a project was praiseworthy but unnecessary because so few held newspaper jobs until retirement.[63]

While such systems of underpayment and overwork may have kept labor costs low, they reduced the quality of the newspaper. Experienced reporters left the business. Bonuses for sensational or exclusive stories created incentives for the reporter to get stories at any cost. One San Francisco reporter, Carrie Cunningham, posed as a consoling friend to an accused murderer; she extracted his story and reported it despite her fervent promise of confidentiality.[64]

One writer noted that this system of pay was "an ever-standing invitation for the reporter to exaggerate and fake."[65] Indeed, fabrications to obtain higher pay or to produce stories quickly were not uncommon.[66]

The experience of one young journalist demonstrates how labor policies distorted news. John W. Fox left his North Carolina home for New York City in the middle 1880s with the dream of becoming a great reporter and man-about-town. He was excited about living in a city rich with theater, artists, and educated people, and he planned to graft himself onto the life of refinement through his writing and new acquaintances. He became a reporter, but he found he had "no time for study or for social pleasures." He worked long hours—at times from 10 A.M. until after midnight—seven days a week. In his lonely letters to friends back home, he wrote, "I am cut off, you see, from all social pleasures as theaters, in fact from any kind of amusement." Newspapers were not what he had expected, and journalists often failed to get the news. Indeed, news was a highly malleable entity. Space payment, he discovered, led to exaggeration, fabrication, and padding. "Men write 'for space' and with no higher aim it is no wonder that there is little regard for the truth." And despite his own perturbation, he found himself engaging in the same deceits—in part just to save time: "I find I am falling into the habit of tinging things and of trusting to my imagination. I am frequently forced to this because I have no time and because it is often impossible to make personal investigation. I know that this is dangerous and that one will become so that he is unable to describe things as they really are, that finally he will actually deceive himself without knowing it."[67]

H. L. Mencken once described his experiences at the turn of the century when he worked for a Baltimore newspaper. He and two other reporters faced the difficult task of writing a story about a long-shoreman who had drowned. The task was simplified when they joined in fabricating an identity for the deceased. Over beers at a nearby saloon, they created the details so that their editors would find the various accounts consistent.[68] Similarly, interviews often were faked. As one writer said, journalists "write interviews with people they never saw; put words in the mute lips of dying men," all in the rush for a good story.[69]

The resulting news was vivid if not altogether true. The *Brooklyn Weekly* noted that stories "are dressed up and high spiced and all sorts of imaginary conversations and episodes are introduced."[70] The Scripps-McRae papers promised to blacklist anyone who fabricated stories, but many in the industry (although they condemned it) believed the practice was widespread and unlikely to end unless the space system was scrapped.[71]

Through all this, as historian Ted Curtis Smythe notes, reporters had an economic incentive to wrap the news in sensationalism and to fabricate facts when time was short or the task difficult. The entire system—of keeping labor costs low and eventually producing slovenly reporting, sensationalism, or outright fabrication—rested upon this relatively new vision of the American newspaper as a money-maker. Certainly, antebellum political editors watched expenses, but they were not totally consumed by a business mentality that put the bottom line ahead of the news. Rather, they were consumed with a partisan mentality that valued news for its political function.

Reporters were not the only workers whose wages worried publishers. If the proceedings of the American Newspaper Publishers Association (ANPA) and of various state publishers groups are indicative of general concerns, publishers' greatest worries centered on printing and production workers (compositors, typographers, and other skilled mechanical workers), who seemed far more likely than reporters to organize trade unions in the late nineteenth century. In 1895, ANPA members discussed methods to increase productivity among compositors and typographers while avoiding collective bargaining.[72] Publishers agreed on the necessity of a united front within the newspaper industry to fend off unions.[73] In 1899, ANPA members discussed strategies to avoid "labor dictation."[74]

At smaller papers, the effort to keep costs low meant that editors supplemented their local news coverage with syndicated material. A newspaper in Iowa City, Iowa, for example, could buy a full-page of articles on Lincoln's birthday from the American Press Association at a relatively low price, because the APA sold that package to thousands of other newspapers across the country.[75] The Franklin Illustrated News Service for Daily and Weekly Newspapers offered a variety of features in the 1890s, including reports on the Commission of Inquiry into the Pullman strike, the "palatial home" of boxing champion Jim Corbett, and various international intrigues (e.g., "Spies of the Mikado [Japan] Put to Death in China").[76]

This reliance on relatively low-cost news supplied by others was a significant development for late nineteenth-century journalism. The information purchased ranged from the up-to-date news provided by the Associated Press to features (such as fiction, fashion, and personality profiles) provided by companies such as the American Press Association.[77] Mass-produced "news" usually was far cheaper than home-produced news, so many newspapers relied upon so-called newspaper unions (unrelated to labor unions) to provide them with half or more of each issue's content. The unions produced an eight-page paper, filling some pages with general news, innocuous editorials, and other material. The number of preprinted pages varied from perhaps as few as three to as many as six. The format also varied, with some papers containing "patent insides," others containing "patent outsides." The remaining pages were blank. These partly completed papers were shipped to local editors, who filled the blank pages with local news and ads.[78] As one trade journal noted, this process was popular because it saved money.[79] Thousands of weeklies did this. *Printers' Ink* estimated in 1894 that more than 7,000 U.S. weeklies relied upon five of the newspaper unions: Western Newspaper Union (with 2,484 clients), A. N. Kellogg Company (1,962 clients), Chicago Newspaper Union (1,400), Atlantic Coast Lists (1,450), and the San Francisco and Northern Pacific Union (192). In all, the leading newspaper unions provided copy to about three-fourths of the nation's weekly newspapers in the latter decades of the nineteenth century.[80] In 1892, *Newspaperdom* said that small dailies, too, relied on the unions extensively, although it did not estimate how many did so.[81]

These patent insides (or outsides) benefited both the newspaper unions and local publishers—at least financially. The unions bought paper and other materials in large quantities at reduced rates, generally rewrote news published elsewhere to minimize news-gathering costs, and sold advertising for the preprinted pages to enhance profits. The unions then sold the half-full newspaper to local publishers for about the cost of what the publisher would have paid for blank paper alone. That actually saved the publisher money, because he didn't have to pay for composition and other production costs on the preprinted pages. The patent insides and outsides let publishers increase the size of the paper without additional costs for reporting or production.

Many publishers and some industry observers argued that the use of mass-produced articles helped to sustain the weekly or small-city daily, allowing it to offer a variety of features and other articles without bankrupting the local publisher. W. S. Cappeller of the *Mansfield News* (Ohio) said that the material was fresh and that he used it extensively.[82] A writer in *Newspaperdom* in 1892 noted that such services greatly expanded the local press: "A vast mine of literary and news matter is opened up for the use of any publisher who desires to buy it; and the cost is so trifling that the richest treasures are within easy reach of the poorest."[83]

However, newspaper quality suffered. The same writer noted that the newspaper unions at first seemed to be "a blessing," but "underneath the pleasant exterior there is an insidious danger which has sent more than one unlucky editor to his doom." Editors had only a very loose control over the kinds of material they received. An editor could select fiction, articles on social events, sports, and so on, but had no control over specific articles. "Sometimes entire pages are made up of available and desirable articles; but more frequently, they contain one or more columns that the editor does not want, but which he has to buy in order to get the one or more columns that he does want. And it is herein that the editor begins to find himself between the devil and the deep sea."[84]

Many editors discovered, to their chagrin, that the so-called news itself was recycled. One Ohio editor contended that such articles were just rewritten news that 70 percent of all readers had already seen in other newspapers or magazines.[85]

In 1900 and 1901, the trade publication *Inland Printer* ran a series of articles entitled "Establishing a Newspaper," written by O. F. Byxbee. He noted that the greatest argument in favor of the ready prints was their cheapness but that editors essentially gave up control of their newspapers to outsiders when they relied on the newspaper unions: "The character of the matter is frequently not what would be selected to appeal to the particular needs of a community, is often unattractively presented and poorly made up, and in the advertising are included many ads that should not be in a family newspaper."[86]

The patent insides did, indeed, include a fair number of ads. The April 10, 1891, issue of the *Oakland Observer* (Oregon) carried newspaper union articles on its second and third pages; inserted among them were ads for various patent medicines, such as Hamburg Breast Tea, Dr. Judd's Electric Belts, and California Fig Syrup. Reading notices also were common.[87]

Troubling, too, was the fact that a neighboring newspaper would contain the same stories from the same newspaper union. In 1891, the editor of the *McMinnville Telephone Register* (Oregon) said he received 17 newspapers via exchanges that had identical reading matter word for word with three of these duplicate newspapers from the same county. "These boiler-plate concerns should kick to their owners, the patent-makers of Portland . . . It is about as legitimate a business as piracy or smuggling."[88] Yet the newspaper unions thrived. Publishers apparently found that the benefits outweighed the costs, despite problems with freshness or redundancy.[89] The editor of the *Monmouth Democrat* (Oregon) defended ready-prints from the McMinnville attack: "The 'patent' arrangement enables the country publisher to give his readers more reading matter than he could pay for having set up in his own office, and as it is miscellany or general news (and well selected), it makes no difference where it is set up."[90]

The consequence of such mass-produced news, so well attuned to the cost-cutting mentality of the newspaper business, could be seen most clearly in the kind of news produced. As Nathaniel Fowler noted, the need to produce fairly timeless, inoffensive news for thousands of newspapers (and millions of readers) produced bland content. "It must be uncompromising to the extreme," he wrote.[91]

One issue of one newspaper (the McMinnville, Oregon, *Daily Campaign* of April 3, 1886) provides an example of this kind of content. The paper that day had these newspaper union articles: "A Chinese Barber in New York City," "Sea Sickness," "Widows of India," "The Chrysanthemum" (and its growing popularity), "A Persian Street," "How Starch Is Made," and "The Lamp: Its Origins."[92] The Toledo, Oregon, *Yaquina Post* for January 26, 1901, carried the newspaper union stories "The Blouse Beautiful" and "A Harvard Man's Surrender—Prof. Frye Captured by the Bright Eyes of a Cardenas Maid." The *Oakland Observer* (Oregon) on April 10, 1891, carried the newspaper union stories "How the French Serve Beef," "Earliest Use of Forks," and jokes:

Hotel Porter: Will you please refrain from spitting on the floor, sir?
Western Granger: What, do you expect me to hit the wall from here?[93]

A Predictable Product

Predictability is essential to successful and profitable mass production, and predictability in both supply and product was the goal in late nineteenth-century American business in general. For instance, as the American tobacco industry grew in the 1880s and 1890s, entrepreneurs acted to ensure a steady supply of high-quality tobacco. To guarantee such a supply, James B. Duke and others in the industry began to produce their own tobacco rather than relying solely on market sales from farmers. This increased predictability of supply, in quality and cost. Similarly, predictability in the product was desired, and mechanization made this possible. Before extensive mechanization in the early 1880s, cigarettes were rolled by hand. Naturally not all were identical in size or shape. Such an unpredictable product naturally defied systematic packaging or marketing. The Bonsack machine made cigarettes uniform in the 1880s, so one could know how many cigarettes could actually fit in the prepared container.[94]

A measure of predictability came to characterize the newspaper industry as well, and from a business perspective, such predictability was as necessary for newspaper manufacturers as it was for cigarette manufacturers.

For county weeklies and small dailies, the patent insides and outsides were important parts of a predictable news product. These smaller newspapers also relied extensively on correspondents to provide them with a cheap and steady supply of news.[95] Hugh Wilson, an editor from Abbeville, South Carolina, said that most newspapers could get fairly reliable local and regional correspondents for little or no pay.[96]

Metropolitan newspaper publishers and editors also wanted a predictable news product. Like other business people of their era, they wanted a steady supply of the raw materials for their commodity. And the ultimate raw material was news itself, so papers began planning news events. In big cities, where newspaper competition was often fierce and scoops could mean lucrative street sales, *waiting* for news wasn't always the best financial strategy. W. A. Swanberg notes that William Randolph Hearst's first big splash in San Francisco journalism came from coverage of a spectacular hotel fire in Monterey, California. But as Swanberg writes, Hearst couldn't expect a spectacular fire every day, so he turned to cultivating his own news.[97]

One reporter who was well-known for creating news was Elizabeth Cochrane Seaman, who wrote for Joseph Pulitzer's New York *World* under the pseudonym Nelly Bly. She first secured a job on Pulitzer's paper by feigning a mental collapse to gain entry to New York's Bellevue Hospital. After 10 days there, she escaped and exposed the cruel treatment of its inmates. In other pursuits, she jumped off ferry boats to test the readiness of rescue teams (they didn't do very well, but she survived), and she posed as a young immigrant to expose fraudulent employment agencies. Her newspaper reports forced public attention on social problems and spurred reform.[98] But she was significant not just for the evil her reports exposed. She was also the catalyst for events about which her paper could report. Her activities provided for a steady supply of newspaper raw material.

The role of the newspaper as a catalyst of events led not just to articles about social ills but also to articles valued for their vividness and color. Nelly's famed race against the fictional Phineas Fogg—she went round the world in 72 days, eight days faster than Phineas' record—was for fun and excitement. It generated both attention for Nelly and circulation for the *World*. For nearly 10 weeks, the *World* had a predictable supply of news that would capture the readers' attention.

Nelly's successes inspired others. In San Francisco and later in New York, William Randolph Hearst employed writers such as Winifred Sweet (Annie Laurie) to copy Nelly's escapades.[99] The *Chicago Herald* sponsored its own expedition to the North Pole and covered it extensively, until ice crushed its ship ("The *Herald*'s Arctic Ship, the Ragnvald Jal, Ground to Pieces in the Polar Region").[100] And the *Pittsburgh Leader* hired its own detective to track down a murder suspect.[101] (The detective bungled the case; the suspect recognized him and escaped.)

Other newspapers around the country sent their reporters to inspect public hospitals, insane asylums, and jails, at times undercover and at times with permission of officials involved. Sometimes there was a thin line between this reformist zeal and transgressions of the law. One Los Angeles reporter, feigning insanity, was committed by a judge to an asylum. The reporter later confessed his deceit to win release (and write about his experiences), but the judge cited him for contempt for "unlawful interference with the administration of justice."[102] In Chicago, a reporter tried to steal a body from the city morgue to expose slipshod security. But security wasn't all that bad after all, and the reporter was arrested.[103] A *Cincinnati Tribune* correspondent who was white was even disguised as a black crime suspect to test whether Kentuckians might try to lynch him. Fortunately for the correspondent, no lynching was attempted.[104]

The beat system also provided some predictability to news gathering and production. Reporters went to the same locations to check news each day, frequenting places where news could be expected. This system allowed predictability both in news gathering (the number of reporters covering such routine items would probably not vary greatly from day to day) and in output (news articles would deal with trials, arrests, injuries, fires, deaths, and so on). The extensive coverage of public institutions—courts, police and fire departments, government, hospitals, and asylums—best exemplifies how beats made news predictable. Beat reporting also helped to hold down labor costs; newspapers were collecting information that already had been processed to some degree by someone else. Getting stories from the courts and the police blotter was much more efficient than getting them from the unstructured world at large.

Table 4.1 Percentage distribution of news produced, by type of system

	Chicago Record		*Pittsburgh Leader*
	April 1–9, 1893	April 30–May 4, 1893	March 8–14, 1899
Beat system (%)	82.3	90.7	71
Nonbeat system (%)	17.7	9.3	29
Articles (N)	159	108	324

Note: See note 105 for a breakdown of the complete data for the news categories within each system.

The rationale for government coverage cannot be reduced merely to financial convenience. The notion of the press as protector of the public from official depredation probably contributed even to the routine coverage of city hall or the police. Nonetheless, it is important to consider the financial benefits of such a system of news gathering. A content analysis of the *Chicago Record* (in 1893) and of the *Pittsburgh Leader* (in 1899), as shown in table 4.1, demonstrates the reliance on a beat system.[105]

Some newspapers' coverage depended almost entirely on a beat system. The *Portland Recorder* (Oregon), for example, in 1893 had five reporters. Usually they were deployed to routine sources of information: the courts, city hall, police department, jails, morgue, hotels, and train depot. On Sundays, religious services were given extensive coverage.[106] In a lengthy article in 1896, the Salem, Oregon, *Capital Journal*, a daily newspaper, outlined its major sources of news. All were part of a regular beat system: police, courts, city government, county government, state capitol, and the town's chief hotel.[107] In a business where many papers bragged of their resourcefulness in bringing readers the freshest news, a lot of content was routine.

In the late nineteenth century, some American newspapers—particularly in metropolitan areas, where news-gathering costs were greatest—began operating city news associations to cover the most basic beats. In the early 1890s, the Baltimore News Association had one reporter at each police station, with a phone to a central office where all member newspapers could obtain news.[108] Boston newspapers established the Boston City Press Association in 1891 to save money by providing common coverage of standard news items, such as the courts, statehouse, and city hall.[109] *The Journalist* reported that New York City had two similar associations in the early 1890s.[110]

Marketing the Product: Newspaper Self-Promotion

As in other late nineteenth-century businesses, competition necessitated advertising. Most publishers did not advertise in other publications, but they certainly trumpeted their accomplishments in their own columns.

Readers were reminded often of the vast resources and efforts of newspapers. The *St. Louis Republic* touted its Texas bureau as evidence of its far-flung news operations.[111] The *Pittsburgh Leader* noted that its telegraphic services and Associated Press reports "make it what it is today, a model American newspaper."[112] Sometimes, news events and how they were covered were blurred in the rush toward self-promotion. Headlines in the *Cincinnati Tribune* on December 2, 1893, read:

ACROSS THE RIVER
The *Tribune* Again Complimented
on its Accuracy
NEWPORT COUNCIL MEETING
Quote from the Kentucky
Sister Cities in the Make Up
of Cincinnati's Reliable
Family Newspaper

After a series of articles on street improvements, the *Tribune* noted that it was "looking after the welfare of the people of Cincinnati . . . We have already saved the city thousands of dollars by directing attention to reckless expenditure of the people's money and we propose to do a good deal more in this line."[113] And, following the Republican League Convention in Cincinnati in 1895, the *Tribune* claimed it published the best account of the event, while professing "the *Tribune* is not inclined to boast often or noisily of its own enterprise."[114]

The *Chicago Herald* devoted a full page to itself on its thirteenth birthday. The headlines read: "Some of the Purposes of a Great and Successful Newspaper—Its Principles Restated and Its Remarkable Development Briefly Outlined."[115] The *Herald* also printed small notices, interspersed in its news columns, that praised the quality of its sports coverage.[116] In October 1894, it noted that its reporting during the previous week was without rival: ". . . THE HERALD reports everything that is of human interest that concerns a respectable number of the people, and does it in a manner that leaves nothing further to be desired."[117]

Newspaper self-promotion emphasized not just the quality of its news but also its *quantity* (in pages, circulation, and ad lineage), its *speed* in news gathering (the scoop), and its *delivery*. All were central to the paper's success as a business.

When Joseph Pulitzer was building the New York *World* in the 1880s, the paper extolled each new milestone passed in circulation or ad lineage. When ad lineage topped all New York City competitors on December 1, 1884, the paper called it "an Event in Journalism" ("It was, in fact, a red letter day for *The World*, from a business point of view."). In particular, the *World* bragged that "it is an event to outstrip the *Herald* as an advertising medium and we must be excused for calling attention to it."[118] The *St. Louis Republic* reported on the growth of its advertising lineage in 1889, calling it a "midsummer marvel."[119]

The *Pittsburgh Leader* boasted of its efforts in covering the Knights Templars meeting in 1898, running a long article with this headline:

NEWS OF THE CONCLAVE
HOW THE "LEADER" HANDLED THE GREAT LOCAL EVENT
Rivals Were Not Merely Outclassed; They Were Overwhelmed—
Readers Let Into the Inside Work of Taking Care
of a Great News Item

The article noted that the *Leader* was *first* in publishing "the correct information on the great parade . . . Other afternoon newspapers merely reproduced the formation in the official program, giving a few additions which were mostly inaccuracies."[120]

The *St. Paul Globe* trumpeted its scoop in reporting the capture of an escaped criminal in 1885: "The Globe has a contract with the public to furnish all the latest and most authentic news."[121] The *Globe* also claimed to be the first paper in that city with the news of General U. S. Grant's death.[122]

The *St. Louis Republican* praised its work in covering the 1884 election, noting: "Like Washington of glorious memory, THE REPUBLICAN is first in war, first in peace and first in the hearts of its countrymen. It is also first in the field of news and invariably first in carrying the intelligence of any great event to the waiting thousands of the great Mississippi Valley and the Southwest."[123]

The rush to be first with the news led to some inaccurate claims of scoops. As one trade publication noted in 1898, five different New York newspapers each reported that *its* tug boat first hailed the Spanish cruiser *Vizcaya* conveying the news of the *Maine* disaster.[124]

Newspapers also promoted themselves by publicizing their speedy delivery, both within their own regions and to outlying areas. The New York and St. Louis newspapers stressed the use of trains in delivering the news to distant readers. The *New York Times* bragged that its special trains to Syracuse twice beat the competition (the *World* and the *New York Herald*) with special editions of the paper published during the state Democratic convention.[125] In 1888, the *St. Louis Republic* chartered a special train to speed its election edition to its subscribers and called the train an immense success.[126]

The *Chicago Herald* trumpeted its "FAST MAIL SERVICE," noting that the newspaper reached Ashland, Wisconsin, in 15 hours, bringing "the remote points of the far northwest within a day's reach of the metropolis" and putting the *Herald* "upon the tea table of residents and summer resorters the day of its issue."[127]

Marketing and the News

At times, marketing permeated the news itself. In New York City in 1885, a jealous husband (a Dr. Tauszky) tried to kill his wife. Failing, he tried to commit suicide, but he proved equally inept at this. The attempted murder-suicide attracted attention, and the New York *World* managed to interview the wife's mother, a Mrs. Rosenthal. She recounted that her daughter was resting after her trauma. Incidentally, Mrs. Rosenthal noted: *"The World's account of the terrible affair is the most accurate of any of the morning papers. We have read them all."*[128]

A *Boston Globe* article on life-saving stations along Cape Cod included a testimonial from one of the life-savers. He said that the *Globe* "seems to be the only paper that takes any interest in the life-saving service, being ever ready to report its doings in cases of shipwreck and disaster."[129] The *Cincinnati Tribune* used a story on health hazards in a local canal for its own self-promotion. On May 29, 1893, the paper ran a front-page story in which a Cincinnati health officer commented on the situation—and praised the *Tribune's* coverage. "By the way," he said, "the *Tribune's* article on the canal was the best and most complete thing I have seen, and I have it in my desk and am constantly referring to it in my work of investigation."

These first three business strategies (low operating costs, predictability in supply and output, and marketing) all directly influenced newspaper content. Business concerns also led to cooperation among publishers, even among competitors. The prime vehicle for such consultations was the various trade associations—local, state, regional, or national business groups—which grew in the middle and latter decades of the century.[130]

Newspaper Trade Associations

Beginning as early as the 1850s, editors and publishers in various states began meeting to discuss common general professional and business concerns. These state press associations also organized annual excursions for the editors and their spouses. In 1893, several press associations sponsored trips to the Chicago World's Fair.[131] In 1889, members of the Associated Ohio Dailies and their spouses went on a boat trip on Lake Huron, mixing business with sight-seeing. On that trip, the entertainment on the steamer *City of Alpena* included a sing-along of a composition written especially for the occasion ("Good Bye," sung to the tune of "Auld Lang Syne") and ended with the singing of the doxology.[132] But entertainment was only the backdrop for these gatherings, which addressed the general problems and business of journalism. The proceedings of these groups provide a glimpse of the issues publishers and editors faced and of the advice and assistance they sought from their peers. Most meetings included a lecture or discussion on the role of the press in American democracy and extensive discussions and presentations on day-to-day business matters.

State and regional publishers and editors organized the earliest newspaper trade associations. The founders of the Ohio Editorial Association, begun in 1849, touted it as a nonpartisan business organization.[133] The first meeting of the Wisconsin Press Association, in 1853, dealt with advance payment of subscriptions, increased rates for legal printing, state printing contracts, and uniform prices for job work.[134] In 1857, the Wisconsin Press Association attempted to set guidelines for advertising rates for member newspapers and to get the legislature to raise rates for printing state laws.[135] One of the founders of the New York Press Association said that publishers had established this organization mainly to try to set uniform advertising rates and, thus, to present a united front to advertisers.[136]

The Associated Ohio Dailies first met in 1885 to bring together the business managers and publishers of daily Ohio newspapers "for a free discussion of the many questions of mutual concern, including the best method and systems for successfully conducting the business interests of a daily paper."[137] The first meeting focused on circulation, advertising rates, and methods of newspaper accounting.[138]

Trade associations developed for all sizes of newspapers. For weeklies, there were county and regional organizations (Livingston [New York] Press Association; Elkhorn Valley [Nebraska] Editorial Association, Connecticut Valley Press Association; Hocking Valley [Ohio] Editorial Association; and the Buckeye [Ohio] Weekly Press Association).[139] For weeklies and small-city dailies, there were the state press associations (New York Press Association, New Jersey Editorial Association, Wisconsin Press Association, and others). Dailies were also served by several trade groups, including the American Associated Dailies, established in 1892 to combat fraudulent advertising,[140] and the Associated Ohio Dailies. On a national level, the American Newspaper Publishers Association (established in 1887) and the National Association of Managers of Newspaper Circulation (established in 1899) focused on big-city newspaper concerns,[141] while the National Editorial Association (established in 1885) represented small dailies and weeklies.[142]

These trade associations all shared business concerns, but they had specialized purposes, too. The county organizations concentrated on setting uniform advertising rates and buying newsprint in bulk at reduced rates. C. K. Sanders of the Livingston Press Association noted: "National and state press associations are of great benefit and much enjoyed, but for practical utility, the county associations can get nearer to a business basis and work together for mutual interests."[143] The state press associations tackled statewide issues, particularly relating to libel laws, legal advertising, and patent medicines. National organizations, such as the American Newspaper Publishers Association and the National Association of the Managers of Newspaper Circulation, were more attuned to metropolitan newspapers' needs. But all served the business of journalism.

The most common concerns at trade association meetings were advertising,[144] circulation,[145] technology,[146] and labor.[147] Some advertising issues included placement (where ads appeared in a newspaper),[148] foreign advertising (rates and collection procedures for non local advertisers),[149] advertising agents,[150] newspaper directories,[151] substitution (of generic for brand-name products),[152] and collecting ad revenues.[153]

Some trade associations helped inculcate business methods. In 1897, the president of the Nebraska Press Association praised county press associations, saying that they helped rid the industry of unbusinesslike methods.[154] One Ohio publisher exhorted his colleagues in the early 1890s to set aside their political differences when it came to business: "You Democrats and Republicans can fight all you want to in your papers, but for heaven's sake, when it comes down to business, when we are meeting on a common platform, let us go hand in hand and accomplish that which will be of benefit to us all."[155] An Illinois editor in 1890 praised the Illinois Press Association, saying that it had helped to advance the business interests of its members:

[Editors] are no longer the prey of patent medicine men and advertising sharks. They no longer accept cigars and free lunches as an equivalent for a puff in the paper, but charge a stated price for all business notices, collect the same promptly, buy and pay for the necessaries as they require and such luxuries as they want and can afford. Two or three free tickets to the circus or theater no longer secure the insertion of fifty or a hundred lines of readers [reading notices] and a reduction on the rate for a regular advertisement in addition.[156]

United Action

A. D. Hosterman, publisher of the *Springfield Republic Times* (Ohio), noted that the publishers and editors who started the Select List of Ohio Dailies in 1893 did so to promote unity in action regarding advertisers and paper supplies. The Select List made combined purchases of newsprint and printing materials for its members. Hosterman recalled: "It was found that publishers were paying a variety of prices, the smaller ones being charged what was thought to be an exorbitant amount . . . Some papers then were getting their newsprint at three cents a pound, while others were charged four cents."[157]

The American Associated Dailies was established in 1893 by newspapers from 13 states[158] to coordinate information and policies on advertising. The association's first circular promised to give "information whereby each member may be informed of the fraudulent advertising schemes, irresponsible advertising agents and foreign advertisers who do not pay their contracts" and to provide information about advertisers "who are about to send out large amounts of advertising, with such other information as may be of advantage to the members of the Association."[159]

Members of the Chicago Daily Newspaper Publishers' Association agreed to cooperate on advertising rates, return privileges, and distribution. *Newspaperdom* noted that the agreement "simplifies and reduces the cost of handling papers in the city and obtains special facilities for out-of-town delivery, by mail and express. Working single-handedly, newspapers are too often dictated to by railroads, news companies and others, to the evident disadvantage of newspapers as a whole, and this a local publishers association renders practically impossible."[160]

Uniform Advertising Rates

Many trade associations, including those in Wisconsin, New York, Maine, Missouri, Indiana, Nebraska, and Ohio, were established to obtain uniform advertising rates in order to limit costly interpress rivalry and rate-cutting.[161] E. W. Stephens, of the *Columbia Herald* (Missouri) and president of the Missouri Press Association in 1889, praised uniform-rate agreements and denounced publishers who cut ad rates to lure advertisers. "However bitter the rivalry, no editor is hungering to deplete his pocket book on account of it."[162] In 1892, Henry Neill, of the Madison, South Dakota, *Leader,* argued that publishers must cooperate with one another in setting uniform ad rates.[163]

C. K. Sanders of the Livingston Press Association said that trade associations were established "to attack as well as to eradicate disastrous internal competition."[164] The Livingston Press Association had five bylaws, four of which specifically set advertising rates (e.g., for announcements, obituaries, etc.); the fifth was a provision for amendments.[165] The Associated Publishers of Washington, D.C., agreed in 1888 to charge uniform rates for advertising and to avoid price-cutting in ads.[166]

This concern over advertising rates characterized all newspapers. Walt Elder, of the Clarion, Iowa, *Wright County Democrat,* and a member of the Upper Des Moines Editorial Association, said that his county organization helped stabilize advertising and job-printing rates. "Our object should be to protect ourselves from extortion, not to extort from others."[167] At the 1884 New York Press Association meeting, Beman Brockway of the *Watertown Times* recalled that the primary object of the first New York meeting was "to compare notes and reach nearly uniform rates of advertising, it having been too much the custom to allow advertisers to dictate rates."[168] E. P. Call of the *Boston Herald* called for uniformity in advertising rates at the 1888 meeting of the American Newspaper Publishers Association.[169] In 1890, one member of the Illinois Press Association decried wide variations in ad rates in Illinois, noting that some publishers were getting a pittance compared with others.[170]

Trade associations attempted to set uniform rates, but they were not always successful. The continuing exhortations about ad rates at association meetings throughout the 1890s seemed to indicate that not all publishers were cooperating. Some did, and it may well have been the small county organizations (e.g., the Livingston Press Association) that were most successful in getting agreement and consistent compliance on advertising rates. Hugh Wilson, editor of the Abbeville, South Carolina, *Press and Banner,* noted in 1892 that he and his cross-town rival had adopted uniform subscription prices and advertising rates in the 1860s and had stuck to that agreement for 25 years.[171] At that level, working with no more than a few other editors, such agreements might well have worked. Larger organizations with both large and small newspapers, weeklies and dailies, faced a difficult task of coming up with an acceptable rate system.

Fighting Competition

The rationale behind uniform advertising rates was to reduce costly internewspaper business rivalries. No one suggested that newspapers would cease competing for news, circulation, or advertising lineage. Rather the notion was that self-destructive competition (as in the lowering of rates to win advertising contracts) should be eliminated. Publishers also wanted to thwart attempts to establish new newspapers and to fight off other businesses that might siphon advertising revenues. Publishers were convinced that billboards, circulars, pamphlets, street car and railroad advertising, and even church bulletins and theater playbills were stealing their advertising. Milton McRae exhorted his fellow publishers: "Anything that we can do to stop them legitimately is bound to be for our own interest."[172]

Publishers were wide-ranging in their desire to stop competitors' advertising. They wanted to prevent distribution of advertising handbills in mailboxes.[173] They argued that advertising on lampposts, wagons, and sandwich boards tended to obstruct sidewalks.[174] The *Chicago Herald* denounced that city's plan to lease patrol boxes for advertising, arguing that ads would crowd the sidewalks.[175] Publishers also wanted to ban door-to-door advertising and sales.[176]

Some publishers tried to stop advertising on street cars. R. B. Brown, editor and publisher of the *Zanesville Courier* (Ohio) in the 1890s, argued, "Every dollar of which so expended detracts and subtracts from the revenues of the newspaper."[177] He claimed that the newspaper had a right "to hold a restricted field and to 'taboo' all sorts of fake advertising which seeks to win away from it the support that it must have."[178] Another publisher estimated that ad placards in Columbus, Ohio, street cars brought in $4,000 a year, money "that ought to go to the Ohio State Journal, the Columbus Dispatch and other newspapers in that city."[179]

In 1890, ANPA publishers agreed that they would try to stop street car and railway advertising,[180] but they realized they should proceed carefully. Victor Lawson of the *Chicago Daily News* urged his fellow publishers to tailor their action to win public support. Rather than complaining that street car advertising took revenues away from newspapers (although he agreed that was the problem), Lawson suggested that the publishers question the legality of such advertising under the public franchises that regulated street cars. "It is proper for us to consider it, not the damage it is to us, of course it is a damage to us, but as before the public we are perfectly justified in calling attention to and stopping what we see to be an illegal action of this corporation."[181] In 1893, the Associated Ohio Dailies appointed a committee to test the legal right of street cars to carry ads. The committee was "to urge on the local papers of each city to contest the case in each city." The committee also was supposed to ask the state's attorney general to rule against such advertising.[182] That same year, the New York Press Association lobbied the legislature and city governments to pass laws forbidding advertising on elevated railroads and horse cars.[183]

In their zeal to monopolize advertising, some publishers even sought to ban billboards. At various trade meetings, publishers denounced billboards for taking revenues from newspapers.[184] In 1890, the publisher of the *Brooklyn Eagle* lamented that billboards took away from newspaper advertising revenues. "Of course, there is a large amount of advertising we would like to abolish, which we cannot," he said.[185] In 1900, several San Francisco publishers petitioned the mayor and the board of supervisors for a ban on billboard and sign board advertising.[186] Some billboards were unsafe. Some fell down. Others obstructed traffic. Therefore, many objections to them were legitimate, but these objections served merely to obscure the principal objection of some publishers, which centered on the financial threat of billboards. Newspapers appear to have followed Lawson's advice. The *Chicago Herald* editorialized in 1894 that flimsy billboards were dangerous to public safety and that billboards hid building law violations. However, the *Herald* did not advocate leaving billboards up if such abuses were corrected. Rather, the paper argued that "public propriety demands abolition of the billboard because of the nefarious ends it is chiefly used to promote."[187]

In some areas, competing newspapers cooperated to exclude new newspapers. In 1896, the major Cincinnati newspapers organized a boycott that killed the fledgling *Cincinnati Record*. The established papers organized the regular news dealers and newsboys to boycott the *Record*. Advertisers avoided the paper because of the boycott. Lacking sufficient capital to create an entirely new distribution system or to sit out the boycott, the *Record* failed after 10 days.[188]

The five major Boston newspapers in the 1890s created their own delivery system, the Hotel and Railway News Company, which was both economical (the five papers divided the costs) and designed to keep out potential competitors. Thomas Downey, circulation manager of the *Boston Globe,* said new papers could not use the system and, thus, faced the expensive task of establishing their own delivery routes to the suburbs and outlying areas. Downey said, "The result is that we have driven everybody out of the field that has attempted to come in there."[189]

Downey also noted that the Boston newspapers controlled the sale of papers on local trolleys. That way they could exclude papers from other towns, such as New York. He admitted: "That does away with one element of opposition. It seems a little hoggish to do that, but it is business. We pay for it and if we pay for it we ought to enjoy all the rights and privileges we can get out of it."[190]

Political Activism in Pursuit of Business Goals

Trade associations also served their members through their political clout. Publishers relied on trade associations, particularly on the state level, to create political leverage to advance their business goals. That power came from the fact that legislators faced reelection and needed the newspapers' support. One Ohio publisher urged his colleagues to remind legislators of that.[191] By the 1880s, most state newspaper trade associations had standing legislative committees to promote favorable legislation and to stop any harmful legislation.[192] At the national level, the ANPA and the National Editorial Association kept close watch on legislation, too. In the 1890s, the ANPA lobbied members of Congress over bills on tariffs and postal rates.[193]

Publishers believed that their lobbying often was successful in halting unfavorable legislation. The legislative committee of the New York Press Association reported in 1891 that no laws favorable to the press had been passed in the legislature. But it had defeated all bills unfavorable to the press, too.[194]

For small-city dailies and country newspapers, an important source of revenue was "legal advertising." Throughout the nineteenth century, state and local governments had contracted with newspapers to print their announcements and reports—new laws, tax rates, sheriff's sales, county commissioners' reports, and municipal or county official notices. Legal advertising still provided income even at century's end, despite the general decline of partisan subsidies to the press. Because state laws usually determined the amount, rates, and placement of such ads, state, regional, and county press associations were particularly attentive to this issue.

Legal advertising could be quite lucrative. In Ohio, for instance, the legal advertising for just one item, the taxation rates in a county (usually run for six weeks), could bring $300 cash to the newspaper.[195] In Oregon, state law in the 1890s stipulated that two newspapers in each county run county and state printing notices (e.g., land sales, calls for bids for state agencies). The law gave such printing to the newspapers with the largest bona fide yearly circulation, as determined by the local county court.[196] The Salem, Oregon, *Independent* estimated that these printing contracts could bring $1,200 a year to a small country daily or weekly.[197] In Ohio, government printing usually went to newspapers in the county seat, and was not based on circulation. Rather, it was divided between a Democratic and a Republican newspaper.[198] Government advertising also came with very few strings attached: placement or reading notices were not an issue.

Publishers fought attempts to alter legal advertising rates or procedures. State press associations in South Dakota, New York, Illinois, Indiana, New Jersey, Wisconsin, Nebraska, Texas, California, Minnesota, Missouri, New Hampshire, Arkansas, and Ohio all assailed legislative proposals designed to lower public printing costs in the 1880s and 1890s.[199]

Publishers worried that changes in the legal advertising process might nurture competition. When the Ohio legislature was considering a low-bid system in 1893 (to replace the awards by party), one publisher denounced it as a potential support for new newspapers.[200] When both Cleveland and Cincinnati were considering similar changes in their local legal printing, one publisher warned of the danger of "publications that might be started for the sole purpose of getting such patronage."[201] The Minnesota Press Association resolved that "only well established journals of recognized merit as newspapers" should obtain official or legal advertising.[202]

Various legislative proposals to regulate the patent medicine industry also drew opposition from publishers. Patent medicines were an important source of advertising revenue for newspapers across the country in the 1880s and 1890s. Even small rural weeklies received ads from patent medicine companies. Consequently, publishers often viewed any attempt to regulate patent medicines as a threat to newspaper profits. Various states considered proposals on patent medicines. Patent medicine sellers saw proposals to license physicians and medical practitioners as attempts by a fledgling medical establishment to control the market. That argument had some merit.[203] The trade journal *Advertising Experience* claimed that the laws in most states were pushed "at the instigation of the associations of so-called regular physicians who are finding that competition of patent medicines is cutting into their trade."[204]

The intent behind the bills is unclear. What is clear, however, is that publishers identified the well-being of their newspapers with that of the patent medicine companies. John Mack of the *Sandusky Register* (Ohio) condemned one licensing bill as "vicious legislation" that would harm the patent medicine manufacturers and would have "robbed the newspapers of Ohio annually of tens of thousands of dollars of advertising patronage as legitimate as that of the local merchant."[205]

Patent medicine manufacturers and newspapers assailed bills that would have required patent medicine labels to list contents. Patent medicine manufacturers worried that trade secrets would be released and cheap substitutes would flood the market. However, the attack on labeling laws occurred partly because some medicines contained alcohol. Patent medicine sales were extremely strong in the Bible Belt and other temperance areas. Labeling laws were perceived as possibly fatal to business there. Alcohol was not the only potential problem arising from labeling proposals. Some patent medicines contained poison, and the manufacturers rightly concluded that the public might look askance at a little belladonna in a bottle.[206]

Patent medicine manufacturers found a welcome forum at many press trade association meetings in the late nineteenth century. A representative for the J. C. Ayer Company, a major patent medicine manufacturer, spoke at the 1899 ANPA meeting and warned about "hostile legislation."[207] The Ayer representative reminded publishers (quite unnecessarily) that laws that harmed the patent medicine business also harmed newspapers. He specifically complained that one New York proposal would require that, "if a medicine happens to contain a small modicum of poison, it must be put up in a certain colored bottle."[208] He invited publishers to attack such "vicious, pernicious and vexatious" legislation:

We don't ask for lengthy editorials, which may sow seeds of suspicion in the minds of the people, who would never have thought of harm in their favorite household remedy, but for such newspaper notoriety as you might give; but in the sphere of each of you there is an opportunity with your own Senator and representative to defeat the ends of these men who live by blackmail, of those, too, who see in the compelling of each proprietor to publish his formula an open door to every man who desires to sell a substitute.[209]

Some publishers attacked such legislation directly in their news columns. And trade associations lobbied legislators against such laws.[210] A. D. Hosterman of the *Springfield Republic Times* (Ohio) said that newspapers must attack patent medicine regulations because their enactment would lessen newspaper advertising.[211] Some patent medicine advertising contracts with newspapers specified that newspapers had an affirmative duty to support the patent medicine businesses editorially.[212] Newspapers in Ohio and Wisconsin did so by opposing labeling laws in the 1890s.[213]

Not everyone in the newspaper industry was subservient to the patent medicine industry, but many were. As the *Journalist* noted in 1892, New York City newspapers reacted with unanimity in attacking a pure food and drug bill in New York State, demonstrating once again that "the big advertiser whistles and the editor dances."[214]

Conclusions

Business concerns shaped the operation of the newspaper and consequently the news itself in the late nineteenth century. The need for capital and profit became the driving force of the newspaper. Day-to-day operations simply had to conform to those needs.

Newspapers held down operating costs by keeping wages low and by guaranteeing a stable, predictable product (even in an industry where such predictability would seem impossible). This "commodity" then was marketed to the consuming public.

That newspapers were businesses and that business strategies shaped day-to-day operations are no surprise. The crucial point, though, is to see the impact of this business orientation on news. Some methods, such as the beat system, produced news that continually focused on the various agencies of government. Other methods, such as the ready-print syndicated materials common in country weeklies and small dailies, provided standardized news and features that were entertaining if not very timely. Still other methods were less informative, though equally entertaining. Attempts to maximize circulation led to fabrication and sensationalism, trivializing the newspaper's role in providing information to the public. The marketing of the newspaper elevated a narcissistic type of news to prominence. Newspapers focused on themselves and devoted news columns to praising the wonders of their reportage, advertising lineage, or scoops. Some of this was subtle, some not. But it was pervasive. J. A. Woodson, of the *Sacramento Record Union,* noted in 1892 that the "bane of the editorial department, more so than ever before, is the counting room." Woodson contended that business interests within the newspaper shaped the news not just in large metropolitan newspapers but in country newspapers as well.[215]

Business concerns also led to widespread cooperation throughout the newspaper industry, which further fostered the business mentality within each newspaper. The trade associations created a forum for discussions of business issues and a springboard for industrywide cooperation in obtaining more lenient libel laws or, for small county trade associations, merely buying bulk newsprint at reduced prices.

However, trade associations also helped to propel the commercialization of the news. At trade meetings, publishers learned to cloak their economic self-interest in the guise of advocacy for the public good. They lobbied on behalf of their own advertisers, whom they also promoted in their news columns. They attacked a wide variety of efforts to regulate the patent medicine industry, even labeling laws, in a move that clearly equated their private revenues with the public good.

One industry trade journal writer noted in 1891 that the newspaper "wasn't a missionary or a charitable institution . . . and it is rather desirable to make receipts meet expenditures.[216] It had long been desirable to make receipts meet expenditures, and certainly antebellum partisan editors were not immune to notions of profit and loss.

But by the late nineteenth century, the issue went beyond assuring that receipts met expenditures with some profit left over. The issue became for many an overriding vision that exalted the financial success of the newspaper.

One newspaper publisher noted in 1893 that "it will be a sorry day for journalism if our leading papers pass out of the control of trained, professional newspaper men, and their policy be dictated and guided by men who look upon the business of journalism as the pork packer does upon his."[217] But, indeed, that had occurred. Some publishers had come to see their newspapers just as any other commodity: something to be shaped and sold at the lowest cost possible to the largest number of consumers.

Newspapers did many great things, to be sure, but news was gathered, valued, and disseminated within the context of the newspaper-as-business. C. F. Chapin of the *Waterbury American* (Connecticut) gave an address in 1891 to his local YMCA, entitled "The Newspaper: An Editor Tells the Public Some Things Which His Newspaper Can Hardly Say for Itself." Chapin saw the newspaper as a heroic institution, but one that operated within specific business concerns:

People do not buy . . . papers because they like the editors nor out of curiosity to see what they may say, but because their contents have a market value to them for which they are willing to pay. These editors and publishers are not primarily engaged in defending morality in the community, attacking corruption in the State, upholding a social or political or religious principle. *Incidentally they are probably doing one or all of these things, but their chief aim is to make a paper which people will buy and read.* And they are doing it simply for the money it brings and the power and influence it gives.[218]

Chapter Five

Shaping and Packaging the News: Luring Readers and Advertisers

Our Subscribers Have Money
You Have Goods
Don't You Want to be Introduced?
—*Bates and Morse,* Advertiser's Handy Guide for 1893

The business orientation of the newspaper industry in the late nine-teenth century dictated that publishers and editors pay heed to two audiences: advertisers and readers. Advertisers supplied the biggest share of newspaper revenue, and readers, with their numbers and buying power, attracted advertisers. The need to appeal to these two audiences was central to defining news.

The desire to lure advertisers and readers propelled the commer-cialization of news. Publishers and editors shaped and packaged the news to increase its marketability, and in doing so they emphasized content that was interesting, entertaining, and diverting. News was not simply a reflection of the day's events. It was a selected account chosen for its ability to please both advertisers and readers.

Luring the Advertiser

Publishers and editors lured advertisers by producing a newspaper that ad-vanced advertisers' marketing interests. They scrutinized circulation and the demographic profile of the reading audience. They printed vast amounts of editorial matter that praised particular businesses and local advertisers. And they printed special editions that would be popular vehicles for advertising.

Circulation and Demographic Concerns

Advertisers worried most about circulation, given their desire to sell goods to as many people as possible. Newspaper advertising rates reflected this priority: as circulation grew, so did advertising rates. A writer in the *Newspaper Maker*, a newspaper industry trade journal, noted in 1896 that, for the publisher, "circulation is circulation, no matter how obtained. The larger he can make the figures which the sales show, the broader the basis on which he may adjust his rate card."[1]

Publishers and editors boasted of their circulation. Some newspapers turned to public relations stunts to dramatize their circulation or their preeminence in their market. The *St. Louis Post Dispatch* appointed a committee of prominent citizens (including the Missouri secretary of state, the state auditor and comptroller, and a department store manager) to inspect its books over a four-month period to verify its circulation claims.[2] The *Cincinnati Tribune* challenged its rival, the *Commercial Gazette*, on February 24, 1893, offering a $500 donation to the Cincinnati Children's Home if its circulation was smaller than the *Gazette*'s. Of course, the burden of proof was on the *Gazette*. The *Nashville Banner* offered $1,000 to charity if anyone could prove it did *not* have the largest "bona fide circulation" of any Nashville daily.[3] The *Chicago Record* offered $10,000 to charity if its rival, the *Chicago Tribune*, had correctly stated its circulation claims.[4] Stephen O'Meara, publisher of the *Boston Journal*, said he would donate $1,000 to a hospital if the circulation of one of the *Journal*'s competitors was within 50,000 of what it claimed. The *Journal*'s business manager later wrote that the offer accentuated the newspaper's large circulation and increased advertising.[5] In an effort to discredit the Milwaukee *Journal*'s claim of a 47,000 daily press run, its rival, the *Evening Wisconsin*, published a photo of a delivery wagon full of unsold *Journal* papers.[6]

In circulation, bigger was better, all else being equal. But all things were seldom equal. Advertisers needed *buyers*. This emphasis on purchasing power focused attention on middle and upper classes rather than on the poor. One trade journal writer warned that advertisers had no need for newspapers that went to the poor, unless the advertisers sold trash or intended "to deceive the unwary and the ignorant."[7]

Circulation concerns focused attention on the demographic profile of a paper's audience. Attention to demographics helped commercialize the news. Demographic concerns defined readers primarily by their ability (or lack of ability) to purchase goods. News would respect that view.

Advertisers and publishers valued "quality" readers—a byword for up-scale readership. Adolph Ochs promoted his *New York Times* in

1896 by stressing its high-class readership. "Qualitas, non Quantitas" rather than "quantitas non qualitas," he proclaimed. A "high class paper" had its value, he noted.[8] Other publishers echoed Ochs's claims. The Oakland, California, *Evening Enquirer* promised that "the best class of people" composed its readership.[9] The *San Francisco Evening Bulletin* warned advertisers not to be misled "by newspapers of a much inferior grade, but claiming larger circulation, for in reaching the *purchasing class*, the BULLETIN HAS NO COMPETITOR, it is peerless as an advertising medium among the evening papers" in San Francisco.[10]

"Quality" could make a difference in ad rates. In the 1890s, the New York *Evening Post*, with 25,000 circulation, charged 20 cents a line for ads, while the New York *World*, with a circulation 25–30 times as large, charged only 40 cents a line. These rates reflected the fact that the *Post*'s readership was more affluent than that of the *World*, and was more valued by advertisers.[11]

Metropolitan newspapers were not alone in focusing on the buying power of readers. The publisher of the weekly *Bucyrus Journal* (Ohio) noted that his paper "includes among its subscribers the wealthiest, the most intelligent and the most enterprising of our citizens."[12] One New York newspaper directory, in its 1893 and 1895 editions, carried ads from a variety of small daily newspapers, all promoting the purchasing power of their readers.[13]

Even religious publications stressed the purchasing power of their readers. In advertising trade journals, publishers of religious newspapers noted not their ethereal goals but their advertising effectiveness. The Church Press, a printing house in Chicago that produced more than 30 religious newspapers, promised that its papers went to "neither 'ristocrat nor rabble, but to prosperous family people."[14] The Chicago *Advance*, a Congregational paper, reached "the very best class of people."[15] The Religious Press Association, based in Philadelphia, claimed that its seven religious weeklies were ideal for advertisers, because the newspapers went to "people who have money for their needs." These newspapers "talk in the Protestant denominations to people who have homes to keep up; children to rear, clothe, doctor and educate."[16] A group of Methodist newspapers claimed in one advertising trade journal that "Methodists are big consumers," and "always have money to spend for good things."[17] On another occasion, the same publications promised that "Methodists are liberal givers of Christmas presents" and that "each member of the many Methodist families is a buyer at this season."[18]

These characterizations of readers as consumers were ecumenical in nature; newspapers spanning the diversity of American religion— Unitarian, Roman Catholic, and Baptist—pledged they could deliver willing consumers to businesses that advertised.

Religious publications represented just one special audience. The foreign-language press also sought advertising revenues and consequently emphasized readers' purchasing power. The St. Louis, Missouri, *Anzeiger des Westens*, a German newspaper (published daily, Sunday, and weekly), told advertisers that it had "masses of thrifty German-Americans" among its readers.[19] Ads in one advertising trade journal for a group of Chicago German-language newspapers extolled their readers' finances: "Did you know there are over 400,000 Germans in Chicago who are a thrifty well-to-do class of people and have money to spend for worthy articles?"[20]

Targeting the Family

Some advertisers found the religious and foreign-language presses valuable as marketing tools, but most turned directly to the urban daily newspaper to reach the ideal consuming audience: the family. The appeal to hearth and home was purely pragmatic. The simple reality was that families were the key purchasers of basic consumer goods that marked the growing national marketplace in the late nineteenth century (baking soda, soap, department store goods, and the like). Consequently, the publishers of daily newspapers stressed their ability to link these particular consumers to advertisers.

The *Oakland Tribune* (California) stressed the value of its family readership in the 1890s, claiming that "one copy of a newspaper that reaches the home is worth more for purposes of advertising than three that don't."[21] The *Tribune*, fortunately, was just such a paper, "a distinctively family paper" reaching "people who buy merchandise, build houses, pay taxes and generally support the substantial interests of a community."[22] Another Oakland daily, the *Evening Enquirer*, followed suit, promoting itself as "a clean family paper" that circulated "among the best class of people in Oakland, its suburbs and Alameda County."[23] Across the bay, the San Francisco *Call* was "clean—reliable—independent—it has long stood pre-eminent as the GREAT FAMILY PAPER of the Pacific Coast. It goes *into the homes of the people* and for 38 years has possessed their confidence."[24] A few years later, the *Call* relied on an advertiser's testimonial to stress its value as a link to the family circle. That advertiser said he had used the *Call* for more than 20 years as "the means of *directly reaching the home circle.*"[25]

Women as Consumers

Within the family, women emerged as the key demographic target. Newspapers earlier in the century had not particularly geared content toward women,[26] but the desire to increase circulation in general led to a desire to exploit this relatively untapped audience. Milton McRae of the *Cincinnati Post* noted that he had found "that one of the greatest secrets of large circulation is to interest the women."[27]

Advertisers valued women as readers because women generally managed household operations and purchased the goods for the family. In the early 1890s, one trade journal writer estimated that women bought six-sevenths of what came into the home.[28] The *Cincinnati Tribune* estimated that "eighty percent of all domestic buying is done by women of the household."[29] The *Dry Goods Economist,* a leading department store trade journal, advised department store owners to "start out with the assumption that nine-tenths of the money earned by man is spent by woman."[30] One newspaper wrote: "Experienced advertisers know that women are the principal buyers not only of food products and household articles, but also of many things that are not directly connected with the household menage. They influence sales where they are not themselves actual purchasers."[31]

As consumers, women were ideal targets for advertisers. Nathaniel Fowler, a prolific writer on newspaper operations and advertising methods toward the end of the century, argued that women paid more attention to advertisements than men did. As we read of him earlier, Fowler said that ads appealed in a special way to women: "A woman who does not read advertisements would not be a woman, consequently all women read advertisements." Fowler went on to cite practical reasons for women's preoccupation with advertising: "Women are the buyers of everything everywhere . . . Woman is the pivot which turns trade."[32]

Certainly this view of the reader as consumer marked a substantive change in the American newspaper from the early years of the century, when editors viewed readers as voters. Whatever the nature of a newspaper's readership—whether it was Methodists, farmers, Swedes, or families in Cleveland or Woodland, Oregon—newspapers promised advertisers a link with consumers. "Prosperous" farmers read the *Atlantic Telegraph* (Iowa); the *Brooklyn Citizen* circulated "among those who have the MEANS OF BUYING"; the *Leavenworth Standard* (Kansas) went to "money spenders"; the *Lewiston Journal* (Maine) reached "the bulk of the purchasing class"; the *Cincinnati Tribune* went to "the home buyers at first hand"; and the readers of the *Buffalo Courier* were "people who have money to spend."[33]

News about Business

Publishers and editors lured advertisers by promoting them within their news columns. Jason Rogers, the former editor of the New York *Mercury* and a commentator on press management in the 1890s, argued that newspapers should use their *news* columns to stay chummy with advertisers and to get new accounts. According to Rogers, the way to lure advertisers was to create flattering news stories about them:

A publisher should with a spirit of broad minded liberality, make a regular daily feature of news from the store. If one of the large stores has just received a new consignment of imported goods, and yet is not a regular user of the advertising columns of your paper, a well-written news story on the woman's page will convincingly prove the value of the paper as an advertising medium, entirely aside from the display of liberality and fair play involved.[34]

In 1894, S. S. Rogers of the *Chicago Record* and *Chicago Daily News* told ANPA members that the battle for advertising dollars was constant. Accordingly, the wise newspaper manager was sure to do all he could to keep advertisers happy.[35]

Exactly how many editors took his advice is not clear. But some got the message. In the early 1890s the *Boston Traveller* began a new department, "Shopping," which was aimed at women readers.[36] The *St. Louis Republic* ran an *editorial* in 1889 calling a local department store a "model advertiser" after it had contracted for full-page ads weekly for a year. "No mercantile concern is better known to the people of this city; none has had a more rapid and remarkable growth . . ."[37] The *Detroit News Tribune* published "practical talks" with advertisers and the consumers. One trade journal writer praised the series, noting: "A recent talk on mail order business is just the sort of material advertisers wish to have pounded into the public. It shows how mail order business is done and thereby helps to make new mail order customers for its advertisers."[38] The *Chicago Herald* called its regular advertisers "solid and substantial."[39] The *St. Paul Globe* ran profiles of various businesses on Seventh Street ("Seventh Street: The Great Ten Mile Thoroughfare of the City of St. Paul. A Notable Exponent of the Increasing Business and Wealth of the City").[40] Such interviews usually focused on the notable achievements of such businessmen and the wonderful stores they owned. The *Boston Globe* ran a special business edition on January 1, 1885, and during the next two days extensively quoted local businessmen who praised the edition as valuable to business interests. The New York *World* ran an "index" to New York businesses in 1885; conveniently, those businesses on the index also happened to be *World* advertisers. The *Chicago Herald*, seeking endorsements for Paine's Celery Compound, deployed its own reporters to interview druggists who attended the Chicago World's Fair.[41] In all, the reporters interviewed 102 pharmacists, and each one extolled the virtues of the compound. The interviews filled five news columns and were located next to two full columns of ads for the compound.

Some of this content was just part of editors' promotions of their home towns. The Chambersburg, Pennsylvania, *Public Opinion* carried an editorial saying that a good newspaper "never lets pass a good opportunity to advocate the interests of its home enterprises."[42] The *Cincinnati Tribune* urged its readers to "talk up your town" to help business.[43] The *Kansas City Times* printed a special edition (320,000 copies) in 1895, extolling the city's banks, railroads, and other businesses. The paper paid the expenses of 35 businessmen who traveled to New York City to promote Kansas City with bankers and captains of industry.[44]

The primary beneficiary of articles about business appears to have been department stores, the largest advertisers in many newspapers. The *Chicago Herald* noted the opening of a new department store in 1894, calling it a public event.[45] On the day before a new department store opened in Brooklyn in 1885, the New York *World* devoted a full page to the store and its wondrous stock, headlining it as: "An Immense Establishment Surpassing in Beauty Anything Ever Produced in This Country" and "THE GRANDEST DRY GOODS STORE IN BROOKLYN."[46] In Boston, the *Globe* gushed in similar fashion over one of its major advertisers, Jordan, Marsh and Company. What appeared to be a regular news story[47] noted "their colossal sale" which was the "topic of general conversation everywhere." The article detailed some of the items on sale at the store and praised the "pluck, grit, perseverance" of the management:

> Limited space, however, precludes the possibility of our enumerating all the lots offered, and it will thus remain for the readers of THE GLOBE to peruse the advertisements this firm has placed on the fourth, fifth and sixteenth pages of this issue, or better, to call in person at the store of Jordan, Marsh & Co., early Monday morning and inspect in person the remarkable values this most popular house is offering.[48]

And, two months later, the *Globe* noted that "the indefatigable energy and persistent activity that this firm shows is really something marvelous."[49]

In St. Louis, a sale at Humphrey's department store in 1888 drew similar newspaper support from the *Republic*. An article noted that the sale would continue for another week or so, and "if there is anybody in St. Louis, or out of it, who is in search of a genuine bargain in clothing and gents' furnishing goods, all he will have to do to find what he wants is to visit Humphrey's."[50] The *Chicago Herald* printed a story on Christmas shopping with a fictional "Mrs. Goodhusband," mentioning the city's major stores (by name and location) and describing the goods carried there.[51]

Some of these articles on business (such as the one about Paine's Celery Compound and some of those on department store sales), presented as news articles, were probably reading notices. All appeared in the regular typeface of the newspaper among news stories. Furthermore, the *Globe* had a policy against reading notices, so it seems unlikely that the articles on Jordan, Marsh and Company were paid for by the store itself. Rather, those articles were part of the overall business strategy of praising advertisers and, as Jason Rogers had urged, making them aware of newspapers' power as a marketing tool.

Special Editions

In addition to laudatory reports on business, newspapers also lured advertising by publishing special editions. These editions might be topical (e.g., on bicycles, a popular item in the late nineteenth century)[52] or seasonal (e.g., Christmas and Easter). Special editions (often 40 pages or longer, with color supplements) were quite popular with readers and thus commanded high advertising rates.[53] One publisher noted that the business value of special editions derived from their ability to increase advertising.[54]

Christmas special editions were most common, linked as they were to a key shopping season. Christmas editions appeared in the late nineteenth century in both large and small communities (*New York Herald, New York Journal,* and New York *World,* Louisville *Courier Journal, Milwaukee Journal, Aurora Daily News* [Illinois], *Albany Argus* [New York], Alameda, California, *Semi-Weekly Argus,* Newport News, Virginia, *Daily Press, Lawrence Daily Journal* [Kansas], *Salina Daily Republican* and *Evening News* [Kansas], *Abilene Daily Reflector* [Kansas], *Winfield Daily Courier* [Kansas], and *Winona Herald* [Minnesota].[55]

Luring the Reader

Readership was central to newspaper revenues. Advertisers wanted to reach consumers, and circulation determined advertising rates. Consequently, newspapers worked hard to produce news that would attract large numbers of readers. Editors diversified content, deemphasized politics when it seemed prudent to do so, and offered prizes and contests to create customer loyalty.

Diversified Content

In 1892, a writer in the trade journal *Newspaperdom* noted that "news columns must be made brighter, better, newsier"; stories must be "vivid, bright, pyrotechnic enough" if circulation is to be maintained "and value as an advertising medium preserved."[56] The editor of the *Buffalo Times* argued that successful newspapers studied constituents' tastes and likes "with the same care that a successful merchant does," printing items that readers would enjoy.[57] The editor of the *Richmond Times* (Virginia) said that "the man who manufactures the newspaper must as surely cater to the public taste as he who manufactures tobacco, or neckties, or candies, or groceries, or any other article of consumption."[58] And still another editor said, "The successful publisher knows what the public demands and serves it to them accordingly, whether he thinks it is what they ought to have or not."[59]

The first step toward a better and brighter newspaper was to provide content so diverse that everyone would want to buy the paper. One trade journal writer noted that the "modern newspaper" had become "like a great hotel . . . No guest expects to go through the whole bill of fare. . . . One reader turns to the stock market, another to politics, another to baseball, another to book reviews, another to musical and theatrical notices, another to a sermon or lecture (especially if it is his own) and so on . . ."[60]

In 1898, one Sunday's edition of the *Pittsburgh Leader* provided articles on how to eat with chopsticks, gold speculation in British Columbia, big game hunting, identical twins in Michigan, spring fashions for men, gossip about former president Grover Cleveland and his family, fashions (including "April wraps: Novelty coats and capes that captivate feminine fancy" and the startling news that "the all-conquering blouse has suffered its first defeat and threatens to disappear altogether"), women polar explorers, amateur baking, egg farming, women fire fighters, traveling in Europe, prominent species of American trees, insect life, and fiction.[61] The American newspaper had become a cafeteria of information: it contained something for everyone.

Sunday papers, in particular, were stuffed with features and prepared in advance to allow production of an edition two to three times larger than the average daily paper.[62] But the weekday paper differed from its counterpart only in scale. An article in the *Pittsburgh Leader* outlined a philosophy that dictated content every day of the week. "No matter in what you are interested, you will find the subject of your hobby duly exploited . . . in fact, whatever you like most to read, you will find the Leader's departments are the most carefully prepared, the most complete and the most interesting."[63]

All the newspapers analyzed offered highly diverse content to readers, particularly compared with antebellum newspapers. Diversity of content was most obvious in metropolitan newspapers, but it was also found in newspapers outside the big cities. Table 5.1 shows this diversity, noting the median percentage in each content category.[64]

Half the content of antebellum metropolitan newspapers dealt with politics, whereas postbellum newspapers devoted proportionately much less attention to politics and much more attention to crime and courts, accidents, society and women, and leisure activities. Table 5.2 compares antebellum and postbellum newspapers, showing the median percentages in these content categories.[65]

The trend in metropolitan newspapers toward news about things other than politics was most apparent in the 1890s among newer newspapers. The three metropolitan newspapers established before 1830 diversified content considerably by century's end, but they continued to devote a substantial amount of content to politics. In contrast, those metropolitan newspapers established after 1870, as table 5.3 shows, devoted more attention to other content.

This change through the century also was evident in newspapers outside the metropolitan areas, as table 5.4 shows.

Table 5.1. Diversity in newspaper content in the 1890s: Percentage distribution of contents (in medians), by category of news

	Eight metropolitan newspapers 1897[a]	Five small-city/ large-town newspapers 1893/1897[b]	Three small-town newspapers 1897[c]
Politics	19.4	42.7	22.9
Crime and court news	7.5	10.6	6.6
Accidents and deaths	7.8	7.9	11.2
Society and women	6.3	8.3	2.5
Leisure activities	17.5	7.5	6.8
Business and labor	18.0	12.6	20.6
Religion	4.5	3.2	1.2
Science and education	3.1	3.7	8.8
History	0.5	1.6	0.2
Weather	0.4	0.5	0.1
Comics and jokes	1.4	0.4	2.5
Other	2.9	2.7	3.6

[a]See appendix 2, table A2.3, for identification of the newspapers examined and a breakdown of the data for each.

[b]See appendix 2, table A2.4, for identification of the newspapers examined and a breakdown of the data for each.

[c]See appendix 2, table A2.5, for identification of the newspapers examined and a breakdown of the data for each.

Table 5.2. Changes in newspaper content between metropolitan ante- and postbellum papers: Percentage distribution of contents (in medians), by general category

	Five antebellum metropolitan newspapers 1831–32[a]	Eight postbellum metropolitan newspapers 1897[b]
Politics	50.5	19.4
Crime and courts, accidents, society and women, leisure activities	11.6	39.1

[a]See appendix 2, table A2.1, for identification of the newspapers examined and a breakdown of the data for each.

[b]See appendix 2, table A2.3, for identification of the newspapers examined and a breakdown of the data for each.

Content changes reflect societal changes. Articles on sports followed the start of baseball leagues and intercity rivalries in the 1870s.[66] Articles on books, fashion, and theater coincided with increases in leisure time, publishing, education, literacy, and money for entertainment and the arts.[67]

Table 5.3.   Diversity in newspaper content in 1897: Percentage distribution of contents (in medians), by general category and the period established

	Three metropolitan newspapers Est'd. by 1830[a]	Three metropolitan newspapers Est'd. after 1870[b]
Politics	22.1	15.1
Crime and courts, accidents, society and women, leisure activities	31.6	49.8

[a]The papers were the *Boston Daily Advertiser,* the *Charleston Courier,* and the New York *Evening Post.* See appendix 2, table A2.3, for a breakdown of the data for each newspaper.
[b]The papers were the *Boston Globe,* the *New York Journal,* and the *Pittsburgh Leader.* See appendix 2, table A2.3, for a breakdown of the data for each newspaper.

Table 5.4.   Changes in newspaper content between ante- and postbellum nonmetropolitan papers: Percentage distribution of contents (in medians), by general category, 1830s to 1890s

	Four antebellum nonmetropolitan newspapers 1831–32[a]	Five postbellum small-city/large-town newspapers 1893/1897[b]	Three postbellum small-town newspapers 1897[c]
Politics	72.6	42.7	22.9
Crime and courts, accidents, society and women, leisure activities	14.4	34.3	27.1

[a]See appendix 2, table A2.2, for identification of the newspapers examined and a breakdown of the data for each.
[b]See appendix 2, table A2.4, for identification of the newspapers examined and a breakdown of the data for each.
[c]See appendix 2, table A2.5, for identification of the newspapers examined and a breakdown of the data for each.

Content changes also reflected the realities of newspaper finance and management. Diverse content drew large numbers of readers and thus was useful in luring advertisers. Jason Rogers, a former editor, worked hard to promote the idea that diversified content could increase circulation and raise advertising rates. Rogers argued that some readers with strong interests in one or two topics (such as music, fashion, cooking, or sports) would buy the newspaper just to read about those interests. Some would buy the paper solely for its serialized romance stories, others for its local news or baseball or boxing results. Attention to a myriad of subjects, including railroads, agriculture, dry goods, produce, and plumbing, might draw some readers away from specialized trade publications. Rogers endorsed articles on shorthand, bookkeeping, and dressmaking, for instance, because "the educational feature makes home circulation; home circulation is most valuable and sought after by advertisers."[68]

Rogers was no lonely voice. A prospective publisher in the 1870s announced that he saw diversified content as a business proposition. He planned to start a newspaper in New York City and proposed articles on hotels and steamships "for the purpose of securing a large line of advertisements of exceptional character. Music, the drama and fashion departments are likewise contemplated for similar business advantages."[69] The New York *Mail and Express* touted its diversity as a drawing card. "People who read a newspaper because it gives daily special departments of peculiar interest to special classes, and particularly women, like *The Mail and Express*." Topics included music, society, books, women, children, railway men, real estate, horses, and sports.[70]

As the content analysis shows, reports of politics continued to be part of the American press. But other content changed greatly from early in the century. Later on, sports coverage was common.[71] Fiction was common in all 1890s newspapers; weeklies and dailies regularly ran short stories or serialized longer works.[72] Seasonal fiction was popular, such as the flurry of Irish tales around St. Patrick's Day in the *Cincinnati Tribune* in 1893 ("A Connemara Miracle: A Delightful Story of Irish Life and Superstition" and "Shamrocks: Little Stories of Irish Life and Irish Folk," both by Frank Mathews).[73] The *Pittsburgh Leader* promoted S. R. Crockett's "Isle of Winds" as "a story of adventure. From the first to last the action is breathless and told with all the author's fire and force."[74] And the *Boston Globe* promoted a Bret Harte story in 1885, noting, "The Ladies are delighted with it."[75]

Content for Women

Because advertisers so valued women readers, the omnibus press naturally catered to their interests. Women's pages and sections were common in Sunday newspapers by the 1880s. Articles about society news and other content for women appeared most days in the American press. Fashion dominated the Sunday women's sections. Other articles gave advice on what to buy—hints on Christmas shopping, tips on home decorating (including curtains, furniture, carpets, and lamps). Recipes were popular, too. The *Chicago Herald* offered a "cooking school" in the Sunday paper, and the *Pittsburgh Leader* ran recipes daily next to its editorials.[76] Some articles were practical, giving advice on how to sew, how to get rid of carpet beetles, and how to adjust old clothes to new styles. The *New York Tribune* offered women a course in shorthand.[77] The trade journal *Newspaperdom* advised country editors to invite women to contribute "short, practical articles on household methods, household economy and the hundred other matters that are of special interest to house keepers."[78]

It was not because of any sense of women as intelligent members of society that publishers, editors, and advertisers valued them as readers. For the newspaper industry, a woman's charm was purely financial. One trade journal writer advised that women had such short attention spans that editorials should be kept under 200 words.[79] The special women's section of the *St. Paul Globe*, "The Woman's Globe," carried an article in 1885 warning of the "evils attending the right of suffrage among women." The article noted that giving women the right to vote led to divorce, and "this is the highway to the dissolution of the family altogether." This attack on suffrage appeared with what apparently were more logical topics for women: "How to Prepare Geraniums for Winter, Fall Bonnets, some fashion talk that is extremely timely, gastronomic gossip; maxims on manners."[80]

Content for women appeared largely because advertisers wanted women to read their ads and buy their products. The newspaper industry's reluctance to hire women as reporters only underscores this point. One trade journal writer noted that women could work under intelligent direction on articles dealing with the household and society. But, "if left to herself her innate prejudices, a marked characteristic of the sex, lead her into indiscreet and intemperate utterances." The writer argued that women simply couldn't be fair ("The feminine mind inclines strongly to bias"), arrived at conclusions all too hastily, and colored her reports with imagination. The writer praised women for their loyalty and emotionalism, but said that such traits were inappropriate to journalism.[81]

Women made some headway into the newspaper industry late in the century,[82] but many publishers hired women only in the fashion or society sections. The publisher of the *Atlanta Journal* noted that women employees were vital to a newspaper, "so necessary that every newspaper should have *at least one* woman on its staff."[83] The publisher of the *Boston Globe*, General Charles H. Taylor, told the Massachusetts Press Association that women in journalism were "both useful and ornamental."[84]

Others were more direct. One editor said that it was permissible to have a few women on a newspaper to deal primarily with fashion and the women's pages, but that such innovations should be carefully controlled. He urged that women devote their attention not to journalistic careers but to their social clubs, where "they can indulge their love of power and desire to rule." The vast majority of women were intended for the home, he said. Whatever journalistic successes women have had come through "the counsel and direction of their chief," the male editor.[85]

The De-emphasis on Politics

The relationship between newspapers and politics changed during the century. In the 1890s, newspapers continued to present news about politics, endorse candidates, and urge people to go to the polls on election day. Some editors and publishers continued to enjoy patronage appointments. (President William McKinley, for example, rewarded faithful Republican editors with postmasterships and ambassadorships. Democratic and Republican editorial associations endured, and partisans—such as Free Silver advocates—established newspapers to espouse their causes.)[86] But the nature and extent of newspaper partisanship changed markedly in the nineteenth century, and many newspapers no longer identified themselves primarily as party organs. One Maine editor noted in 1885 that most newly established newspapers were independent in politics. "They occupy a growing field and one in which much good may be accomplished by the diffusion of general information."[87]

The antebellum political editor of the New York *Evening Post*, William Cullen Bryant, would have been surprised to see an editorial in his own newspaper in 1898 which announced that partisan news-papers could not be "fair and truthful." Readers avoided such papers, it argued, so partisan papers were "apt to have a short life."[88]

Increasingly, newspapers in the late nineteenth century claimed to be *independent* politically. Historians estimate that 95 percent of all newspapers in the Jacksonian era were partisan.[89] Such partisanship clearly declined toward the end of the century. A survey of newspapers in 25 leading cities,[90] based on *Pettingill's Newspaper Directory* for 1877, showed that 39.8 percent of them claimed to be independent.[91] In 1899, the percentage of independent newspapers in those same 25 cities had risen to 50 percent.[92]

Some newspapers touted their independence. The weekly *Woodburn Independent* (Oregon) noted in 1888: "It is not our intention to devote much time or space to politics, but rather to that which will most interest an agricultural community . . . Standing, as we do, distinctly apart from all political parties, we reserve the right to criticize or condemn the tenets of any or all parties, and will exercise this right without fear or favor."[93] The Salem, Oregon, *Independent* promised to be independent "in politics as in everything else."[94]

A substantial number of newspapers still claimed some political affiliation. Yet even publishers and editors with deep political preferences argued that they were not going to be dictated to by the party. They pledged loyalty, not to party personnel or party machinery, but to party ideals that they alone would determine. The editor of the *St. Louis Republic* proclaimed in 1888 that his paper was Democratic, but he noted that his newspaper would "neither profess nor tolerate the partisan fanaticism that creates a party into a church, a lapse from whose creed is held to imperil the soul's salvation." Democratic party officials and candidates would not escape scrutiny and criticism where justified. "In short, the *Republic* will remain a staunch Democratic newspaper but it will discuss men and measures, parties and principles, in such a spirit of candor and fairness as will prove informing *to Democrats and Republicans alike and will repel or offend no good citizen.*[95] B. J. McKinney, editor of the *Marietta Times* (Ohio), said his paper was Democratic and would support the party's nominees "whenever true Democrats and worthy, honest men are nominated." However, if the nominees don't measure up, "my paper is under no obligation to support them."[96]

Other newspapers did not eschew all partisan views, but did play down politics. The Drain, Oregon, *Echo*, a weekly newspaper, told its readers: "We do not expect to run a political organ, but when election times come, we expect to vote the Republican ticket."[97]

This view of newspaper partisanship, so different from the political newspapers of the Jacksonian era, derived in part from changes in politics and in the definitions of the newspaper's role in society. (The notion of the press as the Fourth Estate, keeping a watchful eye on public officials, grew in importance amid the various governmental scandals of the 1860s and 1870s.)[98] But the vision of independence in partisan affairs was also a business matter. Rather than wooing *voters*, many newspapers had come to woo *consumers*, whose numbers would lure advertisers. Partisanship was integral to the antebellum paper, which identified the reader primarily as voter. Such partisanship was hardly relevant for newspapers whose readers were identified less for their beliefs and voting behavior than for their ability to consume. Simply put, many publishers had come to believe that overt partisanship was a financial liability. Publishers recognized that neither advertisers nor readers might like a highly partisan newspaper. In 1892, the new proprietors of the Harrisburg, Pennsylvania, *Morning Call* noted the business rationale for eschewing partisanship. They said: "The experience of former publishers of this paper admonishes us that it is neither pleasant nor profitable for a newspaper to become an organ of the politicians."[99]

Many other publishers and editors likewise saw a financial liability in partisanship. In 1895, the publishers of the *Cincinnati Tribune* declared that nine-tenths of the successful newspapers of the day were independent and that the "old time servile party organs are neither profitable nor influential. The newspaper which is independent, and which is not merely partisan in its utterances, is sure to be the most profitable, for the reason that it enjoys the largest degree of popular approval."[100] Hugh Wilson, the publisher of the Abbeville, South Carolina, *Press and Banner,* warned that a partisan paper would be a financial failure.[101]

Many within the newspaper industry suggested that press nonpartisanship was necessary because the populace itself was becoming more independent. One trade journal writer observed in 1893 that more and more readers wanted their politics "straight."[102] Another writer warned that endorsements would hurt circulation and eventually ruin a paper.[103] And still another trade journal writer contended that the *St. Louis Dispatch* had lost many subscribers in the middle 1890s because of its "exceedingly partisan free-silver attitude."[104] Some Ohio publishers argued that candidates should pay for press coverage because it was tantamount to advertising.[105] There is no evidence that they ever acted on this conviction. One Chicago paper did, though, on a limited scale. During the 1893 city mayoralty election, the *Chicago Record* carried announcements for party rallies in its classified advertising columns.[106]

Newspaper political affiliation varied. Some newspapers retained a strong partisan stance, while others refused even to endorse candidates in nonpartisan municipal elections. These variations reflected a wide variety of concerns and beliefs. But newspapers often claimed independence when it was most advantageous economically. Similarly, where partisanship was most advantageous economically, it was more common.

An examination of all English-language newspapers in California and New York in 1899[107] shows the following trends: small-town weeklies were predominantly independent; newspapers in small cities and larger towns (particularly county seats) were usually partisan; and metropolitan newspapers were more evenly divided between partisanship and independence. Figure 5.1 represents New York in 1899; figure 5.2 represents California in 1899. Both figures show where independent newspapers are most likely to appear, with the number of newspapers per town serving to indicate town/city size. (See note 108 for the complete data.)

Independence was most common among small weekly newspapers, particularly when they were the only newspaper in a town. In one-newspaper towns in New York, 64.5 percent of all newspapers claimed to be independent (which was greatly different from the experience in two-newspaper towns, where nearly nine-tenths of all newspapers claimed a political affiliation). See figure 5.1. Business considerations figured prominently in political affiliation. Small towns had a limited potential readership and a very limited advertising base, both from businesses and from government printing. Partisanship might offend readers, hindering circulation growth or provoking a rival newspaper. Small towns seldom had enough advertising to support two newspapers, so establishing a second newspaper could have been disastrous financially. In 1895, one trade journal writer advised editors in one-newspaper towns to avoid overt partisanship if they wanted to avoid financial ruin.[109] Augustus J. Munson's *Making a Country Newspaper,* published in 1891, advised small-town newspapers to be neutral or nonpartisan: "Newspaper politics belongs to metropolitan journalism where a field sufficiently large to support it can be found.[110]

There's no evidence that people in small towns lacked partisan feeling. But partisanship could not appeal to a large enough group of readers to be financially attractive to advertisers, and thus such partisanship was de-emphasized.

Partisanship was most pronounced in small cities and large towns both in New York and California.[111] A variety of explanations exist here, but clearly a financial incentive existed for partisanship in these places. Reading audiences were larger in small cities and large towns, so partisan newspapers had a better chance of attracting sufficient readers. In addition, governmental patronage printing contracts went to newspapers in state capitals and county seats (which were usually small cities or large towns). In some states (Oregon, New Jersey, New

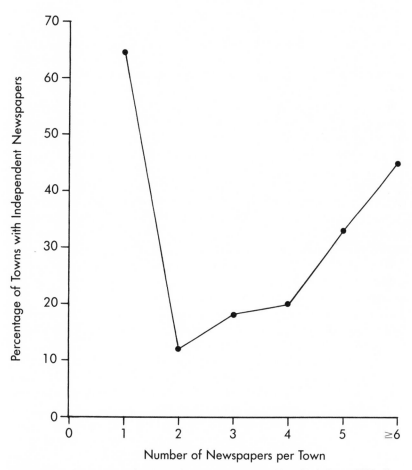

Figure 5.1.   Occurrence of independent newspapers in New York State, 1899. (See note 108 for the complete data.)

York, and Ohio), public printing contracts provided an extremely important form of newspaper advertising revenue for smaller newspapers, and those contracts were awarded along party lines. For example, Democratic officials would award Democratic newspapers in Ohio. In New York, state law required that two newspapers of different parties get county printing contracts.[112] In Oregon, county and state printing appeared in the two largest newspapers in each county, and paid about $900 a year.[113]

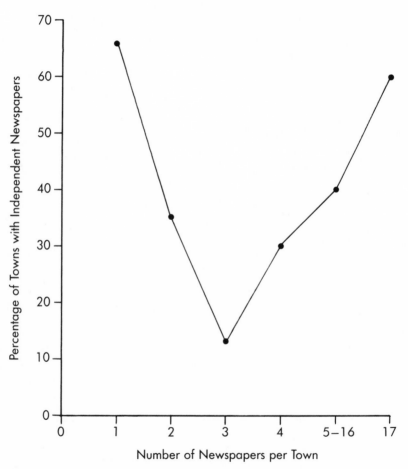

Figure 5.2.   Occurrence of independent newspapers in California, 1899. (See note 108 for the complete data.)

In New York and California, large towns and small cities that were county seats were more likely to have partisan newspapers than were similar-sized towns that were not county seats. See table 5.5.

County-seat patronage clearly nurtured competing partisan newspapers in large towns and small cities. As table 5.6 shows, in two-newspaper towns, New York Democratic and Republican newspapers reached parity *only* in county seats. In two-newspaper towns that were not county seats, Republican newspapers outnumbered Democratic papers almost two to one (as was common in other large towns and small cities in the state). (County seat patronage appears to have nurtured partisanship in small one-newspaper towns as well. Of the 274 small one-newspaper towns in this study, only 5 were county seats, and all 5 had partisan newspapers.)

In metropolitan areas, both partisanship and independence were common, reflecting the political interests of readers as well as market

Table 5.5. Percentage distribution of partisan and independent newspapers in large towns and small cities in New York State and California, 1899

	New York		California	
Nature of newspaper	County Seats	Not county Seats	County Seats	Not county Seats
Partisan	81.3	67.8	70.7	51.0
Independent	18.7	32.1	21.4	46.1
Other	0.0	0.0	7.9	3.0
	100.0	99.9	100.0	100.1
N of newspapers	139	286	140	102

Note: For the purpose of this analysis, in New York, large towns and small cities were defined as those having from 2 to 6 newspapers; in California, as those having from 2 to 10 newspapers.

Table 5.6. Percentage distribution of newspapers in two-newspaper towns, by political affiliation, New York State, 1899

	% Democrat	% Republican	% Independent	N of newspapers
County seats	47.0	50.0	3.0	32
Not county seats	23.4	40.1	35.8	194

considerations. Charles Austin Bates, an advertising agent in New York City in the 1890s, noted that advertisers in general preferred independent newspapers but that each metropolitan market could support a few overtly partisan newspapers. Bates argued that the *Chicago Chronicle*, as "the only Democratic newspaper of any pretensions" in its circulation territory, was valuable to advertisers because it had a potential reading audience of a million people, a constituency "that cannot very well be reached through any other medium." Bates added that advertisers saw the *Chronicle* merely as a business proposition and did not support the paper because of its political views.[114]

In metropolitan areas, two patterns emerge in newspaper partisanship. First, circulation appears to be related to partisanship. Smaller papers tended to be partisan and larger papers to be independent, reflecting the general notion at the time that larger circulations could be built primarily by avoiding or downplaying politics.[115] Second, evening newspapers were more likely than morning newspapers to be independent,[116] reflecting changes in reading patterns and advertisers' preference for evening newspapers. One advertising trade journal writer said that the evening paper "is the advertising medium of all advertising media and must forever be."[117]

Many department stores, usually the largest local advertisers in big cities, usually preferred evening newspapers. One New York City department store relied on evening newspapers exclusively on weekdays. One furniture-store owner said he preferred to advertise in evening newspapers because they were more likely to be read by women, "which is an object in my business."[118] The department store owner John Wanamaker preferred evening to morning newspapers in New York because evening newspapers went into the home and, thus, were a better advertising medium: "I believe that in New York the evening papers are the thing to advertise in, as they are taken home and read by the entire family."[119]

Partisanship reflected newspaper market variations. Where partisanship paid, in county seats in large towns and small cities, it flourished. Where partisanship was a potential liability, in small towns or among the large evening newspapers in metropolitan areas, it was less common.

Contests and Premiums

To lure readers (and to build loyalty to the newspaper "product"), publishers and editors ran contests and offered prizes. The kinds of

contests varied widely, from readers nominating their favorite fire-
man (police officer, railway guard, prize fighter, servant) to guessing
election results.

Contests could boost circulation. The *Chicago Record*'s circulation
rose 25 percent (from 132,000 to 165,000) during a four-month flurry
of contests in 1895. However, such circulation gains could be ephemeral; the *Record*'s circulation dropped to 129,000 when the contests
ceased. But the newspaper's management did not judge the circulation decline as proof of contests' limitations. Rather, management
saw the drop as a sign that *more* contests were needed. In the first six
months of 1896, the paper sponsored additional contests, and circulation rose to 207,000.[120] Contests endured, in part, because many
publishers and editors believed that they added permanent readers.
M. R. Freel, of the *New York Recorder*, claimed that circulation gained
during contests "can be permanently depended on."[121]

Papers sponsored many kinds of contests. The *St. Louis Star* offered
cash prizes for essays by schoolchildren on "critical moments" in the
life of George Washington. Both the *Memphis Commercial Appeal* and
the *Chicago Record* paid readers for short stories in the 1890s (the
Record promised to spend $20,000 in 1895 alone). Some newspapers
printed serialized stories and gave cash rewards to readers who could
solve the mysteries in each story. Real life imitated fiction, too; the
Philadelphia Inquirer offered $1,000 to anyone who could solve an ac-
tual murder and help capture the killer.[122] The *Cincinnati Tribune* offered a free trip to the 1893 Chicago World's Fair to the "ten most
popular pastors" (and their wives, if they were married).[123] The *Tribune* also sponsored one contest for women only and received 100,000
entries.[124] The *Detroit News* offered $70 in prizes for the best loaf of
bread ($25 for first prize) and 2,000 bread makers showed up with
6,000 loaves.[125] The *Cincinnati Commercial Gazette* offered prizes ranging from one to five dollars for the best item of news furnished by any
boy or girl under the age of 16.[126] The *Dallas News* and the *Birmingham
Age Herald* offered sewing machines for a year's subscription.[127] And
the *Nashville Banner* gave prizes for readers who could find a particular word printed in its classified columns.[128]

Some contests required coupons from the newspaper. The idea was
that readers would have to buy the newspaper to get the coupon. The
New York *Evening Telegram* sponsored a "favorite teacher" contest in
1897. The five teachers with the most coupon votes won a trip to
Queen Victoria's diamond jubilee celebration and a five-week tour of
the Continent.[129] When the *Albany Argus* (New York) sponsored a

most-popular-teacher and brightest-student contest in 1897, the paper received 600,000 coupon ballots.[130] The winner of the New York *Evening Telegram*'s 1897 trip to the Klondike had more than 200,000 coupon votes when the contest closed.[131]

Not all contests ran smoothly. During the 1897 *Albany Argus* brightest-student contest, young boys grabbed newspapers from readers on trolleys and street corners, tore out the coupons and then returned the despoiled papers to enraged readers. The New York *Evening Telegram* contest in 1896–97 was such a fiasco that it landed the newspaper in court. The newspaper promised a world tour to the person who came closest to predicting the winner's votes in the 1896 presidential election. William S. Bass of Brooklyn bought 30,000 copies of the newspaper and used a mathematical system to fill in all the coupons. Bass won the contest. One of his entries missed William McKinley's number of votes by just one. But the *Evening Telegram*'s management didn't like Bass's multiple entries and refused to give him the trip. He sued, demanding $10,000. The court sided with Bass and ordered the newspaper to give him the trip or the money. The paper offered the trip but stipulated that he depart within 10 days. He wanted the money (probably to defray the cost of 30,000 copies of the *Evening Telegram*). The outcome is unclear.[132]

Outside of the metropolitan areas, contests and premiums may not have been as common, but they existed. In Elmira, New York, the two competing newspapers used coupon schemes to compete for circulation. The *Elmira Star* offered a variety of prizes (for contests nominating the most popular police officer, letter carrier, and street car employee), while the *Elmira Advertiser* awarded suits of clothes and season tickets at a local theater to individuals chosen from its roster of subscribers.[133] The Drain, Oregon, *Echo*, a weekly newspaper, offered prizes for stories from its readers in 1885 and 1886.[134] The *Wasco News* (Oregon), another weekly, gave a bottle of Dr. Kilmer's Swamp Root for each new subscription or renewal.[135] The *Lima Advertiser* (Ohio) sponsored an annual picnic for its subscribers in the 1890s.[136] The *Lynn Daily Press* (Massachusetts) offered free theater tickets to its readers.[137] And the Salem, Oregon, *Capital Journal*'s coupon contests offered such prizes as books, china sets, silver cutlery, plows, sewing machines, suits, hats, watches, furniture, stoves, guns, and fruit trees.[138]

Some editors shied from these contests. The *Pittsburgh Leader* generally did not sponsor such contests, yet in 1899 it promoted a coupon contest "for good government." Editors urged readers to clip out coupons from the paper pledging their loyalty to "clean popular government" rather than corrupt "ring government."[139]

Conclusions

In an 1890 article in *Printers' Ink,* T. H. Cahill declared that newspapers had moved well beyond their original mission of "collecting and disseminating current intelligence." In their new role, they were the "agent and servant of the advertising spirit." The wise publisher valued advertising: "He well understands where the reliable supports of his business prosperity lie."[140]

Cahill was writing for a trade journal produced by advertising interests, but he aptly characterized the environment within which news was defined. News was not solely "current intelligence." Rather, news had become a commodity to be shaped and packaged with an eye toward the goal of increasing circulation and subsequently advertising revenues.

The environment of news was clearly a commercial one. Demographic concerns focused on the purchasing power of the reading audience. The rush to flatter advertisers (potential and existent) produced articles glorifying businesses, their operations, their advertising, and even their sales. Newspapers concocted special issues—generally unrelated to current events or breaking news—simply because they were ideal for advertisers. General content was "whatever you most like," accompanied by an avoidance of troubling political issues that might offend readers and advertisers. A steady offer of prizes was akin to the barker's cry at a circus—luring in the new customers or enticing others to return.

All this produced a good deal of newspaper content that was quite interesting, to be sure. But it came at a certain cost. One journalist noted that the circus of newspaper contests and prizes had little or nothing to do with journalism. "What has a chromo lithograph or a voting contest as to the most popular typewriter or handsomest police captain to do with journalism?" he asked.[141] Some journalists were concerned about the space devoted to contests, fearing that they preempted or detracted from the real purpose of the newspaper. The editor of the *Boston Daily Advertiser* complained that contests and other prizes distracted everyone from the pressing issues of the day.

"What are the financial questions, what are presidential elections, what is the silver issue, in comparison with the delicious joy" of getting paper dolls in the Sunday newspaper? he asked.[142]

Highly diverse content, articles for women, flattering articles on businesses and advertisers—all these were produced with an eye to increasing revenues. The purpose of much newspaper content was, first, to assemble the largest "quality" audience, and second, to attract advertisers who would pay high advertising rates to reach those quality readers. Current intelligence was only one definition of news; the commercial value of content was certainly another.

The commercialization of news did not go unnoticed in the late nineteenth century. Whitelaw Reid condemned widespread press commercialism, "which sacrifices principles and morality to the cash drawer and makes the newspaper not the exponent of principles but the coiner of money."[143] William Cullen Bryant, a longtime political editor, probably best characterized this trend in American journalism when he criticized penny press pioneer James Gordon Bennett. Bryant said that Bennett was not an editor in the model of Horace Greeley or others from earlier in the century, but a news *vendor*.[144] Earlier in the nineteenth century, editors and politicians shaped news with an eye to politics. By century's end, advertisers, publishers, and editors joined to shape news with an eye to revenues and profits.

Chapter Six

The Commercialization of News

In 1900, American newspapers bore little resemblance to the small journals that had so earnestly debated politics in the 1820s and 1830s. Newspaper owners and editors were no longer primarily political activists obsessed with winning elections and filling their newspapers with political argument. Some publishers proudly saw themselves as businessmen rather than party activists, and most everyone in the newspaper industry claimed to be independent of party dictation. In 1900, American newspapers contained more than news of politics and business; they were a colorful amalgam of general news, sports, entertainment, comics, and even fiction.

The transformation of the American newspaper during the nineteenth century is one of the sweeping changes within American society. Industrialization and urbanization altered the face of the nation. Moreover, they created an environment within which a new kind of newspaper evolved. The growth of advertising—one result of industrialization—provided a major source of revenue for newspapers in the late nineteenth century. Advertising emerged as the chief financial supporter and shaper of the press. Urbanization created the need for a newspaper that went beyond political advocacy and attempted, instead, to make sense of a dispersed community.

Against the backdrop of these broad social developments, the newspaper itself changed. New definitions of news emerged. Many came to see the newspaper as a business rather than a political tool. Publishers and editors realized that they could make large profits by pitching newspaper content to the masses and then selling their huge audiences to advertisers. Advertisers were quick to reinforce this vision of the newspaper as a marketing vehicle.

Day-to-day operations of the press fueled change within the industry, too. Political patronage began to decline just as newspaper costs began to soar. Newspaper owners were forced to think about alternative sources of revenue and to accommodate themselves to providing a newspaper that met the needs of the new patrons who provided those alternative sources. These changes were most evident at midcentury in metropolitan areas, and particularly in the large dailies of that era. But other publishers and editors, in smaller cities and towns across the nation, saw the tremendous success of the metropolitan press and copied some, if not all, of its methods.

How Commercialization Came About

What was the precise nature of the changes in nineteenth-century newspapers? In many ways, what figures most prominently in all the newspapers is the growth of news as a commodity, as a commercial product, to be shaped, packaged, and marketed with a constant eye to profit. Early in the century, the paper and its editor existed to win power, to contest elections, to argue about politics and programs. Certainly profits were part of the economic calculus of editors then, but the *raison d'être*—so clear from content and from discussions about the press in that era—was political. By century's end, although many editors and publishers retained links to party, the newspaper had emerged as a business, dedicated to presenting information within the parameters of profitability. Editors introduced certain categories of news primarily because doing so could make money. The notion of the omnibus press—having something for everyone—was as much a strategy for marketing as it was for disseminating information. Content that was entertaining (comics, jokes, serialized fiction, and so forth) appeared because of its marketing value. Content for women stemmed from commercial considerations, as well. Advertisers wanted to reach women, who were thought of as the principal shoppers, so it followed that they wanted content aimed at women. Such content would lure women to read the newspaper, where they would see ads. The purpose of this commercialized news is clear: it linked advertisers with consumers. It attracted readers, who lured advertisers, who provided profits for the newspaper.

Older types of content, such as political news, depended on business considerations as well. Strong partisanship existed primarily where it was profitable. The most partisan newspapers were in county seats, where political patronage was most plentiful. Elsewhere, editors feared that partisanship would alienate readers and advertisers. Trade journals in the advertising and newspaper industry reinforced this view. Editors did not stop covering politics, and they did not stop taking political stands. But they approached the world of politics gingerly; they kept their distance from politicians and political parties. This was an early version of the least-offensive programming that has served to make much of television so banal.

Some of the commercialized content of the newspapers was really advertising hidden under the trappings of news. Reading notices theoretically lulled the reader into absorbing the marketing messages uncritically. Puffs and promotions appeared throughout newspaper columns, endorsing advertisers and their products. But much of the broad content of the newspaper—sports, entertainment, fashion, cooking, books, and serialized fiction—appeared largely because it supported the advertisements around it. It drew the reader into the tent to hear the salesman's pitch.

Early nineteenth-century newspaper editors were unabashed *advocates for political parties*. Late nineteenth-century newspaper editors were advocates as well, *advocates for business*, for their advertisers. Newspaper opposition to patent medicine labeling laws, attacks on the substitution of generics for name-brand products, publication of puffery, and tolerance of ads disguised as news in the form of reading notices are all part of this advocacy. Also, publishers and editors ardently promoted their own business interests. They tried to eliminate competition (attacks on billboard and street car advertising come to mind) under the pretence of promoting the public good. In all these instances, newspapers were advocates for vested business interests rather than for the general public.

The process of commercialization of news poses larger questions and prompts speculation about whether alternative development was possible. Was commercialization itself a necessary component of newspaper survival? Changes in the newspaper and in news were inevitable given the changing pattern of American life and leisure in the nineteenth century. Leisure activities began to figure prominently in American urban life late in the century, and the narrowly partisan newspaper that ignored news of leisure activities (theater, vaudeville, sports, zoos, circuses) would have had trouble keeping its readers' interest. All three of the century-spanning metropolitan newspapers in this study added content that reflected readers' diversifying interests and activities. These newspapers were not as rich in such coverage as was Hearst's *New York Journal*, but they had diversified.

When advertisers emerged as the key constituent for American newspapers, they placed great emphasis on reaching large audiences of people who might buy their products. The newspaper that produced *only* political news simply did not assemble the audience size desired by advertisers. As such, political newspapers could no longer inhabit the mainstream of American journalism. Instead, they moved to the margins as specialized publications, dependent primarily on subscriptions.

Commercialized news was more entertaining than the politicized news of the 1820s and 1830s. The comics, jokes, gossipy stories about society, reports on sporting events, and serialized fiction created a newspaper that provided something for most any taste. Only the narrow partisan who was oblivious of the larger society would fail to find something of interest. Some newspapers, such as the *Chicago Tribune* or the Salem, Oregon, *Capital Journal,* provided this commercialized news alongside more serious and thoughtful political news. Perhaps the commercialized news produced the audience that advertisers demanded and, thus, allowed the remaining political content. In a broad sense, one can argue that newspapers (and thus news) were redefined or reinvented in the middle and latter decades of the nineteenth century. Gunther Barth argues in his book *City People* that metropolitan areas created new roles for the newspaper as the surveyer and synthesizer of the large and dispersed urban population. By 1900, face-to-face communication was less efficient as a means of knowing about important events in one's community. Metropolitan newspapers of the late nineteenth century filled this need to know about one's community, produced large profits, and inspired other newspapers to copy that success. In this sort of analysis, newspapers are not static institutions, but rather ones that are reconstituted from time to time according to societal needs and economic feasibility. In the antebellum era, political parties had a dilemma. They needed to mobilize voters in statewide elections but faced both a tradition that mitigated against self-promotion by candidates and a transportation system that prevented extensive campaigning. The parties' needs created a role for the newspaper and editor as political activist. The partisan newspaper filled a particular need, just as the metropolitan newspaper of the 1890s filled the particular needs of urban readers and advertisers. In the late twentieth century, the newspaper faces further reconstitution as editors and publishers attempt to assure its survival and profitability into the twenty-first century.

The Impact of Commercialization

Whether inevitable or not, commercialization of the newspaper poses questions about the role of the newspaper in the democratic process.

The many legal safeguards for the press in American society are premised on the notion that the press supplies information central to an enlightened electorate, and thus central to democracy itself.

In the early nineteenth century, partisan editors filled their newspapers with partisan essays, argument and counterargument. These newspapers were a vibrant part of the political process. Editors did not debate in some idealistic desire to create a vast marketplace of ideas. Rather, they argued with one another because they wanted power. They were highly opinionated and interpreted events within their partisan ideology. Through all this they defined their readers as voters. Despite their bias, their intolerance of their opponents, and their subservience to political parties, they produced fervent and wide-ranging debate about political issues.

Business considerations conditioned the involvement of newspapers in the democratic process in the late nineteenth century. Editors covered campaigns, endorsed candidates and rejoiced or lamented over election results. But the key constituent of the press, the advertiser, defined readers as consumers and thus contributed to news values that served that view. While the antebellum press's subservience to political parties produced political debate of potential value for the broad public, the late nineteenth-century press's subservience to advertising interests did not. If anything, the desire to please advertisers meant anything except political news and information. Reading notices, puffs, and news created and valued primarily for its commercial payoff did not advance public debate or knowledge. Some editors admitted that they avoided difficult issues for fear of alienating readers. As David Potter noted in *People of Plenty,* such aversion to controversy (as in television's least-offensive programing) is a kind of censorship, for it guarantees that ideas do not reach the public.

Newspapers in the late nineteenth century did not disengage from all participation in the democratic process. But that participation became conditional. The emphasis on demographics, which valued readers as consumers, excluded the poor, who could vote but had little money to spend. Advocacy for advertisers' interests or for publishers' own interests elevated private commercial gain over broad public service. Some aspects of news gathering valued news more for its potential profitability than for its ability to inform. Some of these changes were inevitable for newspapers to survive. Some of these changes in content made newspapers more interesting to larger numbers of people than ever before. But commercialization of the news

had social cost. The low price of the newspaper made it appear to be
a great bargain. But the *real cost* was much higher. Readers paid little
out of pocket for the new newspaper of 1900, but they paid in other
ways. They received mountains of "news" that momentarily enter-
tained but that did not engage them in the reality of their city, nation,
or world. In retrospect, inexpensive newspapers were not a great
bargain.

Definitions of News

The changes in newspaper content across the nineteenth century
underscore the extent to which news is a social construct, varying
from era to era according to the social forces at work at the time. News
is a malleable compound, a synthesis of interests. It is defined
through the relationship of the press and society, through the economic forces that shape newspapers as businesses, and through the
structure and day-to-day operation of the press itself.

First, and foremost, news depends upon the relationship of the
newspaper (or, more broadly, the media) with other institutions, interests, or groups in society. The definitions of news in the antebellum
era depended on the links between press and party. The definitions of
news in the 1890s depended on the links between press and business.
And the nature of these relationships between the press and other
social groups depended, in part, on expectations that those social
groups had for the press. Political parties in the 1820s and 1830s and
advertisers in the 1890s had very specific expectations about how
newspapers could help them. These constituents were major sources
of funding for the press; their needs became part of the background
against which newspapers selected and shaped the information they
offered readers. These constituents had great influence over the press
because they could either withdraw their patronage (at times, they did
so) or reward newspapers with power and money for the "right" kind
of news.

Moreover, editors and publishers were not unwilling partners of
political parties or, later, of advertisers. Within the newspaper itself,
the vision the news processors held of their own role helped to define
news. In 1830, editors defined their readers as voters, and that definition guided news values. In 1890 or 1900, publishers and editors
defined their readers in a more complex way. Some were voters.

Some were people seeking entertainment. But fundamentally all were consumers.

The occupational group to which editors belonged reinforced particular definitions of news. In the 1820s and 1830s, Jacksonian editor Charles Gordon Greene's peers were other Jacksonians, who also valued his newspaper for its political role. By century's end, the occupation group had changed from a party-based one to a group based in journalism and business. Publishers and editors (as well as circulation managers) met with one another (across party lines) in their trade associations to discuss issues of common concern. Those trade associations reinforced a business vision of the newspaper and of news.

The size or scale of a newspaper (or, more broadly, of any medium) also influences news. The antebellum partisan newspaper was usually a highly personal one, the product of literally a few (often just one) party activists. By century's end, the newspaper—particularly in metropolitan areas, but in small cities, too—had become a relatively complex organization. As the newspaper organization grew, news gathering and editing became the work of just some of its personnel. With the growth of multidepartment newspapers (circulation, advertising, production, as well as news editorial), proportionately fewer workers dealt with news itself. The emphasis in departments such as circulation or advertising was on the product: on selling it and on delivering it. The expertise necessary for efficient production and delivery of a 500,000-circulation newspaper (or even a 20,000-circulation small-city newspaper) in the 1890s had little or nothing to do with journalism. Circulation managers defined news in terms of its marketability rather than its ability to inform.

Costs also shape news definitions. The free postal exchange of antebellum newspapers facilitated the spread of partisan news and opinion nationwide. The scissors-and-paste method of excerpting from those exchanges cost little; news was abundant and cheap. Late in the century, costs had risen substantially for all newspapers. The amount of capital needed to establish a newspaper had risen dramatically, as had operating costs. Efforts to contain costs substantively influenced news gathering and processing. For reporters, space pay, job insecurity, and long working hours tilted news away from a faithful representation of events. As the young New York reporter John Fox noted in the 1880s, such a process guaranteed fabrication and exaggeration. Low pay left reporters ripe for bribes from special interests who wanted a puff or who desired to play up or suppress a

story. Cost containment also meant that news which could be antic-
ipated would be the most likely to be covered. The beat system's
value, in part, is in its economic efficiency. For weekly newspapers
across the country, patent insides cost relatively little but provided
substantial amounts of highly diverse content. The nature of the
patent insides generally guaranteed a certain blandness; the time
lapse inherent in production and distribution eliminated much that
was timely.

Competition defines news, as well. The creation of news (for example, reporters jumping off ferry boats to test rescue squads' readiness) could guarantee lively stories and conceivably boost urban
street sales of newspapers. Some newspapers, particularly in the
highly competitive metropolitan markets, devoted a good deal of
space to contests and premiums designed to lure customers.

Other factors no doubt influence news values and definitions. The
changing patterns of news in the nineteenth century point out some
of the major determinants of news. This study of nineteenth-century
newspapers points to two fundamental factors in news values and
definitions: first, the relationships between media and groups within
the larger society, and second, the internal operations of the media
themselves. Both are central to the definition of news.

Appendices

Notes

Selected Bibliography

Index

Appendix 1

Content Analysis Scheme

All nonadvertising content in the newspapers was examined according to its subject and its length. The original subject categories are below; the various tables in appendix 2 demonstrate a collapsed version of these categories.

The original subject categories were derived from a general sense of newspaper content and were altered twice in response to pretesting. The final version of the subject categories was tested for reliability; three different coders utilized the coding scheme, and reliability averaged 93 percent (with one coder, the reliability was 90 percent, the other two, 95 percent).

The papers in the study were chosen to provide a cross-section of U.S. newspapers, by size of city (metropolitan, nonmetropolitan) and by location (region).

Subject Categories

1. National politics, political issues: federal government, Congress, members of Congress, staff, bills, debates and proceedings, executive departments (including cabinet), defense and armed forces, first family, national political parties (e.g., national conventions, campaigns), Supreme Court.
2. U.S. foreign relations.
3. Foreign politics: relations between and among foreign countries (where the United States was not clearly involved), wars, elections, governmental operations, heads of state.
4. Foreign news (not political): general customs and culture.
5. Foreign news: acts of nature (e.g., floods, earthquakes, disasters, famine), shipwrecks, accidents, deaths.
6. Foreign news: society, art, culture, fashion, leisure time (theater, books, sports, music).
7. Foreign news: disease (cholera, plagues).
8. Foreign news: business.
9. Foreign news: crime, trials, police, arrests, jails.
10. Foreign history.
11. U.S. history: commemoration of U.S. historical events (Washington's birthday, Civil War reminiscences), general U.S. history.
12. Natural history (United States or foreign): Ice Age, dinosaurs, etc.

13. State politics (not home state of the newspaper): legislatures, governors, state politicians, politics of cities outside home state (e.g., mayoral elections).

14. State politics (home state and cities in home state, but not home city).

15. Local politics (home county, city, suburbs): city council, mayoralty, city agencies except for police, fire, hospital, mental health.

16. General crime news (not home county, city, or suburbs): police, criminal court news, prisoners (current, past), jails, duels, police investigations, chases, arraignments or trials in criminal cases, confessions, executions, general police news.

17. General crime news (home county, city, suburbs): police and criminal court news, arrests.

18. Civil court issues (not home county, city, suburbs): lawsuits (but not divorce cases or sanity hearings), general law issues (unless concerning crime).

19. Civil court issues (home county, city, suburbs).

20. Accidents (fatal, not fatal) and hospitals (not home county, city, suburbs): train wrecks, explosions, boat sinkings, carriage upsets, injuries.

21. Accidents (fatal, not fatal) and hospitals (home county, city, suburbs).

22. Divorces, adultery, illicit love, romantic triangles, elopements, breaches of promise, romance, etc.

23. Insanity, mental institutions.

24. Suicides, attempted suicides.

25. Fires (not home county, city, suburbs).

26. Fires (home county, city, suburbs).

27. Other local news (home county, city, suburbs).

28. General business and finance news (not home county, city, suburbs): business, finance, railroads, mining, agriculture, real estate, general investment climate, shipping, trade, markets, crop news, fishing, ship and railroad schedules.

29. General business and finance news (home county, city, suburbs): profiles of local businesses, business persons, bankruptcies.

30. Labor (not home county, city, suburbs): working conditions, labor unions, labor talks, strikes.

31. Labor (home county, city, suburbs).

32. Science, education, technology, medicine: inventions, new technology, schools, school children, general health, drugs, general medical news, conventions or meetings in science, education, technology, medicine.

33. Disease, plagues (United States).

34. Weather (United States): daily forecasts, weather reports, storms, etc.

35. Religion, churches, charity, and philanthropy: denominational meetings, the Vatican, philosophical or quasi-religious groups (e.g., the Theosophical Society).

36. Deaths, serious illnesses (not home county, city, suburbs): deaths from general causes (as opposed to accidents, murders), obituaries, wills, funerals, reports on persons dying.

37. Deaths, serious illnesses (home county, city, suburbs).

38. Miscellany.

39. Fashion, society news: parties, dances, reunions, general society, clothes, travel.

40. Recipes, cooking, news about the home (how to decorate, new homes).

41. Women's "work": shopping, cleaning, cooking, women's volunteer work, women's groups or clubs, women's auxiliaries.

42. Women in unusual situations (reporters, physicians, ministers).

43. Fraternal organizations (veterans' associations, Masons, Odd Fellows).

44. General entertainment: theater, news, plays, reviews, interviews with actors and actresses, music (concerts, music festivals, music halls), lectures (chautauqua, general lectures).

45. Reading and art: book reviews, news about books, writers, art, and artists.

46. Other leisure activities (but not sports), vacations.

47. Fiction, verse.

48. Hobbies, games (card games), pets, animals, zoos, circuses, animal protection groups.

49. Sports and adventure: baseball, boating, boxing, golf, horse racing, walking, bicycling, tennis, hunting, miscellaneous sports, adventure (safaris, hunting, animal terror).

50. The newspaper itself: articles about the newspaper (its anniversary, circulation), general promotional articles ("This Sunday's newspaper will have. . .").

51. Newspaper coupons, premiums, contests, patterns, cut-out dolls, etc.

52. Indexes for the newspaper.

53. Journalism in general (not this specific newspaper).

54. Editorials, editorial cartoons.

55. Letters to editors.

56. Editorial-page columns (but not editorials).

57. Articles for children (children's puzzles, literature).

58. Comics, jokes.

59. Oddities: deformities, two-headed people, mad-dog stories, dwarfs, etc.

60. News of states and cities (not home state, county, city, suburbs) other than political.

61. American Indians: traditions, culture (resettlement part of national political news).

62. Advice to the lovelorn.

Appendix 2

Content Analysis Tables

Table A2.1. Metropolitan antebellum newspapers, 1831–32: Percentage distribution of newspaper content, by category

	Charleston Mercury[a]	Charleston Courier[b]	Boston Morning Post[c]	Boston Daily Advertiser[d]	New York Courier and Enquirer[e]	Median percentage
Politics	48.4	62.4	40.3	51.7	50.5	50.5
Crime and courts	1.2	2.1	5.3	2.5	6.2	2.5
Accidents	6.9	3.6	9.8	2.6	2.2	3.6
Society and women	2.5	0.2	5.7	5.1	1.0	2.5
Leisure	0.4	2.8	6.3	0.1	5.4	2.8
Business and labor	36.8	26.4	17.7	22.9	22.9	22.9
Religion	0.7	0.4	0.0	0.6	5.6	0.6
Science and education	1.8	0.5	1.7	1.2	2.8	1.7
History	0.3	0.0	11.8	11.2	0.0	0.3
Weather	0.5	0.2	0.5	1.4	2.3	0.5
Other	0.1	1.7	0.8	0.6	0.8	0.8
N of column inches	952.8	613.2	428.2	764.8	838.0	

Note: Coding dates vary according to availability of newspapers.
[a]Coded for January 16–21, 1832.
[b]Coded for March 5–10, 1832.
[c]Coded for January 16–21, 1832.
[d]Coded for May 10–15, 1831.
[e]Coded for January 17–22, 1831.

Table A2.2.   Nonmetropolitan antebellum newspapers, 1831–32: Percentage
distribution of newspaper contents, by category

	Haverhill, Massachusetts, Essex Gazette[a]	Rutherfordton North Carolina Spectator[a]	Greenville Mountaineer, North Carolina[a]	Albany Argus, New York[b]	Median percentage
Politics	68.2	68.4	70.8	76.9	69.6
Crime and courts	2.2	2.6	0.4	2.5	2.3
Accidents	5.0	11.1	6.3	4.6	4.8
Society and women	1.3	1.7	1.4	0.4	1.4
Leisure	6.3	3.7	7.4	1.0	5.0
Business and labor	1.5	2.5	2.1	6.8	2.3
Religion	9.2	3.8	4.55	3.6	4.2
Science and education	1.9	1.5	1.0	1.0	1.2
History	0.0	0.0	2.6	0.0	0.0
Weather	0.5	0.8	0.6	0.0	0.6
Other	0.7	3.7	2.8	0.7	1.7
N of Column inches	1,285.2	1,538.0	1,101.5	1,139.5	

Note: Coding dates vary according to availability of newspapers.
[a]All weeklies, coded for January 7, 14, 21, 28, 1832.
[b]A daily, coded for January 9–14, 1832.

Table A2.3.   Metropolitan postbellum newspapers, 1897: Percentage
distribution of newspaper contents, by category

	Pittsburgh Leader	New York Evening Post	Boston Daily Advertiser	New York Journal	Chicago Tribune	Charleston Courier	Boston Globe	San Francisco Chronicle	Median percentage
Politics	9.0	36.2	20.6	18.2	20.1	22.1	15.1	16.0	19.1
Crime and courts	6.5	4.9	7.1	12.4	10.0	7.2	6.5	12.8	7.2
Accidents	4.8	4.5	4.8	20.2	7.6	9.1	8.1	11.9	7.8
Society and women	11.4	4.1	4.7	9.9	5.0	5.9	8.1	6.7	6.3
Leisure	34.6	17.1	9.1	14.0	18.0	15.1	25.3	18.5	17.8
Business and labor	16.6	23.2	22.3	7.5	16.4	19.3	11.4	21.9	18.0
Religion	7.4	2.2	0.1	1.9	5.5	5.5	4.6	4.4	4.5
Science and education	5.3	4.9	2.0	0.5	3.9	6.1	2.2	1.6	3.0
History	0.0	0.0	26.6	0.0	2.7	1.4	5.2	0.0	0.7
Weather	0.1	0.3	0.3	0.4	0.6	2.5	0.4	0.6	0.4
Comics and jokes	1.3	0.5	0.5	10.4	2.2	1.0	6.3	1.4	1.4
Other	3.0	2.2	0.8	2.4	2.8	5.0	6.2	4.3	2.9
N of column inches	2,835.3	7,208.4	6,151.3	14,294.3	11,274.3	5,719.5	13,592.3	9,709.0	

Note: All newspapers were coded for October 17–23, 1897.

Table A2.4.   Large-town/small-city postbellum newspapers, 1890s: Percentage distribution of newspaper content, by category

	Salem, Oregon, Capital Journal[a]	Mansfield News, Ohio[b]	Albany Daily Democrat, Oregon[c]	Macon Telegraph, Georgia[d]	The Dalles Chronicle, Oregon[e]	Median percentage
Politics	41.8	23.3	42.9	42.7	45.7	42.7
Crime and courts	11.9	11.3	7.4	10.6	5.3	10.6
Accidents	7.9	9.7	5.8	6.8	13.7	7.9
Society and women	8.3	13.3	10.5	5.6	8.0	8.3
Leisure	4.6	8.6	4.7	7.5	7.5	7.5
Business and labor	18.0	12.7	12.5	14.3	10.4	12.7
Religion	3.2	8.5	3.2	7.7	2.1	3.2
Science and education	3.7	6.7	4.9	2.1	1.1	3.7
History	0.0	1.6	1.9	0.0	0.0	0.0
Weather	0.2	0.1	0.6	0.9	0.5	0.5
Other	0.9	2.7	3.9	1.4	4.8	2.7
N of column inches	1,004.5	1,124.2	406.8	2,729.5	599.0	

Note: Coding dates vary according to availability of newspapers.
 [a]Coded for October 17–23, 1897.
 [b]Coded for October 19, 22, 1897.
 [c]Coded for October 16–20, 189/.
 [d]Coded for October 2, 16, 30, 1893.
 [e]Coded for October 18–23, 1897.

Table A2.5.   Small-town postbellum newspapers, 1897: Percentage distribution of contents, by category

	Woodburn Independent, Oregon[a]	Junction City Times, Oregon[b]	Elgin Recorder, Oregon[c]	Median percentage
Politics	22.9	22.6	42.2	22.9
Crime and courts	6.0	6.6	9.5	6.6
Accidents	9.2	11.2	12.3	11.2
Society and women	0.9	2.5	5.1	2.5
Leisure	6.8	15.7	1.1	6.8
Business and labor	26.7	16.9	20.6	20.6
Religion	1.2	5.1	0.5	1.2
Science and education	8.8	11.3	4.1	8.8
History	1.2	0.0	0.2	0.2
Weather	0.0	0.0	0.7	0.0
Other	5.4	3.6	1.1	3.6
N of column inches	763.0	1,178.2	635.8	

Note: Coding dates vary according to availability of newspapers.
[a]Coded for October 7, 14, 21, 28, 1897.
[b]Coded for October 2, 9, 16, 1897.
[c]Coded for October 22, 29, 1897.

Notes

Introduction

1. New York *Evening Post*, November 1, 1801.
2. Allan Nevins, *The Evening Post: A Century of Journalism* (New York: Boni and Liveright, Publishers, 1922), pp. 9, 11–12, 17, 19, 23–25, 35.
3. New York *Evening Post*, October 18, 1897.
4. David P. Forsyth, *The Business Press in America, 1750–1865* (Philadelphia: Chilton Books).
5. Hazel Dicken-Garcia, *Journalistic Standards in Nineteenth-Century America* (Madison: University of Wisconsin Press, 1989); Jeffrey B. Rutenbeck, "The Rise of Independent Newspapers in the 1870s: A Transformation in American Journalism" (Ph.D. diss., University of Washington, 1990).
6. This dramatic change certainly was not the only one to occur in the American newspaper during the nineteenth century. That period also saw the evolution of the press as a watchdog on government and the rise of journalism as an occupation. Some editors essentially democratized the newspaper by providing content of interest and importance to Americans across class lines—a sharp contrast to the relatively elitist nature of early nineteenth-century newspapers. See Thomas C. Leonard, *The Power of the Press: The Birth of American Political Reporting* (New York: Oxford University Press, 1986).
7. In the antebellum era, only white males had the franchise.
8. Proprietors to Hack and Seaver, October 17, 1832; Green and Willis to Solomon Richmond, October 13, 1832; Samuel Breck to Green and Willis, November 6, 1832; all in "We the People and Old Colony Press Business Records," 1830–1836, American Antiquarian Society.
9. James L. Crouthamel, *Bennett's New York Herald and the Rise of the Popular Press* (Syracuse: Syracuse University Press, 1989), pp. 18, 21.
10. Alfred McClung Lee, *The Daily Newspaper in America: The Evolution of a Social Instrument* (New York: Macmillan Co., 1937), p. 166.
11. Ibid., p. 167.
12. Ibid., p. 166.
13. William E. Ames, *A History of the National Intelligencer* (Chapel Hill: University of North Carolina Press, 1972); Culver H. Smith, *The Press, Politics and Patronage* (Athens: University of Georgia Press, 1977); Carolyn Stewart Dyer, "Political Patronage of the Wisconsin Press, 1849–1861: New Perspectives on the Economics of Patronage," *Journalism Monographs* 109 (Febru-

ary 1989); Milton W. Hamilton, *The Country Printer: New York State, 1785–1830* (New York: Columbia University Press, 1936).

14. In an 1889 journalism primer, *The Ladder of Journalism: How to Climb It* (New York: Allan Forman, 1889), p. 7, T. Campbell-Copeland identifies three types of newspapers: metropolitan dailies, local dailies, and local weeklies.

15. Nevins, *The Evening Post*, pp. 207–41.

16. Commercial, literary, temperance, and religious newspapers all flourished in the antebellum era. See James L. Crouthamel, *James Watson Webb: A Biography* (Middletown, Conn.: Wesleyan University Press, 1969); Ray Billington, *Protestant Crusade* (Chicago: Quadrangle Books, 1964); William Rorabaugh, *The Alcoholic Republic* (New York: Oxford University Press, 1979); Forsyth, *The Business Press in America*.

17. Gerald J. Baldasty, "The Political Press in the Second American Party System: The 1832 Election" (Ph.D. diss., University of Washington, 1978), pp. 140–70.

18. Crouthamel, *James Watson Webb*, pp. 20–47.

19. It can be argued that it is the most commercialized because of Hearst's penchant for sensationalism to attract readers, marketing of the news, and self-promotion of the *Journal* (banner headlines would remind readers that the *Journal* got the news FIRST, through creativity and hustle).

20. Quoted in the *Newspaper Maker* (April 4, 1898), p. 5. The editorial noted that such partisanship would repel readers, meaning that partisan papers were "apt to have a short life."

21. The newspapers examined for content were issued in 1831 and 1832; the variation in dates examined is due to varying availability of the newspapers.

The *metropolitan* newspapers examined were:

New York *Courier and Enquirer,* January 17–22, 1831

Boston Morning Post, January 16–21, 1832

Charleston Mercury, January 16–21, 1832

Charleston Courier, March 5–10, 1832

Boston Daily Advertiser, May 10–15, 1831

The *small-city/large-town* newspapers examined were:

Albany Argus (New York), January 9–14, 1832

Rutherfordton *North Carolina Spectator,* January 7, 14, 21, 28, 1832

The *small-town* newspapers examined were:

Greenville Mountaineer (North Carolina), January 7, 14, 21, 28, 1832

Haverhill, Massachusetts, *Essex Gazette,* January 7, 14, 21, 28, 1832

22. Most of the newspapers examined for content were issued during the third week of October 1897. Variations from that date are due to the varying availability of newspapers in original form or in microform.

The *metropolitan* newspapers examined were:

Boston Daily Advertiser, October 18–23, 1897

New York *Evening Post,* October 18–23, 1897

Pittsburgh Leader, October 17–23, 1897

Chicago Tribune, October 17–23, 1897
New York Journal, October 17–23, 1897
Charleston *News and Courier,* October 17–23, 1897
Boston Globe, October 17–23, 1897
San Francisco Chronicle, October 17–23, 1897
The *small-city/large-town* newspapers examined were:
  Mansfield News, (Ohio), October 19, 22, 1897 (a semiweekly)
  Albany Daily Democrat (Oregon), October 16–20, 1893
  Salem, Oregon, *Capital Journal,* October 17–23, 1897
  The Dalles Chronicle (Oregon), October 18–23, 1897
  Macon Telegraph (Georgia), October 2, 16, 30, 1893 (a weekly)
The *small-town* newspapers examined were:
  Elgin Recorder, (Oregon), October 22, 29, 1897
  Junction City Times (Oregon), October 2, 9, 16, 1897
  Woodburn Independent (Oregon), October 7, 14, 21, 28, 1897
23. Dicken-Garcia, *Journalistic Standards;* Dyer, "Political Patronage of the Wisconsin Press"; John C. Nerone, "The Mythology of the Penny Press," *Critical Studies in Mass Communication* 4; no. 4 (December 1987), pp. 376–404.
24. These studies include: Herbert J. Gans, *Deciding What's News* (New York: Pantheon Books, 1979); Edward J. Epstein, *News from Nowhere: Television and the News* (New York: Vintage Books, 1974); Gaye Tuchman, *Making News: A Study in the Social Construction of Reality* (New York: Free Press, 1978).
25. William Leiss, Stephen Kline, and Sut Hjally, *Social Communication in Advertising: Persons, Products and Images of Well Being* (Toronto: Methuen, 1986), p. 75.
26. Conor Cruise O'Brien has explored some of these ideas in a particularly brilliant essay, "Press Freedom and the Need to Please," *Times Literary Supplement,* February 21, 1986, pp. 179–80. O'Brien notes that the contemporary western press has developed a sort of "Scheherazade syndrome," in which "readers form a kind of collective sultan who conveys the unspoken message: If you bore me, you die."
27. Charles A. Dana, "Power of the Press," address to the Wisconsin Editorial Association; reported in *St. Louis Republic,* July 25, 1888, p. 1.

Chapter 1: American Political Parties and the Press

1. John B. Turner to Samuel Breck, October 10, 1832, Misc. MSS, "P," "We The People and Old Colony Press Business Records," American Antiquarian Society.
2. William H. Seward to Thurlow Weed, November 14, 1832, Thurlow Weed Papers, Rush Rees Library, University of Rochester.
3. Roy F. Nichols, *The Invention of the American Political Parties* (New York: Macmillan Co., 1967); Robert N. Elliot, Jr., "The Raleigh Register" (Ph.D. diss., University of North Carolina, 1953), pp. 71–74, 77–78.

4. Richard P. McCormick, *The Second American Party System: Party Formation in the Jacksonian Era* (Chapel Hill: University of North Carolina Press, 1966), p. 343; Cullen B. Gosnell and C. David Anders, *The Government and Administration of Georgia* (New York: Thomas Y. Crowell Co., 1956), pp. 16–17.

5. Ronald P. Formisano has written two of the best studies of state politics in the Jacksonian era. See *The Birth of Mass Political Parties: Michigan, 1827–1861* (Princeton, N.J.: Princeton University Press, 1971), and *The Transformation of Political Culture: Massachusetts Parties, 1790s–1840s* (New York: Oxford University Press, 1983). Also see Arthur B. Darling, *Political Changes in Massachusetts, 1824–1848: A Study of Liberal Movements in Politics* (New Haven: Yale University Press, 1925).

6. McCormick, *The Second American Party System*, p. 344; Formisano, *The Transformation of Political Culture*, pp. 10, 15.

7. McCormick, *The Second American Party System*, pp. 344–45; William N. Chambers and Philip C. Davis, "Party, Competition and Mass Participation: The Case of the Democratizing Party System, 1824–1852," in *The History of American Electoral Behavior*, ed. Joel H. Silbey, Allan G. Bogue, and William H. Flanigan (Princeton: Princeton University Press, 1978), p. 174.

8. Chambers and Davis, "Party, Competition and Mass Participation," pp. 174–75, quoting Chilton Williamson, *American Suffrage from Property to Democracy, 1760–1860* (Princeton: Princeton University Press, 1960). In New York State, only a third of adult males could qualify for voting for governor in 1820; following constitutional revision in 1821, 80 percent qualified. McCormick, *The Second American Party System*, p. 113.

9. Robert V. Remini, *Andrew Jackson and the Course of American Freedom, 1822–1832*, volume 2 (New York: Harper and Row, 1981), p. 384; Washington, D.C., *National Intelligencer*, October 5, 1832, quoted in Remini, *Andrew Jackson and the Bank War* (New York: Norton, 1967), p. 98. For criticism of self-promotion by candidates, see the *Macon Advertiser* (Georgia), September 30, 1831 (criticizing Wilson Lumpkin for campaigning for governor); Geneseo, New York, *Livingston Register*, September 14, 1825; *Louisville Public Advertiser* (Kentucky), October 3, 1827, July 16, 1828; Baltimore *Niles' Weekly Register*, May 9, 1827, p. 165; *Greensborough Patriot* (North Carolina), June 13, 1829, August 29, 1832; *New Bern Spectator* (North Carolina), July 25, August 1, 1829; Cincinnati *Advertiser*, August 30, September 6, 1828, April 18, 1829; *Penn Yan Enquirer* (New York), November 2, 1831; Batavia, New York, *Republican Advocate*, October 21, 28, 1831; Thomas Ruffin to David L. Swain, October 15, 1829, D. L. Swain Papers, Southern Historical Collection, University of North Carolina, Chapel Hill; Richard Rush to John Binns, October 18, 1828, Society Collection: American Statesmen and Lawyers: Richard Rush, Historical Society of Pennsylvania.

10. Robert V. Remini, *The Election of Andrew Jackson* (Philadelphia: J. B. Lippincott Co., 1963), p. 62.

11. Charles S. Benton to Azariah Flagg, December 12, 1836, Azariah Flagg Papers, New York Public Library.

12. *Greensborough Patriot* (North Carolina), June 13, 1829.

13. *Haverhill Iris* (Massachusetts), January 21, 1832; *Newburyport Herald* (Massachusetts), August 1, 1832; *Newburyport Advertiser* (Massachusetts), November 5, December 14, 1831.

14. *Newburyport Advertiser,* June 22, 1831.

15. Henry Petrikin to George Bryan, January 17, 1823, George Bryan Papers, Historical Society of Pennsylvania.

16. James S. Chase, *Emergence of the Presidential Nominating Convention, 1789–1832* (Urbana: University of Illinois Press, 1973); John C. Vinson, "Electioneering in North Carolina, 1800–1835," *North Carolina Historical Review* 29 (April 1952).

17. In *The Transformation of Political Culture,* Formisano writes that newspapers were essential for parties, facilitating intraparty communication and serving "as a kind of public address system to supporters and sometimes as forums for debating controversial issues." p. 16.

18. Guion G. Johnson, *Antebellum North Carolina: A Social History* (Chapel Hill: University of North Carolina Press, 1937), pp. 95–96.

19. *Louisville Public Advertiser* (Kentucky), June 14, 25, 1828; Concord *New Hampshire Patriot,* August 6, 1828; Harrisburg *Pennsylvania Reporter,* May 25, 1838; *New Bern Spectator* (North Carolina), January 20, 27, 1832; *Savannah Republican* (Georgia), January 20, 1831; Charleston *City Gazette,* December 1, 1830; Winfield Scott to C. K. Gardner, August 7, 1824, Gardner Papers, New York State Library; Theodore D. Jervey, *Robert Y. Hayne and His Times* (New York: Macmillan Co., 1909).

20. Russel B. Nye, *Society and Culture in America, 1830–1860* (New York: Harper Torchbooks, 1974), p. 366.

21. Ibid.

22. Richard B. Kielbowicz, *News in the Mail: The Press, Post Office and Public Information* (New York: Greenwood Press, 1989).

23. Robert K. Stewart, "The Jackson Press and the Elections of 1824 and 1828" (M.A. thesis, University of Washington, 1984).

24. Pinckney was spokesman for the state rights activists in South Carolina; Greene, for the Jacksonian Democrats in Massachusetts.

25. *Proceedings of a Convention of Delegates from the Different Counties in the State of New York, Opposed to Free Masonry, Held at the Capitol in the City of Albany, on the 19th, 20th and 21st Days of February, 1829* (Rochester: Weed and Sprague, 1928), p. 12.

26. Myron Holley to Orville Holley, December 28, 1830, Holly Papers, New York State Library.

27. James Gordon Bennett diary, July 18, 1831, New York Public Library.

28. John C. Calhoun to J. H. Hammond, February 16, 1831, James Henry Hammond Papers, volume 2 (1830–33), Library of Congress.

29. Nicholas Biddle to P. P. F. Degrand, December 22, 1830, Letterbooks, p. 426; Biddle to M. Robertson, April 8, 1831, Letterbooks, pp. 501–2, Nicholas Biddle Papers, Library of Congress.

30. Nicholas Biddle to C. J. Ingersoll, February 12, 1831, Letterbooks, p. 466, Nicholas Biddle Papers, Library of Congress.

31. The median for the five metropolitan newspapers studied here is 50.5 percent of content devoted to politics. A fuller presentation of these data is available in table 1.1 below and in appendix 2.

32. The median for the five newspapers studied here is 22.9 percent of content devoted to business and labor. Please see table 1.1 and appendix 2 for a fuller presentation of these data.

33. Less than half of all revenues derived from advertising. Kobre estimates that about 16 percent of the New York *Courier and Enquirer's* income came from advertising in the 1830s. Crouthamel estimates that less than 50 percent of the revenues of the leading New York City commercial newspapers (the *New York Daily Advertiser*, the *Commercial Advertiser*, and the *Mercantile Advertiser*) came from advertising. Sidney Kobre, *Development of American Journalism* (Dubuque: Wm. C. Brown Co., 1969), p. 170; James L. Crouthamel, *James Watson Webb: A Biography* (Middletown, Conn.: Wesleyan University Press, 1969), p. 16.

34. Seven of the nine New York City commercial-political papers were Whig in the late 1830s; the others, Democratic. Crouthamel, *James Watson Webb,* p. 84.

35. James Crouthamel writes that in 1832 the New York *Courier and Enquirer,* edited by James Watson Webb, was a "consistent" supporter of Jacksonian policies. "It had not become the power in politics that Webb hoped to make it, but it was influential in party circles. It is no exaggeration to say that Webb managed the nation's largest Jacksonian daily in 1832." *James Watson Webb,* p. 33.

36. *Historical Statistics of the United States, Colonial Times to 1970,* volume 1, Series A57-72, "Population in Urban and Rural Territory by Size of Place, 1790 to 1970" (Washington, D.C.: Government Printing Office, 1975).

37. The definition of a metropolitan area for 1830 is open to discussion, and the figure of 25,000 or more in population is suggested here as one possible definition. The population of the nation's leading cities in 1830 were: New York City, 197,112; Philadelphia, 80,462; Baltimore, 80,620; Boston, 61,392; and Charleston, 30,289. U.S. Census Office, *Fifth Census or Enumeration of the Inhabitants of the United States, 1830,* "Aggregate Amount of Each Description of Persons within the United States and the Territories According to the Census of 1830" (Washington, D.C.: Duff Green, 1832), pp. 17, 51, 65, 81.

Cities of 50,000 or more held 3.3 percent of the population; 1.5 percent lived in cities of 100,000 or more (i.e., New York). *Historical Statistics of the United States,* Series A57-72.

38. Robert Remini, *The Election of Andrew Jackson,* p. 77.

39. John Eaton to Overton, November 16, 1824, John B. Overton Papers, Tennessee State Archives, Nashville, quoted in Gabriel L. Lowe, Jr., "John H. Eaton, Jackson's Campaign Manager," *Tennessee Historical Quarterly* 11, no. 2 (June 1952), p. 128.

40. Lowe, Jr., "John H. Eaton," pp. 126–28; Remini, *The Election of Andrew Jackson*, p. 49.

41. Nathaniel J. Palmer to W. P. Mangum, October 21, 1831, pp. 414–15, and C. Fisher to Mangum, August 24, 1832, pp. 571–72, Henry T. Shanks, ed., *The Papers of Willie P. Mangum*, volume 1 (1807–32) (Raleigh: State Department of Archives and History, 1950); *Raleigh Register* (North Carolina), September 29, 1831.

42. *Albany Argus* (New York), quoting the *Baltimore Republican*, December 13, 1831; Worcester, Massachusetts, *Worcester County Republican*, March 4, 1829; John Norvell to B. S. Bonsall, June 4, 1832, Benjamin S. Bonsall Correspondence, Gratz Collection, Case 15, Box 2, Historical Society of Pennsylvania; *Greensborough Patriot* (North Carolina), November 7, 1829, April 14, 1830, June 1 and November 12, 1831; Herbert Ershkowitz, "New Jersey during the Era of Jackson, 1820–1837" (Ph.D. diss., New York University, 1965), p. 103; Russel J. Ferguson, *Early Western Pennsylvania Politics* (Pittsburgh: University of Pittsburgh Press, 1938), p. 267; Marguerite G. Bartlett, *The Chief Phases of Pennsylvania Politics in the Jacksonian Period* (Allentown, Pa.: H. Ray Haas and Co., 1919), p. 30; *Philadelphia Mercury*, September 29, 1827; Philadelphia *National Palladium*, January 8 and September 26, 1827; *Elizabeth City Star* (North Carolina), January 14, 1832.

43. Milton W. Hamilton, "Antimasonic Papers 1826–1834," in *The Papers of the Bibliographic Society of America*, volume 38 (Chicago: University of Chicago Press, 1938), p. 74.

44. Bartlett, *The Chief Phases of Pennsylvania Politics; Boston Daily Advocate*, January 3 and June 12, 1832; Seth Hunt to Thurlow Weed, March 16, 1831, Thurlow Weed Papers, University of Rochester.

45. F. Whittlesey to Thurlow Weed, December 14, 1831, Thurlow Weed Papers, University of Rochester; Myron Holley to William H. Seward, January 2, 1829, William Henry Seward Papers, University of Rochester.

46. Virginia L. Glenn, "James Hamilton Jr. of South Carolina: A Biography" (Ph.D. diss., University of North Carolina, 1964), pp. 146–47.

47. James Hamilton to Waddy Thompson, June 8 and August 31, 1832, James Hamilton Papers, South Caroliniana Library; H. H. Townes to G. F. Townes, March 10 and June 28, 1832, S. A. Townes to G. F. Townes, June 7, 1832, both in Townes Family Papers, South Caroliniana Library; J. Mauldin Lesesne, "The Nullification Controversy in an Up-Country District," *Proceedings of the South Carolina Historical Association* (1939), pp. 18–19; Harry L. Watson, "Early Newspapers of Abbeville District, 1812–1834," *Proceedings of the South Carolina Historical Association* (1940), pp. 28–29, 31; "Letters on the Nullification Movement in South Carolina, 1830–1834," *American Historical Review* 6 (1901), p. 741; *Greensborough Patriot* (North Carolina), December 4, 1830; Camden, South Carolina, *Camden and Lancaster Journal*, March 13, June 22, 1832.

48. *Harrisburg Chronicle* (Pennsylvania), September 10, 1832; Harrisburg *Pennsylvania Reporter*, July 24, 1829.

49. Joseph Sprague to Daniel Webster, January 31, 1830, Daniel Webster Papers, Library of Congress; A. H. Everett to Edward Everett, September 24, 1831, Edward Everett Letters, Hale Family Papers, Library of Congress; Daniel Webster to Edward Everett, August 25, 1831, Edward Everett Papers, Massachusetts Historical Society; *Boston Patriot,* July 20, 1831.

50. S. D. Miller to C. F. Daniels, September 6, 1830, Stephen D. Miller Papers, Duke University. Also see C. F. Daniels to S. D. Miller, September 6, 1830, Chestnut-Miller-Manning Papers, South Carolina Historical Society; C. F. Daniels to James Lawson, November 23, 1830, May 29, 1832, C. F. Daniels Papers, South Caroliniana Library.

51. James L. Crouthamel, *James Watson Webb,* p. 22; Webb to Nicholas Biddle, March 18, 1832, Nicholas Biddle Papers, Library of Congress; John Mumford to Charles Gardner, August 15, 25, 1832, Gardner Papers, New York State Library, Albany; William L. Marcy to Thomas W. Olcott, January 5, 1832, Thomas W. Olcott Papers, Columbia University; John Dix to T. S. Smith, October 20, 1831, John Dix Papers, Columbia University.

52. *Register of All the Officers and Agents, Civil, Military, and Naval, in the Service of the United States on the Thirtieth September, 1833,* comp. William A. Weaver (Philadelphia: Key and Biddle, 1834), pp. 171, 173.

53. William L. Marcy to Martin Van Buren, February 15, 1824, Martin Van Buren Papers, Library of Congress, quoted in Alvin Cass, *Politics in New York State, 1800–1830* (Syracuse: Syracuse University Press, 1965), p. 35; Van Buren to G. Worth, February 22, 1824, Martin Van Buren Papers, Library of Congress; Kalman Goldstein, "The Albany Regency: The Failure of Practical Politics" (Ph.D. diss., Columbia University, 1969), pp. 85–86; *Albany Argus* (New York), June 4, 1824.

54. H. C. Sleight to Henry O'Reilly, March 20, 1873, O'Reilly Collection, Rochester Historical Society, in Milton Hamilton, *The Country Printer: New York State, 1785–1830* (New York: Columbia University Press, 1936), p. 116.

55. *Lynn Record* (Massachusetts), July 17, 1830, November 2, 1831.

56. Herman Norton to Thurlow Weed, March 25, 1829, Thurlow Weed Papers, University of Rochester.

57. Washington, D.C., *Globe,* December 7, 1830; A. C. Flagg to F. P. Blair, January 11, 1832, Gratz Collection, Case B, Box 36, Historical Society of Pennsylvania.

58. Daniel J. McFarland, "North Carolina Newspapers, Editors and Journalistic Politics, 1815–1836," *North Carolina Historical Review* 30, no. 3 (July 1953), pp. 376–77. The best study of the patronage system is Culver H. Smith, *The Press, Politics and Patronage* (Athens: University of Georgia Press, 1977).

59. *Fayetteville Observer* (North Carolina), June 30, 1834, quoted in Herbert D. Pegg, "The Whig Party in North Carolina, 1834–1861" (Ph.D. diss., University of North Carolina, 1932), p. 42.

60. William R. Ransom to Willie P. Mangum, February 8, 1832, Shanks, ed., *The Papers of Willie P. Mangum,* volume 1 (1807–32), pp. 474–76.

61. Pegg, "The Whig Party," p. 42, quoting the *Carolina Watchman* (Salisbury, North Carolina), May 3, 1845.

62. See the Batavia, New York, *Republican Advocate*, September 28, 1827; *Lyons Countryman* (New York), June 6, August 1, 8, 15, November 14, 1832.

63. Johnson, *Antebellum North Carolina*, p. 806; McFarland, "North Carolina Newspapers," p. 377.

64. Hamilton, *Country Printer*, p. 68.

65. Poughkeepsie, New York, *Dutchess Intelligencer*, July 15, 1829, quoted in Hamilton, *The Country Printer*, p. 121.

66. Thurlow Weed, *Autobiography of Thurlow Weed*, ed. Harriet A. Weed (Boston, 1883; reprinted, Da Capo Press, 1970), p. 78.

67. George Bond to Nathan Appleton, January 26, 1832, Nathan Appleton Papers, volume 5 (1832–39), Massachusetts Historical Society.

68. William E. Ames notes that Congress spent about $2.5 million on printing between 1819 and 1846: $1 million to the *National Intelligencer* (with $650,000 more for the American State Papers); $500,000 to Blair and Rives of the Washington, D.C., *Globe;* $400,000 to Duff Green and $258,000 to Thomas Allen of the *Madisonian*. Ames, *A History of the National Intelligencer* (Chapel Hill: University of North Carolina Press, 1972), p. 282.

69. Remini, *The Election of Andrew Jackson*, p. 84; Culver Smith, *The Press, Politics and Patronage*, p. 71; Edward Everett to Duff Green, September 15, 1832, Edward Everett Papers, Massachusetts Historical Society.

70. *Register of All the Officers and Agents . . . of the United States*, 1833, 1835, 1837, 1839, and 1841.

71. The newspapers receiving the largest sums of executive patronage were: Washington, D.C., *Globe* ($163,222.80 from 1831 to 1841); Concord *New Hampshire Patriot* ($18,112.48, 1831–41); *Boston Morning Post* ($63,339.48, 1831–41); *Louisville Public Advertiser* (Kentucky) ($24,639.09, 1831–41); Columbus *Ohio Statesman* ($25,811.38, 1833–41), and Philadelphia *Pennsylvanian* ($17,526.79, 1831–41). *Register of All the Officers and Agents . . . of the United States*, 1833, 1835, 1837, 1839, 1841.

72. Hamilton, The *Country Printer*, p. 120.

73. *Richmond Daily Whig* (Virginia), April 17, 30, May 2, 5, 19, 25, 28, 30, June 1, 5, 9, 12, 13, 19, 27, July 1, 24, and August 4, 1829, January 5 and June 21, 1830; Cincinnati *Advertiser*, April 15, 18, 29, May 6, June 10, and August 15, 1829; *Greensborough Patriot* (North Carolina), June 6, 13, 27, and August 22, 29, 1829; *New Bern Spectator* (North Carolina), June 20 and August 22, 1829, June 26, 1830; Baltimore *Niles' Weekly Register*, June 5, 1830, p. 271.

74. Carolyn Stewart Dyer, "Political Patronage of the Wisconsin Press, 1849–1861: New Perspectives on the Economics of Patronage," *Journalism Monographs* 109 (February 1989).

75. In addition, the special allocation for the printing and binding of the revised statutes (spread over the three-year period of 1828–31) paid Croswell $15,124.59 ($8,205.84 for printing and $6,918.75 for binding). New York State, Senate, Report of the Comptroller, 66th Sess., January 20, 1843, Doc. 12; New

York State, Senate, Report of the Comptroller, 57th Sess., volume 2, March 13, 1835, Doc. 67; Croswell Papers, April 12, 1832, New York State Library.

76. New York State, Comptroller's Office Day Book 22, February 11, 1832 – June 6, 1833; New York State, Comptroller's Office Day Book 20, April 7, 1830 – September 11, 1830; both in New York State Library Manuscripts and Archives, Albany.

77. A. Z. Flagg to F. P. Blair, January 11, 1832, Gratz Collection, Case B, Box 36, Historical Society of Pennsylvania.

78. Samuel Hazard, *The Register of Pennsylvania* (Philadelphia: W. F. Geddes): volume 1 (January 1828), pp. 59–61; volume 3 (January–July 1829), pp. 193–194; volume 4 (July 1829–January 1830), pp. 409–11; volume 6 (July 1830–January 1831), p. 400; volume 7 (January–July 1831), p. 52; volume 8 (July 1831–January 1832), pp. 405–6; *Harrisburg Chronicle* (Pennsylvania), December 16, 27, 1830, February 10, December 12, 1831, December 10, 1832, December 9, 1833.

79. Hazard, *Register,* volume 4, p. 317; Harrisburg *Pennsylvania Reporter,* February 29, 1828; *Harrisburg Chronicle* (Pennsylvania), December 16, 1830.

The allocation for three papers was $15 per legislator (totaling $1,995 for both houses of the legislature).

80. Governor Wolf appointed six printers to various offices in the Pittsburgh area in 1830. The *New Bern Spectator* (North Carolina), March 13, 1830, lists the appointments. Editors usually were justices of the peace or clerks. James A. Kehl, *Ill Feeling in the Era of Good Feeling* (Pittsburgh: University of Pittsburgh Press, 1956), pp. 126, 131.

81. The payments to the *Journal* from 1828 through 1832 averaged about $6,500 annually. State of Georgia, Senate, Journal, 1829, p. 263; State of Georgia, House, Journal, 1829, pp. 390–91; State of Georgia, Acts of the General Assembly, 1831, Appendix, p. 10; State of Georgia, House, Journal, 1831, pp. 8–10; State of Georgia, Senate, Journal, 1832, pp. 356–57.

82. Miller Grieve was secretary to Governor Gilmer in 1830–31 and began editing the Milledgeville *Southern Recorder* a month after Gilmer left office. John Cuthbert, editor of the Milledgeville *Federal Union,* took Grieve's position in the next state administration, serving as the governor's secretary (while still editing his newspaper). State of Georgia, House, Journal, 1831, Appendix, pp. 14, 26; A. B. Caldwell, "Miller Grieve," in *Men of Mark in Georgia,* ed. William J. Northen (Atlanta: A. B. Caldwell, 1910), pp. 104–105; *Memoirs of Georgia* (Atlanta: Southern Historical Association, 1895), pp. 266–67; Milledgeville *Federal Union,* January 1, 1830.

83. *Richmond Daily Whig* (Virginia), June 19, 1829, December 10, 1830.

84. W. R. Gales to David Swain, September 14, 1823, Swain Papers, Southern Historical Collection, University of North Carolina.

85. Dyer, "Political Patronage of the Wisconsin Press, 1849–1861:" 1989, p. 26.

86. Harrisburg, Pennsylvania, *Republican and Anti-Masonic Inquirer,* February 19, 1831.

87. Hazard, *Register,* volume 3, p. 143; Philadelphia *Democratic Press,* March 14, 19, 1828; Milton Hamilton, *The Country Printer,* p. 131.

88. Ernest P. Muller, "Preston King: A Political Biography" (Ph.D. diss, Columbia University, 1957), pp. 33–36.

89. George Bond to Nathan Appleton, January 26, 1832, Nathan Appleton Papers, volume 5, 1832–39, Massachusetts Historical Society; Ershkowitz, "New Jersey during the Era of Jackson," p. 102; E. S. Duryea to David E. Huger, March 24, 1832, Joel R. Poinsett Papers in the Henry D. Gilpin Collection, Historical Society of Pennsylvania.

90. The political nature of these commercial-political newspapers is demonstrated by the *Boston Morning Post,* which devoted only 40.3 percent of its news columns to politics and 17.7 percent to business issues, but was still clearly the Jacksonian state organ. (See appendix 2: table A2.1.) The New York *Courier and Enquirer,* which devoted 50.5 percent of its space to politics and 22.9 percent to business issues, was deeply involved in national banking debates. The *Charleston Mercury* devoted 48.4 percent of its columns to politics, and was edited in the late 1820s and early 1830s by Henry Laurens Pinckney. Pinckney was a legislator, nullification party leader, and mayor of Charleston during his editorial tenure. *Charleston Mercury,* June 18, August 30, September 8, 11, 1830; February 27, April 16, 1832; *Charleston Courier,* February 4, 1863; Granville T. Prior, "A History of the *Charleston Mercury,* 1822–52" (Ph.D. diss., Harvard University, 1946).

91. The figure on competition in New York State is derived from Winifred Gregory, ed., *American Newspapers 1821–1936* (New York: H. W. Wilson Co., 1937); also see *Lyons Western Argus* (New York), December 21, 24, 1831, March 7, 1832; *Cortland Advocate* (New York), October 21, November 4, December 2, 1831, February 17, 24, April 20, May 25, August 10, 1832, for a debate with the Cortland *Anti-Masonic Republican;* also *Cortland Advocate,* November 4, December 2, 1831, April 20, May 4, 11, July 13, October 26, November 4, December 2, 1832, for debate with the Homer *Cortland Observer* and *Homer Globe.*

92. J. L. Petrigru to William Elliot, August 25, 1831, J. L. Petigru Papers, South Carolina Historical Society.

93. In 1832, the three major Washington, D.C., newspapers all received governmental subsidies while pursuing quite different political agendas. The *Globe* received presidential patronage ($39,033.42); the *U.S. Telegraph,* congressional printing ($142,778.65); and the *National Intelligencer,* the American State Papers ($67,376.20). During the Twenty-third, Twenty-fourth, and Twenty-fifth congresses, rival editors held the congressional printing contracts (one for the Senate, one for the House). See *Register,* 1831, 1833, 1835, 1837, 1839, and 1841; Ames, *History of the National Intelligencer,* pp. 127, 151, 158–59.

94. *Register of All the Officers and Agents . . . of the United States,* 1833, 1835, 1837, 1839, 1841; U.S. Congress, House, *Examination of the Post Office Department,* 2d sess., 1835, H. Rept. 103, pp. 779–782, 784–786, 788; U.S. Congress,

Senate, Committee on the Post Office and Post Roads, 23d Cong., 1st sess., 1834, S. Doc. 422; Joseph T. Buckingham, *Personal Memoirs and Recollections of Editorial Life,* reprinted., volume 2 (New York: Arno Pres, Inc., 1970); *Boston Daily Courier* June 26, 1832; Amasa Walker to Pliny Merrick, February 9, 25, 1830, Pliny Merrick Correspondence, Folder 2, American Antiquarian Society; *Boston Daily Advocate,* January 3, 1832; Boston *Columbian Centinel,* January 4, 1832.

95. *Louisville Public Advertiser* (Kentucky), July 9, 1828.

96. Washington, D.C., *U.S. Telegraph,* October 7, 1828.

97. *Lyons Western Argus* (New York), August 1, 1832.

98. *Greensborough Patriot* (North Carolina), quoted in the *Raleigh Register,* July 6, 1832.

99. Haverhill, Massachusetts, *Essex Gazette,* July 16, 1831.

100. This prospectus was published in the Tarborough, North Carolina, *Free Press,* October 18, 1831.

101. *Boston Morning Post,* November 9, 1831.

102. *Macon Advertiser* (Georgia), August 21, 1832.

103. Ibid., September 4, 1832.

104. Columbus, Georgia, *Democrat,* August 4, 1832.

105. *Macon Telegraph,* March 10, June 2, September 9, 14, 1832.

106. Washington, D.C., *Globe,* August 6, 9, 17, 30, September 5, 11, 15, 17, 26, October 2, 1832; Washington, D.C., *National Intelligencer,* August 2, 7, 11, 16, 21, 25, 30, September 6, 13, 1832.

107. *Harrisburg Chronicle,* April 16, 1830.

108. For debates among these Massachusetts newspapers, see: the Salem *Commercial Advertiser,* April 21, June 2, July 7, 21, August 4, 18, September 5, 8, 22, October 24, 1832; *Essex Register* (Salem), April 9, 30, May 31, June 11, 28, July 5, 9, September 13, 30, November 1, 1832; *Essex Gazette* (Haverhill), August 22, 1831, July 18, September 15, 17, October 27, 1832; *Salem Gazette,* January 24, June 12, September 7, 11, and November 13, 1832.

109. For commentary on the tariff, see: Springfield, Massachusetts, *Hampden Intelligencer,* July 27, 1832; Worcester *Massachusetts Spy,* May 9, September 5, 1832; Boston *Independent Chronicle,* June 27, 1832; Concord *New Hampshire Patriot,* November 21, 1831; *Raleigh Register* (North Carolina), September 2, 1830, November 23, 1832; Charleston *Southern Patriot,* July 10, 1832; *Charleston Mercury,* August 25, 1832.

110. Springfield, Massachusetts, *Hampden Journal,* April 11, October 10, 1832; Philadelphia *Democratic Press,* January 8, 19, February 2, 4, 21, March 6, 13, 14, 19, 21, 26, 1828; Boston *Columbian Centinel,* February 1, 3, 11, March 3, 1832; *Boston Daily Advertiser,* May 5, 1832; *Boston Daily Courier,* May 1, August 16, December 13, 1832; *Savannah Republican* (Georgia), May 19, 1832.

111. Washington, D.C., *Globe,* December 18, 1830, January 12, 19, May 16, 1831, January 12, July 12, October 2, 1832; *Harrisburg Chronicle* (Pennsylvania), February 28, 1831; *Albany Argus* (New York), April 12, 1831, January 1,

31, May 9, 11, 15, 16, 17, 24, August 14, 28, 1832; Athens, Georgia, *Southern Banner*, April 3, August 3, 1832; *Savannah Republican* (Georgia), February 4, March 20, July 21, 1832; *Pittsfield Sun* (Massachusetts), September 6, 16, 1832; *Lowell Mercury* (Massachusetts), June 15, August 31, 1832; *Richmond Daily Whig* (Virginia), May 8, 1830; Charleston, South Carolina, *Southern Patriot*, July 17, 1832; Washington, D.C., *National Intelligencer*, March 12, 19, 25, 26, 1831, June 12, July 12, 1832; New Bedford, Massachusetts, *Daily Mercury*, May 8, 12, 21, 31, and June 11, 1832.

112. William B. Fraley, "The Representation Controversy in North Carolina, 1787–1835" (Ph.D. diss., University of North Carolina, 1965), pp. 32–35; Harold J. Counihan, "North Carolina, 1815–1836: State and Local Perspectives on the Age of Jackson" (Ph.D. diss., University of North Carolina, 1971), pp. 135–72.

113. *Richmond Daily Whig* (Virginia), February 16, March 9, 1830.

114. License laws: *Boston Morning Post*, November 10, 11, 14, 16, 18, 24, 1831, February 28, 1832; Boston *Columbian Centinel*, February 4, 1832; church and state: Worcester, Massachusetts, *National Aegis*, February 15, 1832.

115. Troupites versus Clarkites: see the *Columbus Enquirer* (Georgia), July 28, 1832; Milledgeville *Georgia Journal*, March 22, 1830, July 7, 28, August 11, 18, September 15, 1831, June 14, 1832; Milledgeville *Southern Recorder*, July 14, August 4, 11, 18, 25, September 8, 15, 22, 29, October 27, November 10, 17, 24, 1831, January 12, 1832. National Indian policy: see the Milledgeville, Georgia, *Federal Union*, September 4, 1830, March 24, 1831; *Augusta Chronicle* (Georgia), June 16, 1832.

116. *Charleston Mercury*, August 27, 1830; Columbia, South Carolina, *Southern Times*, July 19, August 13, 16, 19, 23, 26, September 2, 9, 1830.

117. *Albany Evening Journal* (New York), March 23, April 29, 1831; *Albany Argus* (New York), June 5, 1829, January 9, 1832; Batavia, New York, *Republican Advocate*, October 2, 1832; Geneseo, New York, *Livingston Register*, November 11, 1828, August 11, September 1, 22, 1830.

118. *Louisville Public Advertiser* (Kentucky), October 18, 1828.

119. Springfield, Massachusetts, *Hampden Intelligencer*, May 2, 1832. For other announcements of meetings, see: Penn Yan, New York, *Yates Republican*, February 17, 1829, July 20, 1830; St. Lawrence, New York, *Northern Light*, September 22, 1831, May 24, August 23, September 6, 13, 1832; *Charleston Mercury*, October 6, 1832; *Boston Daily Advocate*, August 2, 1832; Harrisburg, *Pennsylvania Reporter*, August 7, 1829; Charleston, South Carolina, *Southern Patriot*, October 1, 1831, July 25, 1832.

120. Boston *Columbian Centinel*, September 26, 1832.

121. Penn Yan, New York, *Yates Republican*, August 17, 1830; St. Lawrence, New York, *Northern Light*, August 2, 9, 23, 1832; *Boston Daily Advocate*, November 9, 1832; *Charleston Mercury*, August 31, 1831; *Albany Argus* (New York), October 10, 12, 13, 1829, October 11, 1831, September 20, 26, 1832; Worcester *Massachusetts Spy*, November 7, 14, 1832.

122. *Albany Argus* (New York), October 11, 1831.

123. *Charleston Mercury,* February 24, June 6, August 31, 1831; August 6, 17, 18, 23, 25, September 6, 19, 1832.

124. Milledgeville, Georgia, *Federal Union,* August 16, 23, 30, 1832.

125. Concord *New Hampshire Patriot,* February 28, 1831.

126. Worcester *Massachusetts Spy,* October 24, 1832.

127. *Harrisburg Chronicle,* April 26, 1830.

128. Washington, D.C., *Globe,* November 27, 1837, quoting the St. Louis *Missouri Argus; National Intelligencer,* November 20, 1837, quoting the St. Louis *Missouri Republican.*

129. Daniel M. McFarland, "North Carolina Newspapers," pp. 401–402.

130. Z. McLenegan to Joseph Wallace, October 25, 1831; J. R. Roseburg to Joseph Wallace, May 13, 1832; both in the William Macpherson Papers, Historical Society of Pennsylvania.

131. Batavia, New York, *Republican Advocate,* September 15, 29, 1826, June 29, 1827, February 28, May 30, 1828, September 25, 1829, October 21, 28, 1831; Geneseo, New York, *Livingston Register,* September 8, 1830, September 28, 1831, April 25, 1832; Penn Yan, New York, *Yates Republican,* July 22, November 2, 1828, February 17, 1829, February 2, October 19, 1830.

132. *Lyons Countryman* (New York), June 22, October 5, 1830; January 11, July 26, September 22, 1831.

133. Ibid., October 5, 1830, March 15, May 3, July 12, August 22, 1831.

134. He edited the *Le Roy Gazette* in 1827 and 1828, the Herkimer *Republican Farmers and Free Press* in 1830 and 1831, and the Utica *Elucidator* in 1832.

135. Batavia, New York, *Republican Advocate,* June 29, 1827, May 30, 1828, May 7, 1830, August 14, October 23, 1832; *Lyons Countryman* (New York), March 2, 1830; St. Lawrence, New York, *Northern Light,* November 1, 1832.

136. Lynwood M. Dent, Jr., "The Virginia Democratic Party, 1824–1847" (Ph.D. diss., Louisiana State University, 1974), p. 30; J. C. Calhoun to Francis W. Pickens, March 2, 1832, Pickens Papers, Duke University.

137. Isaac Hill to Levi Woodbury, August 4, 1828, Levi Woodbury Papers, Library of Congress; Col. Henry Orne, *The Letters of Columbus Originally Published in the Boston Bulletin* (Boston: Putnam and Hunt, 1829), pp. 13ff.; *Boston Statesman,* May 11, 13, 1829, November 5, December 3, 1831, March 3, 1832; George M. Dallas to Samuel D. Ingham, February 16, 1825, Dallas Papers, Historical Society of Pennsylvania; *Harrisburg Chronicle* (Pennsylvania), August 27, September 24, 1832, July 29, 1833; Ershkowitz, "New Jersey Politics during the Era of Jackson," pp. 98–102; H. H. Townes to Capt. G. F. Townes, March 10 and August 4, 1831, Townes Family Papers, South Caroliniana Library; Sumter, South Carolina, *Southern Whig,* September 29, 1832; Charleston *Southern Patriot,* September 6, 1832.

138. Harrisburg, Pennsylvania, *Republican and Anti-Masonic Inquirer,* March 6, 1830, June 2, 1831; *Columbia Hive* (South Carolina), September 15, 1832. Editors M. D. Richardson, B. F. Perry, and Richard Yeadon were mem-

bers of the Union and State Rights party Committee of Correspondence in South Carolina; *Harrisburg Chronicle* (Pennsylvania), August 27, 1832; *Philadelphia Mercury,* January 5, 1828.

139. Worcester *Massachusetts Yeoman,* February 25, 1832; Springfield, Massachusetts, *Hampden Intelligencer,* July 25, August 8, 29, 1832.

140. Samuel A. Townes to G. F. Townes, July 5, 1832, Townes Family Papers, South Caroliniana Library.

141. Henry D. Capers, *The Life and Times of C. G. Memminger* (Richmond, Va.: Everett Waddey Co., 1893).

142. *An Oration on the Fourth of July, 1832, at Sumter Court House* (Sumter, S.C.: Gazette Office, 1832).

143. Sumter, South Carolina, *Southern Whig,* August 9, October 6, 1832.

144. *Cortland Advocate* (New York), February 10, 1832.

145. Ibid., February 3, 17, July 20, 27, August 17, September 7, 29, 1832.

146. *Lyons Countryman* (New York), February 16, 1830.

147. Worcester, Massachusetts, *National Aegis,* September 19, 1832; *Boston Daily Advertiser,* September 11, 13, October 13, 1832.

148. *Boston Daily Courier,* April 23, 1832.

149. Jubal Harrington, editor of the *Worcester Republican,* was a delegate to the Worcester County Jacksonian Convention in 1832; he also served as convention secretary. *Worcester Republican,* October 10, 1832. Charles Green, editor of the *Boston Morning Post,* was a delegate to the Jacksonian state convention in late 1831. *Boston Statesman,* August 20, 1831. John B. Eldridge, editor of the Springfield *Hampden Whig,* served as a delegate and as secretary to the Jacksonian state convention in 1831. *Worcester County Republican,* September 7, 1831. Samuel Bowles, editor of the *Springfield Republican,* was secretary of the Springfield National Republican town meeting and chaired the Massachusetts Young Men's National Republican Convention. Springfield *Hampden Journal,* April 18, 1832. Phineas Allen, editor of the *Pittsfield Sun,* chaired the Berkshire County Democratic-Republican Convention in early 1831. *Pittsfield Sun,* March 10, 17, 1831.

150. Green to Calhoun, May 31, 1831; Green to James Hamilton, Jr., November 9, 1831; both in General Correspondence, volume 5, Duff Green Papers, Southern Historical Collection, University of North Carolina. Calhoun was kept informed of political developments in Washington and throughout the nation by Green's letters. See Green to Calhoun, April 21, July 18, 1831, July 9, August 28, October 9, 1832, volume 5, Duff Green Papers.

151. Green to Stephen Simpson, July 17, 28, 1831, General Correspondence, volume 5; Green to James Hamilton, Jr., July 18, 1831, General Correspondence, volume 5; Green to Judge Semple, February 12, 1832, Letterbooks, volume 4, p. 472; Green to J. S. Barbour, July 22, 1831, volume 4, Letterbooks, p. 438; Green to Richard K. Cralle, August 21, September 5, Nov 1, 11, 12, 1831, February 17, 1832, General Correspondence, volume 5; all in Duff Green Papers, Southern Historical Collection, University of North Carolina.

152. Green to Col. A. Storrow, September 3, 1831; Green to James Hamilton, September 4, 1831; Green to D. Russell, July 12, 1831; all in General Correspondence, volume 5, Duff Green Papers, Southern Historical Collection, University of North Carolina.

153. Green to James M. White, August 30, 1832, General Correspondence, volume 5; Green to Joseph Hixie, September 10, 1832, Letterbooks, volume 4, p. 515; Green to F. Whittlesey, September 12, 1832, Letterbooks, volume 4, p. 520; all in Duff Green Papers, Southern Historical Collection, University of North Carolina; Edward Everett to Duff Green, September 15, 1832, Edward Everett Papers, Massachusetts Historical Society.

154. William E. Ames, "A History of the Washington *Globe*," unpublished manuscript, University of Washington.

155. Ibid., pp. 1–2.

156. Ibid., pp. 126, 224, 228–29.

157. T. B. Barnow to Blair, February 10, 1831; Allen A. Hall to Blair, May 7, 1831; Thomas Crawford to Blair, April 13, 1833; and Michael Crider to Blair, April 22, 1844; all in Blair-Lee Papers, Princeton University.

158. Ames, "History of the Washington *Globe*," pp. 157–59, quoting William Thomas Burke to Blair, July 2, 1833; Richard Newcastle to Blair, November 10, 1832; copies in Blair-Lee Papers, Princeton University.

159. Ames, "History of the Washington *Globe*," p. 156, quoting William S. Ranson to Blair, August 12, 1831, copy in Blair-Lee Papers, Princeton University.

160. Ames, "History of the Washington *Globe*," p. 156–57, quoting Joseph E. Hinton to Blair, August 26, 1833; Gerard Banks, Jr., to Blair, November 28, 1831; Richard H. Newcastle to Blair, September 3, 1831; copies in Blair-Lee Papers, Princeton University.

161. Washington, D.C., *Globe*, April 10, May 19, 1832; Sen. A. Bucker to Blair, May 10, 1832, Draper Collection, American States, volume 1, Historical Society of Pennsylvania; F. Ewing to Blair, April 20, 1832, Blair-Rives Papers, Library of Congress.

162. Batavia, New York, *Republican Advocate*, September 11, 1832.

163. Thomas C. Clarke, September 12, 1832, Nicholas Biddle Papers, Library of Congress.

164. Ames, "History of the Washington *Globe*," p. 228, quoting Blair to Kendall, December 24, 1842, copy in Martin Van Buren Papers, Library of Congress; also see Ames, "History of the Washington *Globe*," pp. 241–42.

165. F. Lauriston Bullard, "Nathaniel Green," *Dictionary of American Biography*, volume 4, ed. Allen Johnson and Dumas Malone (New York: Charles Scribners' Sons, 1960), part 1, p. 573; Arthur B. Darling, *Political Changes in Massachusetts, 1824–48*, pp. 41–42; John B. Derby, *Political Reminiscences, Including a Sketch of the Origin and History of the "Statesman Party" of Boston* (Boston: Homer and Palmer, 1835), pp. 12–13.

166. "Letters to John Brazer Davis, 1819–31," Massachusetts Historical Society *Proceedings*, volume 49 (Boston: University Press, 1916).

167. Charles G. DeWitt to A. C. Flag, October 6, 20, 1830; S. J. B. Skinner to Flagg, July 31, 1830; Henry O'Reilly to Flagg, November 11, 1829; Michael Hoffman to Flagg, January 2, 22, December 15, 1827; Jonathan DeGraff to Flagg, December 27, 1827; E. Mack to Flagg, Jan 11, 1832; all in the Azariah Flagg Papers, New York Public Library; Croswell to Charles Butler, September 1, 1824, Charles Butler Papers, Library of Congress; Croswell to Levi Woodbury, April 9, 1832, Levi Woodbury Papers, Library of Congress.

168. M. Cadwallader to Weed, December 14, 1829, and March 26, 1830; Herman Norton to Weed, March 25, 1829; both in the Thurlow Weed Papers, University of Rochester.

169. Walter B. Edgar, ed., *Biographical Directory of the South Carolina House of Representatives*, volume 1, *Session Lists, 1692–1978* (Columbia: University of South Carolina Press, 1974), pp. 292, 298, 304, 309, 313, 316, 322, 326; P. M. Butler to J. H. Hammond, November 21, 1831, James Henry Hammond Papers, Library of Congress; *Charleston Mercury,* August 30, September 8, 1830, February 27, 1832; William L. King, *The Newspaper Press of Charleston, S.C.* (Charleston: Lucas and Richardson, 1882), pp. 148–49; David F. Houston, *Critical Study of Nullification in South Carolina* (New York: Longmans, Green and Co., 1896).

170. Remini, *The Election of Andrew Jackson,* p. 49.

Chapter 2: New Directions in American Journalism

1. *Chicago Tribune,* October 23, 1876, p. 4.

2. *New York Times,* October 20, 1876, p. 2.

3. Ibid.

4. *Chicago Tribune,* October 20, 1876, p. 4; emphasis added.

5. *The Newspaper Maker* (March 15, 1900), pp. 1, 4.

6. Ibid., April 12, 1900, p. 6.

7. Ibid., March 15, 1900, p. 4.

8. John A. Garraty, *The New Commonwealth, 1877–1890* (New York: Harper and Row, 1968); Gunther Barth, *City People: The Rise of Modern City Culture in Nineteenth-Century America* (New York: Oxford University Press, 1980).

9. Charles S. Benton to Azariah Flagg, December 12, 1836, Azariah Flagg Papers, New York Public Library.

10. Robert W. Johannsen, *Stephen A. Douglas* (New York: Oxford University Press, 1973), p. 658.

11. Ibid., p. 665.

12. Ibid., pp. 778–801.

13. Harry J. Brown and Frederick D. Williams, eds., *The Diary of James A. Garfield,* volume 1 (1848–71) (East Lansing: Michigan State University Press, 1968), pp. 342, 348–50.

14. David J. Rothman, "The Structure of State Politics," in *Political Parties in American History (1828–1890)* volume 2, ed. Felice A. Bonadio (New York: G. P. Putnam's Sons, 1974), p. 833.

15. Edgar E. Robinson, *The Evolution of American Political Parties* (New York: Harcourt Brace and Co., 1924), p. 261.

16. John M. Dobson, *Politics in the Gilded Age: A New Perspective on Reform* (New York: Praeger Publishers, 1972), pp. 152–53.

17. Johannsen, *Stephen A. Douglas*, pp. 707–10.

18. Charles Coleman, *The Election of 1868* (New York: Columbia University Press, 1933), p. 293; Lloyd Wendt, *Chicago Tribune: The Rise of a Great American Newspaper* (Chicago: Rand McNally and Co., 1979), p. 121.

19. Coleman, *Election of 1868*, p. 340.

20. Robinson, *Evolution of American Political Parties*, p. 249.

21. Ibid.; Allan Nevins, *The Evening Post: A Century of Journalism* (New York: Boni and Liveright, Publishers, 1922), pp. 464–65, 501, 546; Johannsen, *Stephen A. Douglas*, p. 782.

22. Johannsen, *Stephen A. Douglas*, p. 734, quoting the *New York Herald*, September 9, 1859, and January 12, 1860; emphasis added.

23. Johannsen, *Stephen A. Douglas*, pp. 732–33.

24. Ann Cook, Marilyn Gittell, and Herb Mack, eds., *City Life, 1865–1900: Views on Urban America* (New York: Praeger Publishers, 1973), p. 71, quoting R. A. Woods, ed., *Americans in Process: A Settlement Study* (Boston: Houghton Mifflin Co., 1902), p. 178. Also see Michael E. McGerr, *The Decline of Popular Politics: The American North, 1865–1928* (New York: Oxford University Press, 1986), pp. 23–27.

25. F. B. Marbut, *News from the Capital: The Story of Washington Reporting* (Carbondale: Southern Illinois Press, 1971), p. 69.

26. William E. Ames, *A History of the National Intelligencer* (Chapel Hill: University of North Carolina Press, 1972), pp. 239–41.

27. Ibid.

28. Ibid., p. 254.

29. Ibid., p. 267.

30. Ibid., p. 255; see U.S. Congress, Report on Public Printing, House, 26th Cong., 1st sess., 1841, H. Rept. 298.

31. Ames, *History of the National Intelligencer*, pp. 279–80.

32. George T. McJimsey, *Genteel Partisan: Manton Marble, 1834–1917* (Ames: Iowa State University Press, 1971), p. 168.

33. Marbut, *News from the Capital*, pp. 42–43.

34. Ibid., p. 62.

35. Gerald J. Baldasty, "The Charleston, South Carolina, Political Press and National News, 1808–1847," *Journalism Quarterly* (August 1978), pp. 519–26; Marbut, *News from the Capital*, p. 79.

36. James L. Crouthamel, *James Watson Webb: A Biography* (Middletown, Conn.: Wesleyan University Press), p. 149.

37. McJimsey, *Genteel Partisan*, p. 145.

38. Lloyd Wendt, *Chicago Tribune: The Rise of a Great American Newspaper* (Rand McNally and Co., 1979), p. 197.

39. Ames, *History of the National Intelligencer,* pp. 23, 113–15.

40. Crouthamel, *James Watson Webb,* p. 150.

41. Alfred McClung Lee, *The Daily Newspaper in America: The Evolution of a Social Instrument* (New York: Macmillan Co., 1937), p. 197.

42. Louis M. Lyons, *Newspaper Story: One Hundred Years of the Boston Globe* (Cambridge, Mass.: Belknap Press of Harvard University Press, 1971), pp. 14–15.

43. Crouthamel, *James Watson Webb,* p. 150; Nevins, *The Evening Post,* pp. 421–22.

44.

	1859	1874
Telegraph tolls	$11,679	$ 51,728
Composition	$42,356	$125,883
Editorial work	$43,125	$188,829
Total	$97,160	$366,440

Lee, *The Daily Newspaper in America,* p. 198.

45. Salem *Oregon Statesman,* July 20, 1864, p. 2.

46. William H. Simpson, "The Press: Its Relations to Its Patrons and the Public," *Thirteenth Annual Report of the Proceedings of the Maine Editors and Publishers Association for the Year 1876* (Portland: Brown, Thurston and Co., 1876), p. 13.

47. William E. Gienapp, " 'Politics Seem to Enter into Everything': Political Culture in the North, 1840–1860," in *Essays on American Antebellum Politics, 1840–1860,* ed. William E. Gienapp et al. (College Station: Texas A & M Press, 1982), p. 32.

48. Michael F. Holt, *The Political Crisis of the 1850s* (New York: John Wiley and Sons, 1978), p. 4; also see pp. 133, 135, 137, 167, 175.

49. Although many authors note the general disillusionment with political parties during the middle and latter decades of the century, it is important to note that voter participation actually rose.

50. Formisano, *The Birth of Mass Political Parties: Michigan, 1827–1861* (Princeton: Princeton University Press), p. 327.

51. Holt, *Political Crisis of the 1850s,* p. 175; Formisano, *The Birth of Mass Political Parties,* p. 327.

52. Holt, *Political Crisis of the 1850s,* p. 122; Robinson, *Evolution of American Political Parties,* p. 129.

53. Robinson, *Evolution of American Political Parties,* pp. 129–30.

54. David Loth, *Public Plunder: A History of Graft in America* (New York: Carrick and Evans, 1938), pp. 187–89; Eric F. Goldman, *Rendezvous with Destiny* (New York: Alfred A. Knopf, 1952), pp. 12–14; Matthew Josephson, *The Politicos, 1865–1896* (New York: Harcourt Brace and Co., 1938), pp. 180–213.

55. Vincent De Santis, "The Republican Party Revised, 1877–1897," in *The*

Gilded Age: A Reappraisal, ed. Wayne Morgan (Syracuse: Syracuse University Press, 1963), pp. 81–110.

56. Goldman, *Rendezvous with Destiny,* p. 12.

57. Seymour J. Mandelbaum, *Boss Tweed's New York* (New York: John Wiley and Sons, 1965), p. 47. Also see Edward C. Kirkland, *Dream and Thought in the Business Community, 1860–1900* (Ithaca: Cornell University Press, 1956), pp. 117–18.

58. Allan Nevins, *The Emergence of Lincoln* (New York: Charles Scribner's Sons, 1950), p. 305; Gienapp, " 'Politics Seem to Enter, pp. 200–221.

59. *New York Herald,* June 3, 1840, data reported in Frederic Hudson, *Journalism in the United States from 1690 to 1872* (New York: Harper and Brothers, 1873), p. 460.

60. Nevins, *The Evening Post,* pp. 157–58.

61. *New York Tribune,* June 3, 1872, p. 1, column 6.

62. *New York Times,* June 2, 1872, p. 5, column 2.

63. Hudson, *Journalism in the United States,* pp. 432–33.

64. *New York Herald,* May 6, 1835, quoted in Hudson, p. 433.

65. *New York Tribune,* June 3, 1872, p. 8, column 1.

66. *New York Times,* June 2, 1872, p. 5, column 2.

67. *New York Tribune,* June 3, 1872, p. 8, columns 1, 2, p. 4, column 3. The *Boston Daily Advertiser* noted that Bennett's *New York Herald* "discovered the hunger of the public for detailed and minute information of the commonest every-day occurrences." June 3, 1872, p. 2.

68. *New York Tribune,* June 3, 1872, p. 1, column 6.

69. Ibid., p. 8, column 2.

70. New York *Evening Post,* June 3, 1872, p. 2, column 2.

71. Gerald W. Johnson et al., *The Sunpapers of Baltimore* (New York: Alfred A. Knopf, 1937), p. 22; also see pp. 15, 51–52.

72. Hudson, *Journalism in the United States,* p. 420. Hudson notes that other penny papers in Boston and Philadelphia generally avoided politics. p. 425.

73. Lee, *The Daily Newspaper in America,* p. 181.

74. Nevins, *The Evening Post,* p. 160.

75. Johnson et al., *The Sunpapers of Baltimore,* p. 7.

76. *Historical Statistics of the United States, Colonial Times to 1970,* volume 1, Series A57-72, "Population in Urban and Rural Territory by Size of Place, 1790 to 1970" (Washington, D.C.: Government Printing Office, 1975).

77. Crouthamel, *James Watson Webb,* p. 149.

78. Lee, *The Daily Newspaper in America,* p. 84.

79. Carl N. Degler, *Out of Our Past: The Forces That Shaped Modern America,* 3d. (New York: Harper Colophon Books, 1984), p. 347. Book reading as a form of recreation, the growth of fiction, and publishing houses in major cities, all contributed to an environment in which literacy increased. See Maury Klein and Harvey Kantor, eds., *Prisoners of Progress: American Industrial Cities 1850–1920* (New York: Macmillan Publishing Co., 1976), p. 257.

80. Little local news appeared in antebellum partisan newspapers. A reader of the *Macon Telegraph* (Georgia) could scan that weekly paper through the month of October 1831 (five issues), for instance, and find virtually no news about Macon. The paper instead provided news of the distant world. The issues addressed in the *Telegraph* no doubt had genuine currency for Macon residents (threats of slave insurrections, state rights issues, crop reports from other states, the spread of cholera in coastal areas) but virtually nothing about Macon or nearby towns. See the *Macon Telegraph*, October 1, 8, 15, 22, 29, 1831.

81. Samuel P. Hays, "The Changing Political Structure of the City in Industrial America," *Journal of Urban History* 1, no. 1 (November 1974), p. 8.

82. Barth, *City People*, p. 61.

83. In the late nineteenth century, major cities led the nation in crimes. Arthur M. Schlesinger, Sr., *The Rise of the City 1878–1898* (New York: Macmillan Co., 1933), p. 115.

84. Klein and Kantor, *Prisoners of Progress*, p. 281.

85. During the third week of October 1897, the *Boston Globe* devoted 25.9 percent of all editorial space (N = 13,289 inches) to leisure activities and the *San Francisco Chronicle* devoted 19 percent (N = 9,428.25 inches of editorial space).

86. David Lamoreaux, "Baseball in the Late Nineteenth Century: The Source of Its Appeal," *Journal of Popular Culture* 11, no. 3 (Winter 1977), p. 597; Stephen Freedman, "The Baseball Fad in Chicago, 1865–1870: An Exploration of the Role of Sport in the Nineteenth Century City," *Journal of Sport History* 5, no. 2 (Summer 1978), pp. 38–39.

87. Lamoreaux, "Baseball in the Late Nineteenth Century," p. 597; Klein and Kantor, *Prisoners of Progress*, pp. 276–77; Stan Gelber, "Their Hands Are All Out Playing: Business and Amateur Baseball, 1845–1917," *Journal of Sport History* 11, no. 1 (Spring 1984), pp. 5–27.

88. *New York Times*, May 21, 1888, quoted in *Modern American Cities*, ed. Ray Giner (Chicago: Quadrangle Books, 1969), pp. 92–94.

89. Lyons, *Newspaper Story*, p. 25.

90. Ibid.

91. Wendt, *Chicago Tribune*, p. 218.

92. Nevins, *The Evening Post*, p. 566.

93. Klein and Kantor, *Prisoners of Progress*, p. 279. Also see Arthur M. Schlesinger, Sr., *Political and Social Growth of the American People, 1865–1940*, 3d ed. (New York: Macmillan Co., 1941), p. 290: "The great increase of city dwellers also provided wider patronage for the theater." Also see Nevins, *The Evening Post*, p. 364.

94. Robert Higgs, *The Transformation of the American Economy, 1865–1914* (New York: John Wiley and Sons, 1971), p. 39.

95. Alex Groner et al. (the editors of *American Heritage* and *Business Week*), *American Business and Industry* (New York: American Heritage Publishing Co.,

1972), p. 235; Alfred D. Chandler, Jr., "The Beginnings of Big Business in American Industry," in *New Views On American Economic Development,* ed. Ralph Andreano (Cambridge: Schenckman Publishing Co., 1965), p. 279.

96. Robert Wiebe, *The Search for Order* (New York: Hill and Wang, 1967), p. 8.

97. Sean D. Cashman, *America in the Gilded Age* (New York: New York University Press, 1984), pp. 12–13.

98. Schlesinger, *Political and Social Growth,* p. 60.

99. Ross M. Robertson, *History of the American Economy,* 3d ed. (New York: Harcourt Brace Jovanovich, 1973), p. 340. Also see: Alan Trachtenberg, *The Incorporation of America: Culture and Society in the Gilded Age* (New York: Hill and Wang, 1982), p. 53; Page Smith, *The Rise of Industrial America* (New York: McGraw-Hill Book Co., 1984), pp. 89–112; Alfred D. Chandler, Jr., *The Visible Hand: The Managerial Revolution in American Business* (Cambridge, Mass.: Belknap Press of Harvard University Press, 1977), pp. 81–189.

100. Quaker Oats distributed tens of thousands of free samples around the country to familiarize the public with its product. Morton Keller, *The Life Insurance Enterprise, 1885–1910: A Study in the Limits of Corporate Power* (Cambridge: Belknap Press of Harvard University Press, 1963); Arthur E. Marquette, *Brands, Trademarks and Good Will* (New York: McGraw-Hill Book Co., 1967).

101. Thomas C. Cochran, *The Pabst Brewing Co.: The History of an American Business* (New York: New York University Press, 1948), pp. 129–36; Frank Presbrey, *The History and Development of Advertising* (Garden City, N.Y.: Doubleday, Doran and Co., 1929) pp. 362–63; also see *Chicago Dry Goods Reporter* (March 21, 1896), pp. 11–13.

102. *Advertising Experience* (June 1899), p. iv.

103. East Oregonian Record Books, Oregon Historical Society.

104. New York *Sun,* quoted in *The Newspaper Maker* (May 23, 1895), p. 4.

105. *Profitable Advertiser* (April 1898), p. 423.

106. Ibid., October 15, 1894, p. 215.

107. Nannie M. Tilley, *The R. J. Reynolds Tobacco Company* (Chapel Hill: University of North Carolina Press, 1985), pp. 71–72.

108. Ibid., p. 75.

109. Chandler, *The Visible Hand,* pp. 290–92.

110. Henry R. Boss, *A Brief History of Advertising* (Chicago: Frederick Weston Printing Co., 1886), p. 25.

111. *Printers' Ink* (February 26, 1890), p. 408.

112. *Advertising* (December 1898), p. 135.

113 *Printers' Ink* (January 8, 1890), p. 241.

114. Ibid., September 23, 1896, p. 4. Also see ibid., December 2, 1896, pp. 4–5; *Profitable Advertiser* (June 15, 1899), pp. 33–34.

115. *Printers' Ink* (October 21, 1896), p. 3.

116. *Profitable Advertiser* (June 15, 1893), pp. 12, 21; also see ibid., December 15, 1897, p. 36.

117. Ibid., June 15, 1899, p. 27.

118. Edward C. Kirkland, "Building American Cities," in *Views of American Economic Growth: The Industrial Era*, volume 2, ed. Thomas C. Cochran and Thomas B. Brewer (New York: McGraw-Hill Book Co., 1966), pp. 15–32. The urban infrastructure (street improvements, street cars) expanded the market area beyond a shopper's immediate neighborhood, allowing the concentration of diverse goods in one store distant from the consumer's home. Ralph B. Hower, *A History of Macy's of New York, 1858–1915* (Cambridge, Mass.: Harvard University Press, 1943), pp. 146–47.

119. Hower, *History of Macy's*, p. 148.

120. Chandler, *The Visible Hand*, p. 224.

121. Ibid., p. 223. Also see John W. Ferry, *A History of the Department Store* (New York: Macmillan Co., 1960), p. 16; *Newspaper Maker* (December 16, 1897), p. 8; *Manufacturer* (Philadelphia) (August 13, 1892), p. 5.

122. Department store managers preferred newspapers over magazines. One of the owners of Macy's in the 1890s refused a magazine publisher's bid for advertising, saying the "nature of our business is such that goods will in most instances be closed out before we are able to announce through you that we have them for sale." Hower, *History of Macy's*, p. 268.

123. *Dry Goods Economist* (May 23, 1896), p. 65.

124. Hower, *History of Macy's*, Table 20.

125. Ibid., p. 267.

126. *Profitable Advertiser* (October 15, 1893), p. 142, quoting the New York *World*; also see *Profitable Advertiser* (March 15, 1895), p. 307.

127. *Fame* (February 1897), p. 444. Also see: *Kings' Jester* (April 1892), p. 42; Michael Schudson, *Advertising, the Uneasy Persuasion* (New York: Basic Books, 1984), pp. 150–52.

128. *Advertising World* (September 15, 1897), p. 1.

129. Herbert A. Gibbons, *John Wanamaker*, volume 2, (New York: Harper and Brothers, 1926), pp. 14–15.

130. *Chicago Dry Goods Reporter* (March 25, 1899), p. 53.

Chapter 3: Advertising and the Press

1. Alfred McClung Lee, *The Daily Newspaper in America: The Evolution of a Social Instrument* (New York: Macmillan Co., 1937), p. 718.

2. *Fame* (September 1894), p. 258.

3. Daniel Pope, *The Making of Modern Advertising* (New York: Basic Books, 1983), pp. 5–6.

4. Ernest Elmo Calkins and Ralph Holden, *Modern Advertising* (New York: D. Appleton, 1905), p. 13, quoted in Pope, *The Making of Modern Advertising*, p. 31.

5. Lee, *The Daily Newspaper in America*, pp. 748–49.

6. Ibid.

7. *Proceedings of the Ninth Annual Meeting of the Associated Ohio Dailies,* (Springfield, Ohio: Hosterman Publishing Co., 1894), p. 40.

8. *The Advertising Reporter* (Chicago: Publishers' Commercial Union, 1888), p. 187.

9. *Proceedings of the Ninth Annual Meeting of the Associated Ohio Dailies,* p. 50; also see pp. 51, 53–54.

10. See Quentin J. Schultz, "Advertising, Science and Professionalism, 1885–1917" (Ph.D. diss., University of Illinois, 1978), pp. 79–83.

11. *Pettingill's Newspaper Directory* (Boston: S. M. Pettingill, 1877), p. vi.

12. *Printers' Ink* (October 21, 1896), pp. 3–5. Also see "Honest Circulation," *Printers' Ink* (January 29, 1890), p. 321; "What Is Circulation of a Newspaper?" *Printers' Ink* (December 14, 1889), p. 192; *Advertising Experience* (November 1899), p. 3; (December 1900), p. 14.

13. *Advertising* (May 1897), p. 53; *Advertising World* (February 14, 1899), p. 5; *Printers' Ink* (August 5, 1896), p. 41; *Advisor* (March 1899), p. 3.

14. *Advertising Experience* (December 1900), p. 14.

15. *Advertising* (May 1897), p. 53, quoting the *Newburyport News* (Massachusetts), April 16, 1897; *Fame* (September 1892), p. 203.

16. *Fame* (June 1892), p. 112.

17. *Pettingill's Newspaper Directory,* 1877, p. vi.

18. *Advertising Experience,* June 1899, p. 6.

19. *Kings' Jester* (March 1892), p. 8.

20. *Advertising Experience* (June 1899), p. 6.

21. Ibid., December 1899, pp. ix, xix, xxi; July 1899, p. vi; August 1900, p. xxix; *Kings' Jester* (May 1891), back cover; (February 1892), pp. 205–12; *Advertising* (December 1898), p. 135; (July 1898), p. 77; (May 1897), pp. 52–53; (September 1897), p. 99; *Advertising World* (October 15, 1897), p. 1; *Printers' Ink* (December 15, 1889), p. 187; *Advisor* (March 1899), p. 3; (April 1899), p. 3.

22. *Pettingill's Newspaper Directory,* 1877, p. vii.

23. Charles Austin Bates, *Criticisms* (New York: n.p., 1897), p. 222.

24. *Fame* (August 1896), pp. 222–23.

25. *Printers' Ink* (July 22, 1892), p. 51; emphasis added to signal the devaluation of women through the economic lens of marketing. Also see *Profitable Advertiser* (September 15, 1893), p. 118; *Printers' Ink* (December 15, 1889), p. 189; *Advisor* (March 1899), p. 4. Both of the last two articles warn against cheap newspapers. Regarding women, see: *Profitable Advertiser* (February 19, 1892), p. 287; (September 15, 1893), p. 118; and *Advertising Experience* (November 1899), pp. 3–4.

26. *Advertising Experience* (February 1901), p. 19.

27. Ralph B. Hower, *A History of Macy's of New York, 1858–1915* (Cambridge, Mass.: Harvard University Press, 1943), p. 226.

28. Dr. S. B. Hartman and Co., Advertising Department, to J. Hopley, September 17, 1884, John Hopley Papers, Box 4, Ohio Historical Society. Also see Edwin Alden and Bros. Newspaper Advertising Agency to J. Hopley, 1885, John Hopley Papers, Box 4, Ohio Historical Society.

29. Dauchy and Co. to J. Hopley, September 29, 1880, John Hopley Papers, Box 4, Ohio Historical Society.

30. N. W. Ayer and Son to J. Hopley, April 17, 1885, John Hopley Papers, Ohio Historical Society.

31. N. W. Ayer and Son to J. Hopley, March 21, 1885, John Hopley Papers, Box 4, Ohio Historical Society.

32. Edwin Alden and Brothers to J. Hopley, July 17, 1885; J. Hopley to Edwin Alden and Brothers, July 20, 1885; both in John Hopley Papers, Box 4, Ohio Historical Society.

33. *Advertising Experience* (December 1896), p. 17.

34. O. B. Selfrid of the Lima, Ohio, *Times,* quoted in *Proceedings of the Ninth Annual Meeting of the Associated Ohio Dailies,* p. 45.

35. *Pittsburgh Leader,* October 9, 1897, p. 4.

36. *Cincinnati Tribune,* May 9, 1894, p. 6.

37. *Chicago Herald,* September 14, 1881, p. 1; May 20, 1881, p. 1; May 27, 1881, p. 1.

38. *Chicago Record,* March 21, 1893, p. 5.

39. *McMinnville Telephone Register* (Oregon), October 21, 1897, p. 3.

40. The McMinnville, Oregon, *Daily Campaign* carried reading notices for Dr. Pierce's Prescription and for Hostetter's Stomach Bitters. April 14, 1886, p. 3.

41. *Newspaperdom* (June 1892), p. 14.

42. Quoted in *Printers' Ink* (May 21, 1890), p. 826.

43. S. M. Pettingill and Co. to J. Hopley, December 21, 1870, John Hopley Papers, Box 3, Ohio Historical Society.

44. *Profitable Advertiser* (December 15, 1892), p. 206.

45. Ibid.

46. Ibid.

47. N. W. Ayer and Son to J. Hopley, August 5, 1885, John Hopley Papers, Box 4, Ohio Historical Society. Also see: J. H. Zeilin and Co. to J. Hopley, "Advertising Contract," Dauchy and Co. to J. Hopley, re: Dr. Kennedy's "Favorite Remedy"; Nelson Chesman and Co. (St. Louis) to J. Hopley, July 6, 1885; all in the John Hopley Papers, Box 3, Ohio Historical Society.

48. Dauchy and Co. to J. Hopley, November 11, 1889, John Hopley Papers, Box 3, Ohio Historical Society.

49. John Hopley Papers, Box 4, 1885, Ohio Historical Society.

50. J. Hopley to Edwin Alden and Brothers, September 1, 1885, John Hopley Papers, Box 4, Ohio Historical Society.

51. J. Hopley to Edwin Alden and Brothers, July 20, 1885, John Hopley Papers, Box 4, Ohio Historical Society.

52. J. Hopley to Edwin Alden and Brothers, July 20, 1885, John Hopley Papers, Box 4, Ohio Historical Society.

53. Edwin Alden and Brothers to J. Hopley, July 17, 1885, John Hopley Papers, Box 4, Ohio Historical Society.

54. Dauchy and Company to J. Hopley, December 10, 1880, John Hopley Papers, Box 3, Ohio Historical Society; emphasis added.

55. *Advertising Experience* (January 1899), p. 18.

56. *Advertising World* (December 15, 1898), p. 1.

57. *Printers' Ink* (January 15, 1890), p. 262.

58. A. O. Bunnell, comp., *New York Press Association, Authorized History for Fifty Years, 1853–1903* (Dansville, N.Y.: F. A. Owen Publishing Co., 1903), p. 26.

59. *Ad Sense* (August 1900), p. 34. Also see Orange and Judd to J. Hopley, July 7, 1880, John Hopley Papers, Box 4, Ohio Historical Society.

60. *Printers' Ink* (March 12, 1890), p. 464.

61. Ibid.

62. Ibid., February 2, 1891, p. 153.

63. Ibid., November 28, 1894, pp. 491–92.

64. Ibid., September 9, 1896.

65. *Oakland Observer* (Oregon), April 10, 1891, p. 5. On page 4 was a two-column ad for E. G. Young and Company, general merchants.

66. *Woodburn Independent* (Oregon), October 7, 1897, p. 2.

67. Small-city/large-town newspapers that promoted businesses within their news columns included: McMinnville, Oregon, *Daily Campaign,* June 7, 1886, p. 3; Pendleton, Oregon, *East Oregonian,* February 12, 1876, p. 3; April 9, 1901, p. 3; McMinnville, Oregon, *West Side Telephone,* June 15, 1886, p. 1; *McMinnville Telephone Register* (Oregon), December 9, 1897, p. 4; October 21, 1897, p. 3; *Albany Daily Democrat* (Oregon), January 13, 1891, p. 3. The McMinnville newspapers were Republican, the others Democratic. All were in county seats.

Small-town newspapers that promoted businesses within their news columns included: Drain, Oregon, *Echo,* January 20, 1886, p. 2; August 26, 1887, p. 3; Warrenton, Oregon, *Port Oregon Tribune,* July 24, 1896, p. 2; *Oakland Observer* (Oregon), April 10, 1891, p. 5; *Wasco News,* (Oregon), October 28, 1897, p. 3; *Newberg Graphic* (Oregon), December 22, 1888, p. 3; October 16, 1896, p. 3.

68. *Cincinnati Tribune,* September 23, 1894, p. 2.

69. *Chicago Herald,* May 6, 1894, p. 40.

70. *Boston Globe,* February 8, 1885, p. 5.

71. *The Newspaper Maker* (January 20, 1898), p. 4; (November 19, 1896), p. 3.

72. *Cincinnati Tribune,* September 28, 1894, p. 14.

73. *Printers' Ink* (December 5, 1894), p. 27.

74. Ibid., November 28, 1894, p. 492.

75. Ibid., February 5, 1890, p. 339.

76. Ibid., March 13, 1895, p. 3.

77. *Profitable Advertiser* (June 15, 1899), pp. 69–70.

78. *Printers' Ink* (December 5, 1894), p. 26.

79. *Fame* (June 1897), p. 162.

80. *Ohio Editorial Association Minutes of Annual Meeting, Columbus, February 20, 1901* (n.p., n.d.) pp. 31–37.

81. *Fame* (May 1897), p. 4.

82. *Ohio Editorial Association Minutes, 1901*, p. 37.

83. *The Newspaper Maker* (February 17, 1898), p. 1.

84. Ibid., December 9, 1897, p. 4, quoting the *Cincinnati Post.*

85. Advertising contract, J. H. Zeilin and Company, John Hopley Papers, Box 3, Ohio Historical Society.

86. *Advertising Experience* (July 1898), p. 4.

87. *Fame* (February 1893), p. 455.

88. Ibid.; emphasis added.

89. *Ad Sense* (April 1900), p. 101.

90. *Newspaper Maker* (December 23, 1898), p. 4.

91. Ibid., September 10, 1896, p. 4.

92. Ibid., December 3, 1896, p. 4.

93. New York *Evening Post*, February 9, 17, March 17, April 11, 1899.

94. Ibid., March 17, 1899.

95. Ibid., March 28, 1899.

96. Ibid., March 28, April 12, 1899.

97. Quoted, ibid., April 3, 1899.

98. *Profitable Advertiser* (April 13, 1899), p. 616.

99. *Newspaper Maker* (April 11, 1895), p. 4.

100. Ibid., April 18, 1895, p. 4.

101. *Newspaperdom* (June 1892), p. 9.

102. *Advertising Experience* (December 1896), p. 18.

103. Nathaniel C. Fowler, Jr., "Reaching the Men through the Women," *Printers' Ink* (July 22, 1892), p. 51.

Chapter 4: Newspapers as Businesses

1. *Newspaper Maker* (July 16, 1896), p. 2, quoting the *St. Joseph News* (Missouri).

2. *Newspaper Maker* (October 20, 1898), p. 4.

3. *Proceedings of the Third Annual Convention of the National Association of Managers of Newspaper Circulation, 1901* (Buffalo, 1901), p. 27.

4. C. F. Chapin, "The Newspaper: An Editor Tells the Public Some Things Which His Newspaper Can Hardly Say for Itself," *Journalist* (May 5, 1888), p. 10.

5. Department size and number varied among papers. Metropolitan daily papers had more departments and specialization than weeklies. But even weeklies had some differentiation in news gathering, production, and distribution.

6. Some saw this as the most important department. In 1890, *Printers' Ink* noted, "In the estimation of the newspaper manager, columns of advertising rank out of sight of news in point of solid value." October 22, 1890, p. 405.

7. *Proceedings of the Fourth Annual Convention of the National Association of Managers of Newspaper Circulation, 1902* (Columbus, Ohio: F. J. Heer, 1902), pp. 15–16.

8. *Proceedings of the Third Annual Convention of the National Association of Managers of Newspaper Circulation,* 1901 (Buffalo, 1901), p. 49.

9. *Proceedings of the Fifth Annual Convention of the National Association of Managers of Newspaper Circulation,* 1903 (Columbus, Ohio: F. J. Heer, 1903), p. 44.

10. *Newspaper Maker* (April 12, 1900), p. 6.

11. Ibid., July 18, 1895, p. 3.

12. *St. Louis Republican,* May 16, 1888, p. 7.

13. *Cincinnati Tribune,* April 28, 1895, p. 6.

14. *Newspaper Maker* (May 28, 1896), p. 1.

15. Ibid., April 11, 1895, p. 5.

16. Ibid., January 1, 1895, p. 1; September 10, 1897, p. 3.

17. *Newspaperdom* (July 1892), p. 3.

18. *Newspaper Maker* (January 1, 1895), p. 1.

19. *Journalist* (February 21, 1891).

20. *Newspaper Maker* (May 2, 1895), p. 1; (October 17, 1895), p. 3.

21. *Chicago Herald,* December 3, 1893, p. 29.

22. *Newspaper Maker* (May 2, 1895), p. 1.

23. Ibid., April 24, 1895, p. 1.

24. *Printers' Ink* (May 28, 1890), pp. 869–71.

25. Ibid.; *Chicago Herald,* April 22, 1894, p. 14.

26. Pamphlet, *"Globe-Democrat,* 1896," John Springer Papers, Box 9, University of Iowa.

27. *Printers' Ink* (May 28, 1890), p. 870.

28. Ibid.

29. *Newspaperdom* (July 1892), p. 2.

30. Production staffs increased with organization size, even with high-velocity machines. Although one typesetting machine might do the work of 5–10 people setting type by hand, the complexity of production demanded more workers.

31. *Chicago Herald,* October 1, 1893, p. 20.

32. *Newspaper Maker* (June 27, 1895), p. 2.

33. *Newspaperdom* (July 1892), p. 2.

34. *Ohio Newspaper* 3, no. 4 (January 1933), p. 4, "Recalls Printing Troubles of Other Days."

35. *Chicago Herald,* April 22, 1894.

36. John Mack, publisher of the *Sandusky Register* (Ohio), quoted in *Proceedings of the Eighth Annual Meeting of the Associated Ohio Dailies* (Springfield, Ohio: Hosterman Publishing Co., 1893), pp. 43–44.

37. *Proceedings of the California Press Association at Its Fourth Annual Meeting,* November 15–16, 1892 (Sacramento: Woodson Bros. Print, 1893), p. 18.

38. *Proceedings of the Thirty-third Convention of the Wisconsin Press Association,* 1886 (Lake Geneva: James E. Heg, 1887), p. 41.

39. Address of W. S. Cappeller, 1892 meeting of the National Editorial Association, *The First Decennium of the National Editorial Association of the United States,* volume 1, ed. B. B. Herbert (Chicago: 1896), p. 452.

40. A. H. Lowrie, "The Ethics of Journalism," in *Proceedings of the National Editorial Association of the United States,* 1885–86 (Little Rock, Arkansas: 1886), p. 63.

41. Address of President Hubner, Proceedings of the Nebraska Press Association for 1896, *Nebraska Editor* (February 1896), p. 2.

42. C. W. Smith, *Newspaperdom* (September 1892), p. 8.

43. *Journalist* (August 1, 1891), p. 3.

44. T. Campbell-Copeland, *The Ladder of Journalism: How to Climb It* (New York: Allan Forman, 1889), p. 85.

45. Ibid., pp. 78–79. *Inland Printer* (August 1900, p. 677) noted that small dailies used Linotype machines regularly. Also see O. F. Byxbee, "Establishing a Newspaper," *Inland Printer* (October 1900), p. 67.

46. B. B. Herbert, ed., *First Decennium of the National Editorial Association,* pp. 549, 559.

47. Myron K. Jordan, "The Golden Age of the Press Revisited," research paper, University of Washington, Appendix 6, Table 4.

48. J. J. Browne to Mrs. Browne, September 4, 1896, J. J. Browne Papers, Eastern Washington Historical Society; also see *Spokane Chronicle,* March 25, 1912.

49. Jordan, "Golden Age of the Press," pp. 14–15; Ramey Medicator Company to B. L. Hoard (of Ft. Atkinson, Wisconsin), January 7, August 3, 1893, H. L. Hoard Papers, State Historical Society of Wisconsin.

50. *Woodburn Independent* (Oregon), July 5, 1895, p. 2.

51. *Proceedings of the Tenth Annual Meeting of the Associated Ohio Dailies* (Springfield, Ohio: Hosterman Publishing Co., 1895), pp. 37, 38.

52. "Notes and Query, Machine Composition," by "an Expert," *Inland Printer* (November 1899), p. 265.

53. Nathaniel C. Fowler, Jr., *The Handbook of Journalism* (New York: Sully and Kleinteich, 1913), pp. 74–75, 96–99, 114–18, 124–27; Augustus J. Munson, *Making a Country Newspaper* (Chicago: Dominion Co., 1891). Also see the *Journalist* (March 22, 1884), p. 4; (March 31, 1888), pp. 4, 8; (September 29, 1888), p. 8.

54. *Report of Proceedings of the Ninth Annual Convention of the American Newspaper Publishers Association,* 1895 (New York: ANPA Office, 1895), pp. 54–55.

55. *Journalist* (June 23, 1900), p. 75; (September 1, 1900), p. 157; *Newspaper Maker* (August 23, 1900), p. 6; Fowler, *Handbook of Journalism,* p. 99.

56. *Journalist* (August 14, 1897), p. 133.

57. Ibid., August 18, 1900, p. 139; also see Ted Curtis Smythe, "The Reporter, 1880–1900: Working Conditions and Their Influence on the News," *Journalism History* 7, no. 1 (1980) pp. 3–6.

58. John Williams Fox to M. Fible, March 14, 1886; J. W. Fox to M. Fible, May 11, 1884; J. W. Fox to M. Fible, September 16, 1886; all in the John Fox Papers, Southern Historical Collection, University of North Carolina. *Fourth Estate* (March 9, 1901), p. 396; *Journalist* (October 20, 1900), p. 210; (September 15, 1900), p. 178; Smythe, "The Reporter, 1880–1900," p. 5.

59. *Journalist* (September 1, 1900), p. 157.

60. *Newspaper Maker* (January 9, 1896), p. 5; also see August 2, 1900, p. 6.

61. *Journalist* (September 1, 1900), p. 157.

62. *Newspaper Maker* (April 21, 1898), p. 4.

63. *Journalist* (July 14, 1900), p. 108.

64. *Newspaper Maker*(October 30, 1895), p. 7.

65. *Journalist* (September 1, 1900), p. 159.

66. Ibid.; also see the *Pittsburgh Leader,* April 28, 1898, p. 1, for a cartoon on space pay.

67. John W. Fox to M. Fible, May 11, 1884, John W. Fox, Jr., Letters, John Fox Papers, Southern Historical Collection, University of North Carolina.

68. Henry L. Mencken, *Newspaper Days, 1899–1906* (New York: Alfred A. Knopf, 1941), pp. 262–63.

69. *Newspaper Maker* (December 15, 1898), p. 4. Also see ibid., April 11, 1901, p. 4.

70. *Journalist* (August 14, 1897), p. 134, quoting the *Brooklyn Weekly.*

71. *Newspaper Maker* (October 17, 1895), p. 4; (September 2, 1897), p. 8; (July 28, 1897), p. 5.

72. *Report of the Proceedings of the Ninth Annual Convention of the American Newspaper Publishers Association,* 1895 (New York: ANPA Office, 1895), pp. 28–42, 45–47, 54–56.

73. Ibid., p. 56.

74. *Report of the Proceedings of the 13th Annual Convention of the American Newspaper Publishers Association,* February 15–18, 1899 (New York: ANPA Office, 1899), pp. 23–25.

75. John Springer Collection, "Lincoln's Birthday," supplied by the American Press Association. Other features were available for St. Valentine's Day, St. Patrick's Day, Easter, New Years, and Columbus Day. John Springer Papers, Box 9, 2, University of Iowa.

76. Ibid., Box 9, 1.

77. The *Journalist* estimated that the APA was the "principal" contributor to 600 dailies and 1,200 weeklies. March 27, 1886, p. 10.

78. Ernest E. Calkins and Ralph Holden, *Modern Advertising* (New York: D. Appleton, 1905), pp. 82–83; Charles Floyd [pseud.], "The Country Daily's Opportunity," *Newspaperdom* (August 1892), pp. 7–9; *Printers' Ink* (January 14, 1891), pp. 97, 100; (April 8, 1891), p. 489; (April 22, 1891), p. 551; *Newspaper Maker* (August 29, 1895), p. 3.

79. *Newspaper Maker* (October 6, 1898), p. 4. Also see Fowler, *Handbook of Journalism,* p. 125.

80. Lewis M. Grist, "Use and Abuse of the Plate Service," *Newspaperdom* (March 1892), pp. 6–7. Also see: "A Chance to Drop the Patent Outsides and Make a Home Paper at Nearly the Same Cost," in *Pacific Printer* (April 1880), p. 5; *Pacific Printer* (June 1881), pp. 2, 3; O. F. Byxbee, "Establishing a Newspaper," *Inland Printer* (February 1900), p. 681; and the ensuing response in *Inland Printer* (April 1900), pp. 46–47.

81. *Newspaperdom* (June 1892), p. 4.

82. *Proceedings of the Eighth Annual Meeting of the Associated Ohio Dailies,* p. 86.

83. Grist, "Use and Abuse of the Plate Service," p. 6.

84. Ibid.

85. *Proceedings of the Ninth Annual Meeting of the Associated Ohio Dailies* (Springfield, Ohio: Hosterman Publishing Co., 1894), p. 23.

86. Byxbee, "Establishing a Newspaper," p. 681.

87. McMinnville, Oregon, *Daily Campaign,* April 3, 1886, pp. 2, 3; *Oakland Observer* (Oregon), April 10, 1891, pp. 1, 2, 3, 6, 7. Reading notices were included in the newspaper union material in the *Newberg Graphic* (Oregon), December 22, 1888, p. 4; December 29, 1888, p. 4; July 24, 1896, p. 4 (for Paine's Celery Compound); and on November 6, 1896, p. 4:

> FRIENDS FAILED TO RECOGNIZE HER
> Mrs. Hadix So Changed In Appearance
> that She Hardly Knew Herself.
>
> She says the Secret of the Great
> Change and Her present Good
> Health is Due to the Use of Dr.
> Williams' Pink Pills

88. *Pacific Printer* (December 1891), p. 8.

89. Presbrey, *The History and Development of Advertising* (Garden City, N.Y.: Doubleday, Doran and Co., 1929), p. 274; *Fame* (June 1892), pp. 103–104; *Printers' Ink* (January 29, 1890), p. 314.

90. *Pacific Printer* (December 1891), p. 8, quoting the *Monmouth Democrat.*

91. Fowler, *Handbook of Journalism,* p. 127.

92. Also see Drain, Oregon, *Echo,* May 21, 1885; Warrenton, Oregon, *Port Oregon Tribune,* July 31, 1896, p. 1; Roseburg, Oregon, *Twice a Week Roseburg Review* for 1886; *Oakland Observer* (Oregon), April 10, 1891, pp. 1, 2, 3, 6, 7; McMinnville *West Side Telephone* (Oregon), June 15, 1886, pp. 1, 4; *McMinnville Telephone Register* (Oregon), April 12, 1894.

93. Also see the *Lebanon Express* (Oregon) for March 19, 1897: "History of the Bustle" and "Diamonds Worn by Prominent New York Politicians."

94. Nannie M. Tilley, *The R. J. Reynolds Tobacco Company* (Chapel Hill: University of North Carolina Press, 1985), pp. 70–75.

95. The *Oakland Observer* (Oregon) urged readers to send in material in 1891: "Readers, if you would like to have the happenings of your neighborhood published every week, just send them in." April 10, 1891, p. 4.

96. Hugh Wilson, "Country Journalist and Printer," *Newspaperdom* (December 1892), p. 2.

97. W. A. Swanberg, *Citizen Hearst* (New York: Charles Scribner's Sons, 1961), pp. 59–60.

98. Madelon G. Schlipp and Sharon M. Murphy, *Great Women of the Press* (Carbondale: Southern Illinois University Press, 1983), "Elizabeth Cochrane Seaman," pp. 133–47.

99. Swanberg, *Citizen Hearst*, pp. 59–60.

100. *Chicago Herald,* May 27, 1894, p. 29; July 15, 1894, p. 24; August 3, 1894, p. 1; October 28, 1894, p. 16. The headline is from August 3, 1894, p. 1.

101. *Pittsburgh Leader,* September 15, 1897, p. 1.

102. *Newspaper Maker* (July 25, 1895), p. 4.

103. Ibid., December 6, 1900, p. 4.

104. *Cincinnati Tribune,* January 13, 1895, p. 6.

105. Each story was coded according to its source (e.g., police, city government, hospitals, fire stations, etc.). A more detailed view of the categories of news stories is shown in the table below. "Quasi government" refers to stories clearly not about government operation but rather about the provision of public services. In the coding here, hospitals (which could be publicly or privately owned) were coded as quasi government. "Planned events" were events that a newspaper could anticipate in advance (e.g., a sporting event, nongovernmental meetings, Sunday sermons, etc.). "Bureau" refers to a Chicago newspaper joint news-gathering operation, the World's Fair Bureau in 1893. "Interviews" were coded as nonbeat items. Some of them may have been planned events, if the interview was part of a speech story, for instance, but because it was not clear from newspaper context, all interviews were considered to be outside the beat system. Such coding was used so as not to inflate the number of beat-system stories.

The *Chicago Record* and *Pittsburgh Leader* were chosen because they seemed fairly typical of late nineteenth-century metropolitan newspapers.

Percentage Distribution of News Produced, by Category and Type of System

	Chicago Record		Pittsburgh Leader
	April 1–9, 1893	April 30–May 4, 1893	March 8–14, 1899
BEAT SYSTEM			
Government	36.5	26.9	46.4
Quasi government	2.4	0.0	4.0
Planned events	33.3	30.5	20.6
Bureau	10.1	33.3	0.0
NONBEAT SYSTEM			
Interviews	13.2	1.8	17.0
Other	4.5	7.5	12.0
N of articles	159	108	324

106. Henry L. Pittock Engagement Book, 1893, January 3, 4, August 13, October 29, and November 26, 1893, Oregon Historical Society, Portland.

107. Salem, Oregon, *Capital Journal*, January 1, 1896, p. 2.

108. *Journalist* (March 28, 1891), p. 5.

109. Ibid., April 11, 1891, p. 6.

110. Ibid.

111. *St. Louis Republic*, September 22, 1888, pp. 4, 8.

112. *Pittsburgh Leader*, April 7, 1898, p. 4.

113. *Cincinnati Tribune*, May 24, 1894, p. 4.

114. Ibid., February 14, 1895, p. 4.

115. *Chicago Herald*, May 10, 1894, p. 1.

116. Ibid., September 12, 1894, p. 4.

117. Ibid., October 12, 1894, p. 6.

118. New York *World*, December 1, 1884, p. 3.

119. *St. Louis Republic*, July 29, 1889, p. 4.

120. *Pittsburgh Leader*, October 16, 1898, p. 12.

121. *St. Paul Globe*, May 18, 1885, p. 4.

122. Ibid., July 27, 1885, p. 4.

123. *St. Louis Republican*, November 7, 1884, p. 2.

124. *Newspaper Maker* (February 24, 1898), p. 4.

125. Ibid., October 3, 1895, p. 5.

126. *St. Louis Republic*, November 8, 1888, p. 1.

127. *Chicago Herald*, May 13, 1894; also see January 3, 1895, p. 6; March 1, 1894, p. 4; March 6, 1894, p. 2.

128. New York *World*, January 6, 1885, p. 4, emphasis added.

129. *Boston Globe*, January 16, 1885, p. 1.

130. See Joseph F. Bradley, *The Role of Trade Associations and Professional Business Societies in America* (University Park: Pennsylvania State University Press, 1965), pp. 2–4.

131. *Chicago Herald*, July 25, 28, 1893, p. 3.

132. *Proceedings of the Associated Ohio Dailies*, volumes 1–7, 1885–91 (Youngstown, Ohio: Telegram Printing Co., 1892), pp. 25–31.

133. Harold K. Schellenger, *An Era of Newspaper Organization: Development of the Buckeye Press Association, 1895–1908* (Columbus: Ohio Historical Society, 1939), p. 2.

134. *A Record of the Organization and Transactions of the Wisconsin Press Association* (Whitewater, Wis.: E. D. Coe, 1890), p. 1.

135. Ibid., p. 3.

136. A. O. Bunnell, comp., *New York Press Association, Authorized History for Fifty Years, 1853–1903* (Dansville, N.Y.: F. A. Owen Publishing Co., 1903), p. 122.

137. *Proceedings of the Seventh Annual Meeting, Associated Ohio Dailies* (Youngstown, Ohio: Telegram Printing Co., 1892), p. 3.

138. Ibid., pp. 5–6. Also see: Osman C. Hooper, "How Ohio Newspaper Organizations Began," *The Ohio Newspaper* 2, no. 1 (February 1932), pp. 3–5;

A. D. Hosterman, "How the Select List Originated and Grew," *The Ohio Newspaper* 2, no. 2 (April 1932), p. 6.

139. The publisher of the Yellow Creek, Illinois, *News,* said county associations were common and worked well. *Newspaperdom* (January 1893), p. 16.

140. *Newspaperdom* (January 1893), pp. 14–16.

141. The tenth meeting of the ANPA, in 1896, dealt with efforts by department store owners to force advertising rates lower. *Newspaper Maker* (February 20, 1896), pp. 1, 2; (February 21, 1896),pp. 1, 2; (February 27, 1896), pp. 1, 2. Also see *Proceedings of the Third Annual Convention, National Association, Managers of Newspaper Circulation, Buffalo, N.Y.,* June 17–19, 1901 (Buffalo, 1901).

142. Other groups existed, too: Northeastern Nebraska Press Association; the Western Editorial Association, a "business organization" for editors and publishers of the West (*Nebraska Editor* [June 1896], p. 1); Northwestern Publishers Association, a "protective organization" dedicated to securing advertising (*Newspaper Maker* [June 20, 1895], p. 1); Southwest Press Association (*Newspaperdom* [February 1893], p. 255); Southwest Texas Association (*Newspaperdom* [February 1893], p. 255); and the Pacific Coast Press Association (*Pacific Specimen* [3d quarter, 1880], p. 1).

Some metropolitan newspapers in Chicago, Boston, New York, and Cincinnati joined to advance their business interests. The Chicago Daily Newspaper Publishers' Association was formed to deal with basic business concerns, such as ad rates and return privileges. *Newspaperdom* (August 1892), p. 11. The Associated Publishers of Washington, D.C., agreed to charge uniform rates in advertising. *American Advertiser Reporter* (May 9, 1888), pp. 147–49. The Publishers Association of New York City forbade news dealers from inserting circulars and other advertisements in their newspapers. *Newspaper Maker* (June 9, 1898), p. 2.

143. *Newspaperdom* (April 1892), p. 29.

144. See *Minutes of the Third Annual Meeting of the American Newspaper Publishers Association, 1889* (New York: ANPA Office, 1889), p. 6; *Report of the Proceedings of the Ninth Annual Convention of the American Newspaper Publishers Association, 1895* (New York: ANPA Office, 1895), pp. 6–8, 11–14, 16–18; *Report of the Proceedings of the Twelfth Annual Convention of the American Newspaper Publishers Association, February 16–18, 1898* (New York: ANPA Office, 1898), pp. 14, 16, 17; *Proceedings of the Tenth Annual Meeting of the Associated Ohio Dailies,* p. 37; *St. Louis Republic,* June 6, 1889; *Chicago Record,* March 31, 1893, p. 11; *Chicago Herald,* July 21, 1881, p. 2; February 21, 1894, p. 7.

145. See: *Chicago Herald,* February 21, 1894, p. 7; *Fourth Annual Convention of the National Association Managers of Newspaper Circulation* (Columbus, Ohio: F. H. Heer, 1902); *Fifth Annual Convention of the National Association, Managers of Newspaper Circulation* (Columbus: F. H. Heer, 1903).

146. See: *Proceedings of the Wisconsin Press Association, Milwaukee, March 5–7, 1902* (Jefferson, Wisconsin: Banner Printing Co., 1902); *Seventh Annual Convention of the American Newspaper Publishers Association, 1893* (New York:

ANPA Office). *Proceedings of the Tenth Annual Meeting of the Associated Ohio Dailies*, 1895; *Report of the Proceedings of the Eleventh Annual Convention of the American Newspaper Publishers Association*, 1897 (New York: ANPA Office, 1897); *Chicago Record*, March 31, 1893, p. 11.

147. See: *Report of the Proceedings of the Ninth Annual Convention of the American Newspaper Publishers Association*, 1895 (New York: ANPA Office, 1895), pp. 28–41, 45–47, 54–56.

148. *Fourth Annual Convention of the American Newspaper Publishers Association* (Brooklyn: Brooklyn Times Job Print, 1890), pp. 17–20; *Report of the Proceedings of the Ninth Annual Convention of the American Newspaper Publishers Association* (New York: ANPA Office, 1895), pp. 15, 62; *Report of the Proceedings of the Thirteenth Annual Convention of the American Newspaper Publishers Association*, 1899 (New York: ANPA Office, 1899), p. 20; *Eighteenth Annual Report of the Proceedings of the Maine Press Association, 1881* (Skowhegan, Maine: Joseph Wood, 1881), p. 25.

149. *Journalist* (July 25, 1891), pp. 2–3 (on the 1891 National Editorial Association meeting); *Proceedings of the Illinois Press Association at the Twenty-fifth Annual Session, 1890* (Morris, Illinois: Hayes and Fletcher, Printers, 1890), p. 49; Bunnell, *New York Press Association*, p. 51.

150. *Proceedings of the Wisconsin Editorial Association, 1880* (Whitewater: Whitewater Register Steam Print, 1882), pp. 16–17; *Proceedings of the Wisconsin Press Association, 1890* (Edgerton, Wis.: F. W. Coon, 1890), p. 15; *Proceedings of the Ninth Annual Meeting of the Associated Ohio Dailies, 1894*, pp. 44–45; *Proceedings of the Eleventh Annual Meeting of the Associated Ohio Dailies* (Springfield, Ohio: Hosterman Publishing Co., 1896), p. 75; *Report of the Proceedings of the Thirteenth Annual Convention of the American Newspaper Publishers Association, 1899*, p. 26; *Proceedings of the Illinois Press Association at the Twenty-fifth Annual Session, 1890*, p. 51.

151. *Proceedings of the Ninth Annual Meeting of the Associated Ohio Dailies* (Springfield: Hosterman Publishing Co., 1894), p. 59; *Proceedings of the Wisconsin Press Association, 1890*, pp. 10–17.

152. *Ohio Editorial Association Minutes of Annual Meeting, Columbus, February 20, 1901* (n.p., n.d.), pp. 31, 37.

153. The *Nebraska Editor* in 1896 listed advertisers who were reliable and others who were slow to pay or who had reneged entirely on contracts. *Nebraska Editor* (April 1896), p. 10.

154. Twenty-fifth Annual Session of the Nebraska Press Association, *Nebraska Editor* (February 1897), unpaginated.

155. *Proceedings of the Eighth Annual Meeting of the Associated Ohio Dailies*, p. 22.

156. *Proceedings of the Illinois Press Association at the Twenty-fifth Annual Session, 1890*, p. 29.

157. Hosterman, "How the Select List Originated and Grew," p. 6.

158. The states were: Illinois, Indiana, Kentucky, Massachusetts, Michigan,

Minnesota, Missouri, New Jersey, New York, Ohio, Pennsylvania, Texas, and Wisconsin. *Newspaperdom* (January 1893), pp. 14–15.

159. *Newspaperdom* (January 1893), p. 15.

160. Ibid., August 1892, p. 11.

161. *Proceedings of the Wisconsin Press Association,* 1890, pp. 14–17, 33–35; *Fifteenth Annual Report of the Proceedings of the Maine Press Association, 1878* (Portland: Brown, Thurston and Co., 1878), p. 8; *American Advertiser Reporter* (August 14, 1889), pp. 275–77 (on the Missouri Press Association); *American Advertiser Reporter* (August 29, 1888), p. 277 (on the Northern Indiana Editorial Association); *The Ohio Newspaper* 2, no. 1 (February 1932), p. 3 (on the Ohio Editorial Association); Henry A. Brainerd, *History of the Nebraska Press Association* (Lincoln: n.p., June 1923), pp. 2–3.

162. *American Advertiser Reporter* (August 14, 1889), p. 275.

163. Henry Neill, "Why Country Publishers Should Organize," *Newspaperdom* (December 1892), pp. 10–12.

164. *Thirty-sixth Annual Convention of the New York Press Association, 1892* (Dansville, N.Y.: A. O. Bunnell, 1892), p. 64. Sanders noted that there were four county press associations in New York, as well as ones in Pennsylvania, Texas, Washington, West Virginia, and other states. p. 64.

165. *Newspaperdom* (April 1892), p. 29.

166. *American Advertiser Reporter* (May 9, 1888), pp. 147–49.

167. *Newspaperdom* (February 1893), p. 7.

168. Bunnell, *New York Press Association,* p. 68.

169. *American Advertiser Reporter* (February 15, 1888), pp. 50–51.

170 *Proceedings of the Illinois Press Association at the Twenty-Fifth Annual Session, 1890,* p. 51.

171. Wilson, "Country Journalist and Printer," p. 2.

172. *Fourth Annual Convention of the American Newspaper Publishers Association* (Brooklyn: Brooklyn Times Job Plant, 1890), p. 35.

173. *Newspaper Maker* (April 22, 1897), p. 4.

174. Ibid., July 29, 1897, p. 4.

175. *Chicago Herald,* March 29, 1894, p. 6.

176. *Printers' Ink* (April 9, 1890), p. 603.

177. *Proceedings of the Eighth Annual Meeting of the Associated Ohio Dailies,* p. 20.

178. Ibid., p. 21.

179. Ibid., pp. 21–22. Also see Bunnell, *New York Press Association,* p. 86.

180. *Fourth Annual Convention of the American Newspaper Publishers Association,* pp. 31, 33.

181. Ibid., p. 35.

182. *Proceedings of the Eighth Annual Meeting of the Associated Ohio Dailies,* p. 57.

183. Bunnell, *New York Press Association,* p. 102.

184. *Fourth Annual Convention of the American Newspaper Publishers Associa-*

tion, p. 31. Also see: *Chicago Herald,* November 2, 1894, p. 8; November 7, 1894, p. 6; November 18, 1894, p. 29; December 6, 1894, p. 1.

185. *Fourth Annual Convention of the American Newspaper Publishers Association,* p. 31.

186. *Advertising Experience* (May 1900), p. 4.

187. *Chicago Herald,* November 2, 1894, p. 8; also see the *Herald,* November 6, 1894, p. 6; November 18, 1894, p. 29; December 6, 1894, p. 1.

188. *Newspaper Maker* (December 10, 1896), p. 4.

189. *Proceedings of the Third Annual Convention of the National Association, Managers of Newspaper Circulation* (Buffalo, 1901), p. 51.

190. Ibid.

191. *Proceedings of the Ninth Annual Meeting of the Associated Ohio Dailies,* p. 42.

192. Bunnell, *New York Press Association,* pp. 24, 46–47, 57; *Proceedings of the Missouri Press Association, Thirteenth Annual Meeting, 1896* (Linneus, Mo.: Bulletin Printing House, 1896); *Proceedings of the Tenth Annual Meeting of the Associated Ohio Dailies,* pp. 44–47.

193. *Seventh Annual Convention of the American Newspaper Publishers Association,* 1893, p. 54; *Report of the Proceedings of the Ninth Annual Convention of the American Newspaper Publishers Association,* 1895, pp. 1–3; *Report of the Proceedings of the Thirteenth Annual Convention of the American Newspaper Publishers Association,* 1899, p. 8; *Report of the Proceedings of the Fourteenth Annual Meeting of the American Newspaper Publishers Association* (New York: ANPA Office, 1900), p. 14.

194. Bunnell, *New York Press Association,* p. 102.

195. *Proceedings of the Eighth Annual Meeting of the Associated Ohio Dailies,* p. 18.

196. Salem, Oregon, *Independent,* May 5, 1893, p. 2.

197. Ibid.

198. *Proceedings of the Ninth Annual Meeting of the Associated Ohio Dailies,* pp. 5–8, 22–29.

199. *Newspaperdom* (February 1893), p. 5; *New York Press Association, Thirty-sixth Annual Convention,* 1892, pp. 21–25; *Proceedings of the Illinois Press Association at the Twenty-fifth Annual Session,* 1890, p. 15; *St. Paul Globe,* July 23, July 30, 1885; Kenneth Q. Jennings, "Political and Social Force of the New Jersey Press Association, 1857–1939" (M.A. thesis, Columbia University, 1940), pp. 57–61; *Proceedings of the Wisconsin Press Association, 1st, 2nd, and 3rd Sessions* (Madison: Carpenter and Hyer, 1859), pp. 93, 107–98; *A Record of the Organization and Transactions of the Wisconsin Press Association* (Whitewater, Wis.: E. D. Coe, 1890), p. 1.; *The Nebraska Editor* (November 1898), unpaginated; "The N.E.N. Press Association," *The Nebraska Editor* (March 1896), p. 1; *Proceedings of the California Press Association at Its Ninth Annual Meeting, 1897* (Vallejo: Chronicle Plant, 1897), p. 13; *St. Paul Globe,* July 30, 1885, p. 2; "Publication of State Laws" (on Missouri),

The Nebraska Editor (December 1896), unpaginated; Proceedings of the Arkansas Press Association from Its Organization in October, 1873, to and Including the Fourth Annual Meeting, 1876 (Little Rock: Wm. E. Woodruff, Jr., 1876), p. 39; Proceedings of the Ninth Annual Meeting of the Associated Ohio Dailies, pp. 5–8, 22–29, 31.

200. Proceedings of the Eighth Annual Meeting of the Associated Ohio Dailies, p. 33.

201. Ibid., p. 34.

202. St. Paul Globe, July 30, 1885, p. 2.

203. See Paul Starr, The Social Transformation of American Medicine: The Rise of a Sovereign Profession and the Making of a Vast Industry (New York: Basic Books, Inc., 1982), pp. 97–112.

204. Advertising Experience (May 1899), p. 16. Also see the Newspaper Maker (April 11, 1894), p. 3.

205. Proceedings of the Eighth Annual Meeting of the Associated Ohio Dailies, p. 39.

206. Newspaper Maker (March 16, 1899), p. 4.

207. Report of Proceedings of the Thirteenth Annual Convention of the American Newspaper Publishers Association, 1899 (New York: ANPA Office, 1899), pp. 28, 29.

208. Ibid.

209. Ibid., p. 31.

210. Proceedings of the Eighth Annual Meeting of the Associated Ohio Dailies, p. 29; Newspaper Maker (December 9, 1897), p. 4.

211. Proceedings of the Tenth Annual Meeting of the Associated Ohio Dailies, p. 63.

212. J. H. Zeilin Contract, John Hopley Papers, Box 3, Ohio State Historical Society.

213. Newspaper Maker (December 9, 1897), p. 4; (April 8, 1897), p. 1; (February 17, 1898), p. 1.

214. Journalist (April 9, 1892), p. 8.

215. Proceedings of the California Press Association at Its Fourth Annual Meeting, 1892, p. 17.

216. Newspaperdom (July 1892), p. 3.

217. Proceedings of the Eighth Annual Meeting, Associated Ohio Dailies, pp. 43–44.

218. Chapin, "The Newspaper," p. 10; emphasis added.

Chapter 5: Shaping and Packaging the News

1. Newspaper Maker (May 14, 1896), p. 4.

2. Fame (July 1898), p. 291.

3. Ibid., July 1892, p. 147.

4. Newspaper Maker (November 21, 1895), p. 1; also see October 24, 1895, p. 5; December 5, 1895, p. 1.

5. John A. Thayer, *Astir: A Publisher's Life Story* (Boston: Small, Maynard and Co., 1910), pp. 166–67.

6. *Fame* (July 1898), p. 291.

7. *Newspaper Maker* (May 16, 1895), p. 7.

8. Lyman D. Morse, *Advertiser's Handy Guide for 1896* (New York: Lyman D. Morse, 1896), pp. 706–7.

9. James H. Bates and Lyman D. Morse, *Advertiser's Handy Guide for 1893* (New York: Bates and Morse, 1893), p. 637.

10. Ibid., p. 636. Readership "quality" was a highly variable thing. The publisher of the *Wadesboro Intelligencer* (North Carolina) promoted his paper as "a favorite among all classes of readers (*except negroes and Republicans*) [*sic,* except emphasis added] that will be found a valuable advertising medium." Rev. Levi Branson, ed., *Branson's North Carolina Business Directory for 1884,* 6th ed. (Raleigh, N.C.: n.p., 1884).

11. Addison Archer, *American Journalism from the Practical Side* (New York: Holmes Publishing Co., 1897), p. 3.

12. Flyer, John Hopley Papers, Box 4, Ohio State Historical Society.

13. Bates and Morse, *Advertiser's Handy Guide for 1893,* pp. 719, 762; *Advertiser's Handy Guide for 1895,* carried ads for the *St. Joseph News* (Missouri), *Duluth News Tribune,* Albany *Times Union,* Jersey City *Evening Journal,* Buffalo *Courier,* Nebraska City *Nebraska Press, Tampa Tribune,* Kennebunkport *Open Sea, Bangor Commercial,* (Maine), *Lewiston Journal,* (Maine) *Springfield Republican* (Massachusetts); *New Bedford Evening Journal* (Massachusetts); *Pekin Times* (Illinois).

14. Morse, *Advertiser's Handy Guide for 1895,* p. 674.

15. Ibid.

16. Lyman D. Morse, *Advertiser's Handy Guide for 1899–1900* (New York: Lyman D. Morse, 1899), p. 13.

17. *Advertising Experience* (May 1899), p. xxx.

18. Ibid., November 1899, p. ix.

19. Morse, *Advertiser's Handy Guide for 1899–1900,* p. 681.

20. Ibid., p. 763.

21. Bates and Morse, *Advertiser's Handy Guide for 1893,* p. 633.

22 Ibid.

23 Ibid., p. 637.

24. Ibid., p. 634.

25. Morse, *Advertiser's Handy Guide for 1895,* p. 659, emphasis added.

26. The content analysis for this project demonstrates the small amount of material concerning women in the antebellum newspaper. The category of society and women's news averaged 2 percent of content in metropolitan newspapers; outside metropolitan areas, it averaged 1 percent of content.

27. *Proceedings of the Associated Ohio Dailies,* volumes 1–7, 1885–91 (Youngstown, Ohio: Telegram Printing Co., 1892), p. 67.

Percentage Distribution of Newspaper Content Devoted to Society and Women's News among Selected Antebellum Newspapers, 1830–32

	% of Content	N of Column Inches
NEWSPAPERS IN METROPOLITAN AREAS		
Charleston Mercury, 1832	2.5	952.75
Charleston Courier, 1831	0.2	613.25
Boston Daily Advertiser		
1830	0.4	1,032.00
1831	1.0	659.25
Boston Morning Post, 1832	5.7	428.25
New York *Courier and*		
Enquirer, 1831	1.0	838.00
NEWSPAPERS OUTSIDE METROPOLITAN AREAS		
Sandusky *Clarion,* 1832	0.0	1,716.75
Greenville Mountaineer, 1832	1.4	1,101.50
Albany Argus, 1832	0.4	1,139.50
Rutherfordton *North Carolina Spectator,* 1832	1.7	1,538.00
Haverhill, Massachusetts,		
—*Essex Gazette,* 1832	1.3	1,285.25

28. *Newspaperdom* (March 1892), p. 23.

29. *Cincinnati Tribune,* April 28, 1894, p. 4.

30. *Dry Goods Economist* (January 30, 1897), p. 65. Also see the *Newspaper Maker* (May 16, 1895), p. 7; (June 27, 1895), p. 4; (April 9, 1896), p. 7; (November 5, 1896), p. 3; (November 19, 1896), p. 3; *Printers' Ink* (May 7, 1890), p. 746.

31. Morse, *Advertiser's Handy Guide for 1896,* p. 764.

32. Nathaniel C. Fowler, Jr., "Reaching the Men through the Women," *Printers' Ink* (July 22, 1891), p. 51.

33. Morse, *Advertiser's Handy Guide for 1895,* pp. 671, 701; Morse, *Advertiser's Handy Guide for 1896,* p. 700; *Cincinnati Tribune,* December 1, 1893.

34. *Newspaper Maker* (November 19, 1896), p. 3.

35. *Report of the Proceedings of the Twelfth Annual Convention of the American Newspaper Publishers Association,* 1898 (New York: ANPA Office, 1898), p. 19. Also see the *Newspaper Maker* (October 24, 1895), p. 4.

36. *Profitable Advertiser* (June 15, 1893), p. 12.

37. *St. Louis Republic,* May 5, 1899, p. 4.

38. *Newspaper Maker* (January 20, 1898), p. 4.

39. Ibid., January 12, 1895, p. 9.

40. *St. Paul Globe,* August 10, 1894, p. 10.

41. *Chicago Herald,* May 6, 1894, p. 40.

42. Quoted in the *Newspaper Maker* (June 27, 1895), p. 5.

43. *Cincinnati Tribune*, May 29, 1893.

44. *Newspaper Maker* (August 8, 1895), p. 5.

45. *Chicago Herald*, May 6, 1894, p. 40.

46. New York *World*, February 15, 1885.

47. The article may have been a reading notice, although analysis of the *Globe* appears to show that the paper had already ended them.

48. *Boston Globe*, February 8, 1885, p. 3.

49. Ibid., April 19, 1885, p. 2.

50. *St. Louis Republic*, December 20, 1888, p. 3.

51. *Chicago Herald*, December 17, 1893, p. 14. For other shopping stories see: *Cincinnati Tribune*, September 16, 1893; *Chicago Herald*, November 12, 1882 ("Take the Hint Girls: Presents That the Men Will Like").

52. *Newspaper Maker* (July 22, 1898), p. 4; (April 30, 1896), p. 3; (September 3, 1896), p. 3; (October 24, 1895), p. 4.

53. Ibid., October 24, 1895, p. 4.

54. *Report of Proceedings of the Eleventh Annual Convention of the American Newspaper Publishers Association*, 1897 (New York: ANPA Office), pp. 31–32.

55. *Newspaper Maker* (December 17, 1896), p. 4, (November 11, 1897), p. 4; (January 6, 1898), p. 4, (December 21, 1899), p. 4; *Journalist* (January 3, 1891), p. 13.

56. *Newspaperdom* (June 1892), p. 9.

57. Quoted in the *Newspaper Maker* (July 29, 1897), p. 4.

58. Quoted in the *Newspaper Maker* (June 24, 1897), p. 8.

59. *Newspaper Maker* (March 19, 1896), p. 2.

60. *Newspaperdom* (July 1892), p. 3.

61. *Pittsburgh Leader*, April 3, 1898. For similar content, see the *Pittsburgh Leader*, April 2, 1898; *St. Paul Globe*, October 23, 1895, p. 4 (for index to the Sunday *Globe*).

62. See *Proceedings of the Wisconsin Press Association* (Edgerton, Wis.: F. W. Coon, 1890), pp. 32–33, for a discussion of the Chicago Sunday newspapers.

63. *Pittsburgh Leader*, January 21, 1898, p. 8.

64. Medians are reported here because they appear to be the best available measure of central tendency. Because medians are used, however, percentages in each category do not total 100 percent.

65. Again, medians are reported because they appear to be the best measure of central tendency here. Not all categories of newspaper content are reported here, so the columns do not total 100 percent.

66. Even small-town weeklies touted baseball and promoted their home team's fortunes. *Woodburn Independent* (Oregon), October 7, 1897, p. 2. The *Oakland Observer* (Oregon) helped organize that town's baseball team. *Oakland Observer*, April 10, 1891, p. 5.

67. Metropolitan newspapers provided the greatest amount of such content, but smaller newspapers also covered society, theater, and leisure activities. See McMinnville, Oregon, *Daily Campaign*, April 5, 1886, p. 3; Pendleton, Oregon, *East Oregonian*, April 9, 1901, p. 3; April 10, 1901, p. 3; *Wasco News* (Oregon), October 20, 1898, p. 4.

68. *Newspaper Maker* (November 16, 1896), p. 3; also see: May 28, 1896, p. 2; December 31, 1896, p. 7.

69. E. H. Dunbar to R. Bonner, March 6, 1876, Robert Bonner Papers, New York Public Library.

70. Morse, *Advertiser's Handy Guide for 1895*, p. 726.

71. For sports coverage, see the *Cincinnati Tribune*, January 8, 1893, April 19, June 9, 1894; *Chicago Herald*, May 10, December 25, 1881, June 7, November 12, 1882; *St. Paul Globe*, July 17, 1885; *St. Louis Republic*, December 29, 1888; *Boston Globe*, May 22, 1885; New York *World*, January 8, 9, 13, 15, 1883.

72. Weeklies that carried short stories or serialized fiction include the *Oakland Owl* (Oregon), November 14, 1902, p. 3; December 5, 1902, p. 3; December 12, 1902, p. 3; the *McMinnville Telephone Register* (Oregon), April 12, 1894, p. 4; April 19, 1894, p. 4; April 26, 1894, p. 4; *Woodburn Independent* (Oregon), August 17, 24, 31, September 7, 14, 21, 28, October 5, 12, 19, 26, November 2, 9, 16, 23, 30, 1894, January 11, 18, 25, February 1, 8, 15, 22, March 1, 8, 15, 22, 29, April 5, 12, 19, 26, May 3, 10, 17, 24, 31, June 7, 14, 21, 28, 1895; *Wasco News* (Oregon), September 22, 1898, p. 4; October 6, 1898, p. 4; October 13, 1897, p. 4. Also see C. W. Smith, "Country Dailies," *Newspaperdom* (September 1892), p. 8. Metropolitan newspapers printing fiction include the *Cincinnati Tribune*, July 19, 21, 24, 26, 28, 1893; *St. Paul Globe*, March 8, 15, 1885; *St. Louis Republic*, May 12, 19, 26, June 9, 16, 23, 30, July 14, 1889.

73. *Cincinnati Tribune*, March 9, 1893, p. 8.

74. *Pittsburgh Leader*, December 15, 1899, p. 6.

75. *Boston Globe*, March 22, 1885, p. 7.

76. For articles on society, see the New York *World*, January 25, 1885, p. 20; for articles on society, fashion and cooking, see: the *Cincinnati Tribune*, July 19, 21, 24, 26, 28, September 16, October 19, 23, December 3, 1893, April 22, 29, May 6, 13, 20, 1894; *Boston Globe*, April 5, May 10, 1885; *St. Paul Globe*, May 10, 1885; *Chicago Herald*, June 22, December 25, 1881. The *Pittsburgh Leader* featured a recipe for "Kensington rolls" on April 23, 1898, p. 4.

77. *Newspaper Maker* (July 30, 1896), p. 4.

78. *Newspaperdom* (June 1892), p. 2.

79. *Newspaper Maker* (October 10, 1895), p. 4.

80. *St. Paul Globe*, September 27, 1885.

81. *Newspaper Maker* (January 5, 1898), p. 7.

82. See Myra B. Lord, *History of the New England Woman's Press Association, 1885–1931* (Newton, Mass.: Graphic Press, 1932); *The Newspaper Maker* (July 22, 1897), pp. 2, 3; (June 24, 1897), p. 4; A. O. Bunnell, comp., *New York Press Association, Authorized History for Fifty Years, 1853–1903* (Dansville, N.Y.: F. A. Owen Publishing Co., 1903), pp. 87–88.

83. *Newspaper Maker* (June 24, 1897), p. 4; emphasis added.

84. Ibid., January 27, 1898, p. 5.

85. Quoted, ibid., May 20, 1897, p. 4.

86. *Newspaper Maker* (March 4, 1897), p. 3; (April 22, 1897), p. 1; (May 2, 1895), p. 1; (August 6, 1896), p. 1; (July 25, 1897), p. 3; (October 22, 1896), p. 5; (July 1, 1897), p. 8; (April 4, 1895), p. 3; (November 4, 1895), p. 7; *Pittsburgh Leader,* May 18, 1898, p. 5; November 1, 1899, p. 4; *Chicago Herald,* July 28, 1881. C. A. Moore to St. Clair McKelway, May 7, June 12, 1896, St. Clair McKelway Papers, New York Public Library. *St. Paul Globe,* July 24, December 28, 1884, August 1, 1885, S. A. Armstrong to F. H. Carruth, September 25, 1884; J. T. Blakemore to F. H. Carruth, September 23, 1884; George W. Pierce to F. H. Carruth, September 27, 1884; Phil Skillman to F. H. Carruth, June 29, 1886; all in the Hayden Carruth Papers, New York Public Library.

87. Quoting Edward Elwell (editor of the Portland *Transcript), Twenty-second Annual Report of the Proceedings of the Maine Press Association, 1885* (Bar Harbor: Mount Desert Publishing Co., 1885), p. 28.

88. Quoted in the *Newspaper Maker* (April 4, 1898), p. 5.

89. Michael E. McGerr, *The Decline of Popular Politics: The American North, 1865–1928* (New York: Oxford University Press, 1986), p. 14. Also see Carolyn Stewart Dyer, "Political Patronage of the Wisconsin Press, 1849–1861: New Perspectives on the Economics of Patronage," *Journalism Monographs* (March 1988).

90. The cities were: New Haven, Atlanta, Indianapolis, Des Moines, Cleveland, Denver, San Francisco, Los Angeles, New York, Chicago, Boston, Albany, Detroit, Baltimore, Milwaukee, Minneapolis, Philadelphia, Pittsburgh, Providence, Richmond, Memphis, Nashville, Dallas, Charleston, and St. Louis.

91. Total N = 118 newspapers in 1877.

92. Total N = 126 newspapers in 1899.

93. *Woodburn Independent* (Oregon), December 1, 1888, p. 3.

94. Salem, Oregon, *Independent,* March 18, 1893, p. 3.

95. *St. Louis Republic,* May 31, 1888; emphasis added.

96. B. J. McKinney, "The Newspaper in Its Relation to a Political Party," *Ohio Editorial Association Minutes of Annual Meeting, Columbus, February 20, 1901* (n.p., n.d.), p. 57. Also see Rolf H. Swensen, " 'An Age of Reform and Improvement': The Life of Col. E. Hofer, 1855–1934" (Ph.D. diss., University of Oregon, 1975). Hofer said the Salem *Capital Journal* was an independent Republican newspaper, and added that he was "not prepared to follow the cranky notions, unsound principles and impractical ideas at times advocated by mistaken leaders" even if they were Republicans. *Capital Journal,* January 2, 1891, p. 1.

97. Drain, Oregon, *Echo,* December 17, 1885, p. 2.

98. Speech on the *Hartford Courant* (Connecticut), October 12, 1904; "The Right of Privacy, 1895"; and "In Praise of the Ledger, 1893"; all in the St. Clair McKelway Papers, New York Public Library.

99. Quoted in *Newspaperdom* (December 1892), p. 35.

100. *Cincinnati Tribune,* May 17, 1895, p. 4.

101. *Newspaperdom* (December 1892), p. 1.

102. Ibid., January 1893, p. 24.

103. J. G. Hodgkinson, "What Is an Independent Journal?" *Newspaperdom* (February 1893), pp. 9–10; also see the *Newspaper Maker* (July 29, 1897), p. 4 (quoting *Printers' Ink*), and *Newspaper Maker* (September 3, 1896), p. 4.

104. *Advertising Experience* (December 1896), p. 24.

105. *Newspaper Maker* (July 27, 1899), p. 4; also see October 14, 1897, p. 6.

106. *Chicago Record,* March 28, 1893, p. 6.

107. This analysis is drawn from Pettingill's *National Newspaper Directory and Gazette* for 1899. In New York, 813 newspapers were analyzed; in California, 392. These two states were chosen because their leading cities (New York City, San Francisco) had newspapers that epitomized the new journalism (viz., Pulitzer's New York *World,* Hearst's *New York Journal,* and the *San Francisco Examiner*), and because both had a large rural population, thus providing a view of nonurban America. California was also a relatively new state. In 1860, its population was 380,000, compared with 3.8 million in New York. In 1900, California's population was 1.5 million, compared with 7.3 million in New York. *Abstract of the Twelfth Census, 1900,* 3d ed. (Washington, D.C.: Government Printing Office, 1904), pp. 32, 225, 334–37; Warren A. Beck and David A. Williams, *California: A History of the Golden State* (Garden City, N.Y.: Doubleday and Co., 1972); John W. Caughey and Norris Hundley, Jr., *California: History of a Remarkable State,* 4th ed. (Englewood Cliffs: Prentice Hall, Inc..).

Pettingill was the leading U.S. advertising agency in the 1850s and 1860s, with offices in New York and Boston. Its directory remained important in the advertising industry even after the emergence of major competitors. Frank Presbrey, *The History and Development of Advertising* (Garden City, N.Y.: Doubleday, Doran and Co., 1929); pp. 263, 348.

108. Percentage and Numerical Distributions of Towns with Independent Newspapers, by Number of Papers per Town, in New York State and California, 1899

	NEW YORK STATE						
	Number of Newspapers per Town						
	1	2	3	4	5	≥6	Total
% of towns	64.5	12.0	18.0	20.0	33.0	45.0	
N of towns	274	99	43	11	6	10	443
N of newspapers	274	198	129	44	30	138	813

	CALIFORNIA					
	Number of Newspapers per Town					
	1	2	3	4	5–16	17
% of towns	65.9	35.2	13.1	30.0	40.0	60.2
N of towns	122	54	29	5	5	1	216
N of newspapers	122	108	87	20	38	17	392

109. *Newspaper Maker* (August 4, 1895), p. 5; also see August 4, 1898, p. 5.

110. Augustus J. Munson, *Making a Country Newspaper* (Chicago: Dominion Co., 1891), pp. 26–27.

111. The membership of the New York State Republican Editorial Association in 1895 came almost entirely from large towns and small cities. *Republican Editorial Association of the State of New York* (Dansville, N.Y.: A. O. Bunnell, 1895), pp. 59–60.

112. *Printers' Ink* (February 27, 1895), p. 14; Kenneth Q. Jennings, "Political and Social Force of the New Jersey Press Association, 1857–1939" (M.A. thesis, Columbia University, 1940), pp. 12, 35; *Fame* (February 1898), p. 69.

113. Salem, Oregon, *Independent,* May 5, 1893, p. 2.

114. Charles Austin Bates, *Criticisms* (New York: n.p., 1897), pp. 105, 107–8.

115. Percentage Distribution of Partisan and Independent Newspapers in 25 Major American Cities, by Circulation, 1899

	Circulation		
	0–11,000	12,000–129,000	≥129,001
Partisan	65	50.6	21.4
Independent	35	49.4	78.6
N of newspapers	49	62	14

Source: *National Newspaper Directory and Gazette* (Boston and New York: Pettingill and Co., 1899).

116. Percentage Distribution of Partisan and Independent Newspapers in 25 Major Cities, by Time of Publication, 1899

	Morning	Evening	Both Morning and Evening
Partisan	63.2	41.7	50
Independent	36.7	58.3	50
N of newspapers	49	72	4

Source: *National Newspaper Directory and Gazette.*

117. *Advertising World* (June 14, 1897), p. 1.

118. *Dry Goods Economist* (February 22, 1893), p. 16. Also see *Kings' Jester* (April 1892), p. 59.

119. *Dry Goods Economist* (December 12, 1896), p. 15.

120. *Newspaper Maker* (June 4, 1896), p. 4; also see November 14, 1895, p. 3.

121. *Newspaperdom* (August 1892), p. 13.

122. *Newspaper Maker* (April 4, 1895), p. 4; (April 18, 1895), p. 4; (May 9, 1895), p. 4; (August 23, 1897), p. 4; (February 10, 1898), p. 4.

123. *Cincinnati Tribune,* June 20, 1893, p. 6.

124. Ibid., May 16, 1893, p. 5.

125. *Newspaper Maker* (March 11, 1897), p. 2.

126. Ibid., April 4, 1895, p. 3. The trade journal reported, "The plan is a good one, as it excites interest in the home circle."

127. *Fame* (July 1892), p. 147.

128. Ibid., p. 14.

129. *Newspaper Maker* (July 22, 1897), p. 4.

130. Ibid., May 22, 1897, p. 1.

131. Ibid., December 2, 1897, p. 1.

132. Ibid.

133. *Fame* (April 1898), p. 323.

134. Drain, Oregon, *Echo,* December 17, 1885, p. 2.

135. *Wasco News* (Oregon), November 25, 1897, p. 4.

136. *Fame* (April 1898), p. 334.

137. *Newspaperdom* (April 1892), p. 41.

138. Salem, Oregon, *Capital Journal,* May 1, 1893, p. 2; May 18, 1894, p. 2; May 24, 1894, p. 1; May 21, 1895, p. 2.

139. *Pittsburgh Leader,* June 20, 22, 23, 27, 30, 1899.

140. *Printers' Ink* (October 22, 1890), p. 405.

141. Quoted in the *Newspaper Maker* (April 2, 1896), p. 8.

142. Quoted, ibid., April 23, 1896, p. 7.

143. Quoted, ibid., July 3, 1901, p. 4.

144. *Printers' Ink* (December 29, 1892), p. 869.

Selected Bibliography

Manuscript Collections

Adams Family. Papers. Massachusetts Historical Society, Boston.
Appleton, Nathan. Papers. Massachusetts Historical Society, Boston.
Bailey, John. Papers. New York Public Library, New York City.
Barbour, James. Papers. New York Public Library, New York City.
Bennett, James Gordon. Diary. New York Public Library, New York City.
Berrien, John M. Papers. Georgia Historical Society, Savannah.
Berrien, John M. Papers. Southern Historical Collection, University of North Carolina, Chapel Hill.
Biddle, Nicholas. Papers. Library of Congress, Washington, D.C.
Blair-Rives. Papers. Library of Congress, Washington, D.C.
Bonner, Robert. Papers. New York Public Library, New York City.
Briggs, Willis G. Papers. Southern Historical Society, University of North Carolina, Chapel Hill.
Browne, J. J. Papers. Eastern Washington Historical Society, Spokane.
Bryan, George. Papers. Historical Society of Pennsylvania, Philadelphia.
Butler, Benjamin F. Papers. New York State Library, Albany.
Butler, Charles. Papers. Library of Congress, Washington, D.C.
Calhoun, John C. Papers. Library of Congress, Washington, D.C.
Carruth, Hayden. Papers. New York Public Library, New York City.
Chestnut-Miller-Manning. Papers. Southern Historical Collection, University of North Carolina, Chapel Hill.
Croswell, Edwin. Papers. New York State Library, Albany.
Cushing, Caleb. Papers. Library of Congress, Washington, D.C.
Dallas, George M. Papers. Historical Society of Pennsylvania, Philadelphia.
Daniels, C. F. Papers. South Caroliana Library, Columbia.
Dix, John. Papers. Columbia University, New York City.
Duncan, James H. Papers. Essex Institute, Salem, Massachusetts.
Dunlap, Andrew. Papers. Essex Institute, Salem, Massachusetts.
East Oregonian Record Books. Oregon Historical Society, Portland.
Everett, Edward. Letters. Volume 11, Hale Family Papers. Library of Congress, Washington, D.C.
Everett, Edward. Papers. Massachusetts Historical Society, Boston.
Flagg, Azariah C. Papers. New York Public Library, New York City.
Fort, Tomlinson. Papers. Emory University, Atlanta.
Fox, John. Papers. Southern Historical Collection, University of North Carolina, Chapel Hill.

Galloway-Maxcy-Markoe. Papers. Library of Congress, Washington, D.C.
Gardner, Charles K. Papers. New York State Library, Albany.
Gouverneur, Samuel. Papers. New York Public Library, New York City.
Gratz Collection. Historical Society of Pennsylvania, Philadelphia.
Green, Duff. Papers. Southern Historical Collection, University of North Carolina, Chapel Hill.
Hale Family. Papers. Library of Congress, Washington, D.C.
Hamilton, James. Papers. South Caroliniana Library, Columbia.
Hammond, James Henry. Papers. Volume 2 (1830–33). Library of Congress, Washington, D.C.
Hammond, James Henry. Papers. South Caroliniana Library, Columbia.
Hoard, Halbert L. Papers. State Historical Society of Wisconsin, Madison.
Holley, Orville and Myron. Papers. New York State Library, Albany.
Hopley, John. Papers. Ohio Historical Society, Columbus.
Jackson, C. S. Papers. Oregon Historical Society, Portland.
Kinder, George D. Papers. Ohio Historical Society, Columbus.
Knight, W. D. Papers. Eastern Washington Historical Society, Spokane.
Lawrence, Abbott. Papers. The Houghton Library, Harvard University, Cambridge, Massachusetts.
Lumpkin, Wilson. Papers. University of Georgia, Athens.
Macpherson, William. Papers. Historical Society of Pennsylvania, Philadelphia.
McKelway, St. Clair. Papers. New York Public Library, New York City.
Merrick, Pliny. Correspondence. American Antiquarian Society, Worcester, Massachusetts.
Miller, Stephen D. Papers. Duke University, Durham.
New York State Comptroller's Office Day Books. New York State Library, Albany.
Olcott, Thomas W. Papers. Columbia University, New York City.
Osborne, Henry Z. Papers. Bancroft Library, University of California, Berkeley.
Overton, John B. Papers. Tennessee State Archives, Nashville.
Palfray, Warwick, Jr. Papers. Essex Institute, Salem, Massachusetts.
Petigru, J. L. Papers. South Carolina Historical Society, Charleston.
Pickens, Francis W. Papers. Duke University, Durham.
Poinsett, Joel R. Papers. Henry Gilpin Collection, Historical Society of Pennsylvania, Philadelphia.
Poinsett, Joel R. Papers. South Caroliniana Library, Columbia.
Polhill, Emily N. Papers. Southern Historical Collection, University of North Carolina, Chapel Hill.
Seward, William Henry. Papers. Rush Rhees Library, University of Rochester, Rochester, New York.
Smith, William Henry. Papers. Ohio Historical Society, Columbus.
Springer, John. Papers. University of Iowa, Iowa City.
Starr, Edwin. Papers. South Caroliniana Library, Columbia.

Stone, Melville. Papers. Newberry Library, Chicago.

Swain, David L. Papers. Southern Historical Collection, University of North Carolina, Chapel Hill.

Taylor, Benjamin F. Papers. South Caroliniana Library, Columbia.

Taylor, John W. Papers. New York Public Library, New York City.

Tompkins, Daniel A. Papers. Southern Historical Collection, University of North Carolina, Chapel Hill.

Townes Family. Papers. South Caroliniana Library, Columbia.

Tracy, Albert H. Papers. New York State Library, Albany.

Van Buren, Martin. Papers. Library of Congress, Washington, D.C.

"We the People and Old Colony Press Business Records," American Antiquarian Society, Worcester, Massachusetts.

Webster, Daniel. Papers. Library of Congress, Washington, D.C.

Weed, Thurlow. Papers. Rush Rhees Library, University of Rochester, Rochester, New York.

Woodbury, Levi. Papers. Library of Congress, Washington, D.C.

Wright, Silas. Papers. New York Public Library, New York City.

Wright, Silas. Papers. New York State Library, Albany.

Trade Journals and Newspaper Directories

Ad Sense

Advertisers' Gazette

Advertiser's Handy Guide for 1893. By James H. Bates and Lyman D. Morse. New York: Bates and Morse, 1893.

Advertiser's Handy Guide for 1895. By Lyman D. Morse. New York: Lyman D. Morse, 1895.

Advertiser's Handy Guide for 1896. By Lyman D. Morse. New York: Lyman D. Morse, 1896.

Advertiser's Handy Guide, 1899–1900. By Lyman D. Morse. New York: Lyman D. Morse, 1899.

Advertising (Chicago)

Advertising Experience

Advertising World (Columbus, Ohio)

The Advisor

American Advertiser Reporter

American Journalist

Branson's North Carolina Business Directory for 1884. 6th edition. Raleigh, N.C., 1884.

Charles Austin Bates Criticisms(*Current Advertiser* after May 1900)

Chicago Dry Goods Reporter

Dry Goods Economist

Fame

Fourth Estate

Inland Printer
The Journalist
The Kings' Jester: A Journal for Advertisers and Advertising Men
The Manufacturer
National Newspaper Directory and Gazette. Boston and New York: Pettingill and
    Co., 1899.
The Nebraska Editor
Newspaperdom
The Newspaper Maker
The Ohio Newspaper
Pacific Printer
Pettingill's Newspaper Directory. Boston: S. M. Pettingill, 1877.
Printers' Ink
Profitable Advertiser
White's Sayings

Newspapers

Antebellum Period

Albany Argus (New York)
Albany Evening Journal (New York)
Athens, Georgia, *Southern Banner*
Augusta Chronicle (Georgia)
Augusta Constitutionalist (Georgia)
Baltimore, Maryland, *Niles' Weekly Register*
Batavia, New York, *Republican Advocate*
Boston Daily Advertiser
Boston Daily Advocate
Boston *Columbian Centinel*
Boston Daily Courier
Boston *Independent Chronicle*
Boston Morning Post
Boston Statesman
Camden, South Carolina,*Camden and Lancaster Journal*
Canandaigua, New York, *Ontario Repository*
Charleston City Gazette
Charleston Courier
Charleston Mercury
Charleston *Southern Patriot*
Charleston *State Rights and Free Trade Evening Post*
Cincinnati *Advertiser*
Columbia Hive (South Carolina)
Columbia, South Carolina, *Southern Times*

Columbus, Georgia, *Democrat*
Columbus Enquirer (Georgia)
Cortland Advocate (New York)
Elizabeth City Star (North Carolina)
Fayetteville Observer (North Carolina)
Geneseo, New York, *Livingston Register*
Greensborough Patriot (North Carolina)
Greenville Mountaineer (North Carolina)
Harrisburg, Pennsylvania, *Republican and Anti-Masonic Inquirer*
Harrisburg Chronicle (Pennsylvania)
Harrisburg *Pennsylvania Reporter*
Haverhill, Massachusetts, *Essex Gazette*
Haverhill Iris (Massachusetts)
Lancaster Journal (Pennsylvania)
Lowell Mercury (Massachusetts)
Louisville Public Advertiser (Kentucky)
Lynn Mirror (Massachusetts)
Lynn Record (Massachusetts)
Lyons Countryman (New York)
Lyons Western Argus (New York)
Macon Advertiser (Georgia)
Macon, Georgia, *Messenger*
Macon Telegraph (Georgia)
Milledgeville, Georgia, *Federal Union*
Milledgeville *Georgia Journal*
Milledgeville, Georgia, *Southern Recorder*
New Bedford, Massachusetts, *Daily Mercury*
New Bern Spectator (North Carolina)
New York *Courier and Enquirer*
New York *Evening Post*
Newburyport Advertiser (Massachusetts)
Newburyport Herald (Massachusetts)
Penn Yan Enquirer (New York)
Penn Yan, New York, *Yates Republican*
Philadelphia *Democratic Press*
Philadelphia Mercury
Philadelphia *National Palladium*
Pittsfield Sun (Massachusetts)
Raleigh Register (North Carolina)
Richmond Daily Whig (Virginia)
Rutherfordton *North Carolina Spectator*
St. Lawrence, New York, *Northern Light*
Salem, Massachusetts, *Commercial Advertiser*
Salem Gazette (Massachusetts)
Savannah Republican (Georgia)

Schenectady Whig (New York)
Springfield, Massachusetts, *Hampden Intelligencer*
Springfield, Massachusetts, *Hampden Journal*
Springfield, Massachusetts, *Hampden Whig*
Springfield Republican (Massachusetts)
Sumter, South Carolina, *Southern Whig*
Tarborough, North Carolina, *Free Press*
Ulster Palladium (New York)
Utica, New York, *Elucidator*
Utica, New York, *Oneida Observer*
Washington, D.C., *Globe*
Washington, D.C., *Madisonian*
Washington, D.C., *National Intelligencer*
Washington, D.C., *U.S. Telegraph*
Worcester, Massachusetts, *National Aegis*
Worcester County Republican (Massachusetts)
Worcester Spy (Massachusetts)

Late Nineteenth Century

Albany Argus (New York)
Albany Daily Democrat (Oregon)
Boston Daily Advertiser
Boston Globe
Charleston *News and Courier*
Chicago Herald
Chicago Record
Chicago Tribune
Cincinnati Tribune
The Dallas Chronicle (Oregon)
Drain, Oregon, *Echo*
McMinnville Telephone Register (Oregon)
McMinnville, Oregon, *West Side Telephone*
Macon Telegraph (Georgia)
Mansfield News (Ohio)
Newberg Graphic (Oregon)
New York *Evening Post*
New York Journal
New York *World*
Oakland Observer (Oregon)
Pittsburgh Leader
Roseburg, Oregon, *Twice a Week Roseburg Review*
St. Louis Republican (*Republic* after May 31, 1888)
Salem, Oregon, *Capital Journal*

San Francisco Chronicle
Woodburn Independent (Oregon)

Trade Association Proceedings, Reports

National Associations

The First Decennium of the National Editorial Association of the United States, Volume 1, ed. B. B. Herbert.
Proceedings of the Annual Convention of the National Association of Managers of Newspaper Circulation. 1901–03. Various publishers.
Proceedings of the National Editorial Association of the United States. Little Rock: 1886.
Report of the Proceedings of the Annual Convention of the American Newspaper Publishers Association. 1888–1901. New York: ANPA Office.

State and Local Associations

Arkansas
Proceedings of the Arkansas Press Association, from Its Organization in October, 1873, to and Including the Fourth Annual Meeting, 1876. Little Rock: Wm. E. Woodruff, Jr., 1876.

California
Proceedings of the California Press Association at its Fourth Annual Meeting. Sacramento: Woodson Bros. Print, 1893.
Proceedings of the California Press Association at Its Ninth Annual Meeting, 1897. Vallejo: Chronicle Plant, 1897.

Illinois
Proceedings of the Third Special Session of the Illinois Press Association 1879. Mattoon, Ill.: Gazette Steam Print, 1879.
Proceedings of the Illinois Press Association at the Twenty-Fifth Annual Session, 1890. Morris, Ill.: Hayes and Fletcher, 1890.

Kansas
Proceedings of the Second Annual Meeting, Kansas Editorial Association, 1894. Sterling: Junkin and Steele, Printers, 1894.

Louisiana
Official Proceedings of the First Annual Session of the Louisiana Press Association, 1880. New Orleans: T. H. Thomason, 1880.

Maine

Transactions of the Maine Editors and Publishers' Association, from 1870 to 1874, Inclusive. Wiscasset, Maine: Joseph Wood, 1874.

Fifteenth Annual Report of the Proceedings of the Maine Press Association, 1878. Portland: Brown Thurston and Co., 1878.

Eighteenth Annual Report of the Proceedings of the Maine Press Association, 1881. Skowhegan, Maine: Joseph Wood, 1881.

Twenty-second Annual Report of the Proceedings of the Maine Press Association, 1885. Bar Harbor: Mount Desert Publishing Co., 1885.

Twenty-fourth Annual Report of the Proceedings of the Maine Press Association, 1887. Bar Harbor: Mount Desert Publishing Co., 1887.

Thirty-sixth Annual Report of the Proceedings of the Maine Press Association, 1899. Portland: Maine Coast Cottager Office, 1899.

Massachusetts

Transactions of the Massachusetts Press Association. Rockland: Rockland Standard Press, 1897.

Transactions of the Massachusetts Press Association. Rockland: Rockland Standard Press, 1898.

Minnesota

Proceedings of the Minnesota Editors and Publishers' Association, 1871–1874. St. Paul: Ramaley and Cunningham, 1874.

Mississippi

Proceedings of the Mississippi Press Association from Its Organization, May, 1866 to May, 1884. Jackson, Miss.: Clarion Steam Book and Job Printing Establishment, 1885.

Missouri

Proceedings of the Missouri Press Association, Thirteenth Annual Meeting, 1896. Linneus, Mo.: Bulletin Printing House, 1896.

Proceedings of the Seventh Winter Meeting of the Missouri Press Association, 1900. Trenton, Mo.: Tribune Press Print, 1900.

New Hampshire

Convention of the New Hampshire Publishers, Editors and Printers, 1868. Concord: McFarland and Jenks, 1868.

Proceedings of the New Hampshire Printers' Association. Manchester: Charles F. Livingston's Power Printing House, 1871.

Proceedings of the Editors, Publishers and Printers' Association of the State of New Hampshire. Manchester: C. F. Livingston's Printing House, 1872.

Proceedings of the New Hampshire Publishers, Editors and Printers' Association. Manchester: Charles F. Livingston, 1873.

Proceedings of the New Hampshire Press Association. Concord: Republican Press Association, 1890.

Proceedings of the New Hampshire Press Association. Concord: Republican Press Association, 1895.

Proceedings of the New Hampshire Press Association, 1896–1902. Manchester: John B. Clarke Co., 1902.

New Jersey

Minutes of the Thirty-sixth Annual Meeting of the Editorial Association of the State of New Jersey. Freehold, N.J.: Monmouth Democratic Print, 1892.

Minutes of the Fortieth Annual Meeting of the Editorial Association of the State of New Jersey. Freehold, N.J.: Monmouth Democratic Print, 1896.

New York

Brief History of the Editors' and Publishers' Association of the State of New York. Dansville, N.Y.: A. O. Bunnell, 1874.

Twenty-second Annual Convention of the New York Press Association. Dansville, N.Y.: A. O. Bunnell, 1878.

Twenty-third Annual Convention of the New York Press Association. Dansville, N.Y.: A. O. Bunnell, 1879.

Twenty-fifth Annual Convention of the New York Press Association, 1881. Dansville, N.Y.: A. O. Bunnell, 1881.

Thirty-sixth Annual Convention of the New York Press Association, 1892. Dansville, N.Y.: A. O. Bunnell, 1892.

Republican Editorial Association of the State of New York. Dansville, N.Y.: A. O. Bunnell, 1895.

Ohio

Transactions of the Ohio Editorial Association during the Years 1856 and 1857. Columbus: Ohio State Journal Co., 1857.

Ohio Editorial Association, Annual Meeting, Columbus, February 16, 1894. Toronto, Ohio: Press of the Tribune, 1894.

Ohio Editorial Association Minutes of Annual Meeting, Columbus, February 20, 1901. N.p.,n.d.

The Ohio Editorial Association, Constitution and By Laws Together with a Brief Sketch of Its Past History. Sandusky, Ohio: I. F. Mack and Brother, 1880.

Proceedings of the Associated Ohio Dailies. Volumes 1–7. Youngstown, Ohio: Telegram Printing, 1892.

Proceedings of the Eighth Annual Meeting of the Associated Ohio Dailies. Springfield, Ohio: Hosterman Publishing Co., 1893.

Proceedings of the Ninth Annual Meeting of the Associated Ohio Dailies. Springfield, Ohio: Hosterman Publishing Co., 1894.

Proceedings of the Tenth Annual Meeting of the Associated Ohio Dailies. Springfield, Ohio: Hosterman Publishing Co., 1895.

Proceedings of the Eleventh Annual Meeting of the Associated Ohio Dailies. Spring-field, Ohio: Hosterman Publishing Co., 1896.

Oregon
Annual Reports of the Oregon Press Association, 1899–1902. Rainier, Oregon: Gazette, 1903.

South Carolina
Seventh Annual Meeting of the South Carolina State Press Association, 1881. Green-ville, S.C.: Baptist Courier and Job Office, 1881.

Texas
Charter, Constitution and Bylaws of the Texas Editorial Association. Jefferson, Tex.: East Texas Job Printing Office, 1875.

Vermont
Convention of Vermont Publishers, Editors & Printers, 1867, 1868, 1869. Montpe-lier: J. and J. M. Poland, 1870.

Washington
Annual Proceedings of the Washington Press Association for the Years 1887–1890. Hoquiam, Wash.: Washingtonian Steam Book, News and Job Print, 1891.

Wisconsin
Proceedings of the Wisconsin Press Association, 1st, 2nd and 3rd Sessions. Madison: Carpenter and Hyer, 1859.
Proceedings of the Wisconsin Press Association, 18th Annual Session. Madison: Atwood and Culver, 1875.
Proceedings of the Wisconsin Press Association. Whitewater, Wis.: Whitewater Register Steam Print, 1878.
Proceedings of the Wisconsin Editorial Association. Whitewater, Wis.: Whitewater Register Steam Print, 1882.
Proceedings of the Twenty-third and Twenty-fourth Conventions of the Wisconsin Editors and Publishers Association. Whitewater, Wis.: Register Steam Print, 1883.
Proceedings of the Thirty-third Convention of the Wisconsin Press Association. Lake Geneva, Wis.: James E. Heg, 1887.
Proceedings of the Thirty-seventh Convention of the Wisconsin Press Association. Edgerton, Wis.: F. W. Coon, 1889.
Proceedings of the Thirty-ninth Convention of the Wisconsin Press Association. Edg-erton, Wis.: F. W. Coon, 1890.
A Record of the Organization and Transactions of the Wisconsin Press Association. Whitewater, Wis.: E. D. Coe, 1890.
Proceedings of the Wisconsin Press Association. Edgerton, Wis.: F. W. Coon, 1892.

Proceedings of the Wisconsin Press Association, Forty-seventh Annual Meeting. Jefferson, Wis.: Banner Printing Co., 1900.

Proceedings of the Thirty-seventh Convention of the Wisconsin Press Association. Edgerton, Wis.: F. W. Coon, 1889.

Proceedings of the Wisconsin Press Association. Jefferson, Wis.: Banner Printing Co., 1902.

Other Sources

The Advertising Reporter. Chicago: Publishers' Commercial Union, 1888.

Ambler, Charles H. *Thomas Ritchie: A Study in Virginia Politics.* Richmond: Bell Book Stationery Co., 1913.

Ambramoske, Donald J., "The Chicago Daily News: A Business History, 1875–1901." Ph.D. diss., University of Chicago, 1963.

American Journalism from the Practical Side: What Leading Newspaper Publishers Say Concerning the Relations of Advertisers and Publishers and about the Way a Great Paper Should Be Made. New York: Holmes Publishing Co., 1897.

Ames, William E. *A History of the National Intelligencer.* Chapel Hill: University of North Carolina Press, 1972.

Ames, William E. "A History of the Washington *Globe*." Unpublished manuscript, University of Washington.

Archer, Addison. *American Journalism: From the Practical Side.* New York: Holmes Publishing Co., 1897.

Baldasty, Gerald J. "The Charleston, South Carolina, Press and National News, 1808–1847." *Journalism Quarterly* (August , 1978), pp. 518–526.

Baldasty, Gerald J. "The New York State Political Press and Antimasonry." *New York History* 64, no. 3 (July 1983), pp. 261–279.

Baldasty, Gerald J. "The Political Press in the Second American Party System: The 1832 Election." Ph.D. diss., University of Washington, 1978.

Balmer, Edwin. *The Science of Advertising.* Chicago: Wallace Press, 1909.

Barth, Gunther. *City People: The Rise of Modern City Culture in Nineteenth-Century America.* New York: Oxford University Press, 1980.

Bartlett, Marguerite G. *The Chief Phases of Pennsylvania Politics in the Jacksonian Period.* Allentown, Pa.: H. Ray Haas and Co., 1919.

Benson, Lee. *The Concept of Jacksonian Democracy: New York as a Test Case.* Princeton, N.J.: Princeton University Press, 1961.

Billington, Ray. *Protestant Crusade.* Chicago: Quadrangle Books, 1964.

Bonadio, Felice A., ed. *Political Parties in American History (1828–1890).* Volume 2. New York: G. P. Putnam's Sons, 1974.

Boss, Henry R. *A Brief History of Advertising.* Chicago: Frederick Weston Printing Co., 1886.

Bradley, Joseph F. *The Role of Trade Associations and Professional Business Societies in America.* University Park: Pennsylvania State University Press, 1965.

Brown, Henry. *A Narrative of the Anti-Masonic Excitement in the Western Part of the State of New York during the Years 1826, 1827, 1828 and Part of 1829.* Batavia, N.Y.: Adams and McCleary, 1829.

Buckingham, Joseph T. *Personal Memoirs and Recollections of Editorial Life.* Reprint ed. New York: Arno Press, Inc.

Bunnell, A. O., comp. *New York Press Association, Authorized History for Fifty Years, 1853–1903.* Dansville, N.Y.: F. A. Owen Publishing Co., 1903.

Byxbee, O. F. *Establishing a Newspaper.* Chicago: Inland Printer Co., 1901.

Calkins, Ernest Elmo, and Ralph Holden. *Modern Advertising.* New York: D. Appleton, 1905.

Callow, Alexander B., Jr. *The Tweed Ring.* New York: Oxford University Press, 1966.

Camp, Eugene M. "Journalists: Born or Made?" Paper read before the Alumni Association of the Wharton School, University of Pennsylvania, Philadelphia, March 27, 1888.

Campbell-Copeland, T. *The Ladder of Journalism: How to Climb It.* New York: Allan Forman, 1889.

Capers, Henry D. *The Life and Times of C. G. Memminger.* Richmond, Va.: Everett Waddey Co., 1893.

Carson, James P. *Life, Letters and Speeches of James Louis Petigru: The Union Man of South Carolina.* Washington, D.C.: H. L. and J. B. McQueen, Inc., 1920.

Cass, Alvin. *Politics in New York State, 1800–1830.* Syracuse: Syracuse University Press, 1965.

Chambers, William, and Walter Burnham, eds. *The American Party Systems: Stages of Political Development.* New York: Oxford University Press, 1967.

Chambers, William H., and Philip C. Davis. "Party Competition and Mass Participation: The Case of the Democratizing Party System, 1824–1852." In *The History of American Electoral Behavior,* ed. Joel H. Silbey, Allan G. Bogne, and William H. Flanigan, pp. 174–197. Princeton: Princeton University Press, 1978.

Chandler, Alfred D., Jr. *The Visible Hand: The Managerial Revolution in American Business.* Cambridge: The Belknap Press of Harvard University Press, 1977.

Chase, James. *Emergence of the Presidential Nominating Convention, 1789–1832.* Urbana: University of Illinois Press, 1973.

Cochran, Thomas C. *The Pabst Brewing Company: The History of An American Business.* New York: New York University Press, 1948.

Cochran, Thomas C., and Thomas B. Brewer, eds. *Views of American Economic Growth: The Industrial Era.* Volume 2. New York: McGraw-Hill Book Co., 1966.

Cochran, Thomas C., and William Miller. *The Age of Enterprise.* New York: Macmillan Co., 1942.

Cook, Ann, Marilyn Gittell, and Herb Mack, eds. *City Life, 1865–1900: Views on Urban America.* New York: Praeger Publishers, 1973.

Counihan, Harold J. "North Carolina, 1815–1836: State and Local Perspectives on the Age of Jackson." Ph.D. diss., University of North Carolina, 1971.

Crouthamel, James L. *Bennett's New York Herald and the Rise of the Popular Press.* Syracuse: Syracuse University Press, 1989.

Crouthamel, James L. *James Watson Webb: A Biography.* Middletown, Conn.: Wesleyan University Press, 1969.

Darling, Arthur B. *Political Changes in Massachusetts, 1824–1848: A Study of Liberal Movements in Politics.* New Haven: Yale University Press, 1925.

Degler, Carl N. *Out of Our Past: The Forces That Shaped Modern America.* 3rd ed. New York: Harper Colophon Books, 1984.

Dent, Lynwood M., Jr. "The Virginia Democratic Party, 1824–1847." Ph.D. diss., Louisiana State University, 1974.

Derby, John B. *Political Reminiscences, Including a Sketch of the Origin and History of the "Statesman Party" of Boston.* Boston: Homer and Palmer, 1835.

Dicken-Garcia, Hazel. *Journalistic Standards in Nineteenth Century America.* Madison: University of Wisconsin Press, 1989.

Dobson, John. *Politics in the Gilded Age: A New Perspective on Reform.* New York: Praeger Publishers, 1972.

Durden, Robert F. *The Dukes of Durham, 1865–1929.* Durham: Duke University Press, 1975.

Dyer, Carolyn Stewart. "Political Patronage of the Wisconsin Press, 1849–1861: New Perspectives on the Economics of Patronage." *Journalism Monographs* 109 (February 1989).

Edgar, Walter B., ed. *Biographical Directory of the South Carolina House of Representatives.* Volume 1, *Session Lists, 1692–1978.* Columbia: University of South Carolina Press, 1974.

Elliot, Robert N., Jr. "The Raleigh Register." Ph.D. diss, University of North Carolina, 1953.

Ershkowitz, Herbert. "New Jersey during the Era of Jackson, 1820–1837." Ph.D. diss., New York University, 1965.

Ewing, Gretchen G. "Duff Green: Independent Editor of a Party Press." *Journalism History* 54 (1977), 331–339.

Ferguson, Russel J. *Early Western Pennsylvania Politics.* Pittsburgh: University of Pittsburgh Press, 1938.

Ferry, John W. *A History of The Department Store.* New York: Macmillan Co., 1960.

Formisano, Ronald P. *The Birth of Mass Political Parties: Michigan, 1827–1861.* Princeton: Princeton University Press, 1971.

Formisano, Ronald P. *The Transformation of Political Culture: Massachusetts Parties, 1790s–1840s.* New York: Oxford University Press, 1983.

Forsyth, David P. *The Business Press in America, 1750–1865.* Philadelphia: Chilton Books.

Fowler, Nathaniel C., Jr., *Fowler's Publicity: An Encyclopedia of Advertising and Printing and All that Pertains to the Public-Seeing Side of Business.* Boston: Publicity Publishing Co., 1897.

Fowler, Nathaniel C., Jr. *The Handbook of Journalism.* New York: Sully and Kleinteich, 1913.

Fraley, William B. "The Representation Controversy in North Carolina, 1787–1835." Ph.D. diss., University of North Carolina, 1965.

Gans, Herbert J. *Deciding What's News.* New York: Pantheon Books, 1979.

Garraty, John A. *The New Commonwealth, 1877–1890.* New York: Harper and Row, 1968.

Georgia State. Senate. Journal. 1829, 1832.

Georgia State. House. Journal. 1829, 1831.

Georgia State. Acts of the General Assembly, 1831.

Gibbons, Herbert A. *John Wanamaker.* Volume 2. New York: Harper and Brothers, 1926.

Glenn, Virginia L. "James Hamilton Jr. of South Carolina: A Biography." Ph.D. diss., University of North Carolina, 1964.

Goldman, Eric F. *Rendezvous with Destiny.* New York: Alfred A. Knopf, 1952.

Goldstein, Kalman. "The Albany Regency: The Failure of Practical Politics." Ph.D. diss., Columbia University, 1969.

Gosnell, Cullen B., and C. David Anders. *The Government and Administration of Georgia.* New York: Thomas Y. Crowell Co., 1956.

Govan, Thomas P. *Nicholas Biddle: Nationalist and Public Banker, 1786–1844.* Chicago: University of Chicago Press, 1959.

Green, Fletcher M. "Duff Green, Militant Journalist of the Old School." *American Historical Review* 52 (1947), 246–264.

Gregory, Winifred, ed. *American Newspapers, 1821–1936.* New York: H. W. Wilson Co., 1937.

Hamilton, Milton W. "Antimasonic Papers 1836–34." In *The Papers of the Bibliographic Society of America.* Volume 38. Chicago: University of Chicago Press, 1938.

Hamilton, Milton W. *The Country Printer: New York State, 1785–1830.* New York: Columbia University Press, 1936.

Hays, Samuel P. "The Changing Political Structure of the City in Industrial America." *Journal of Urban History* 1, no. 1 (November 1974), 6–38.

Hazard, Samuel. The Register of Pennsylvania. Volumes 1, 3, 4, 6, 7, 8. Philadelphia: W. F. Geddes, 1828–32.

Higgs, Robert. *The Transformation of the American Economy, 1865–1914.* New York: John Wiley and Sons, 1971.

Hill, Alonzo F. *Secrets of the Sanctum: An Inside View of an Editor's Life.* Philadelphia: Claxton, Remsen and Haffelfinger, 1875.

Hints to Young Editors, by an Editor. New Haven, Conn.: Charles C. Chatfield and Co., 1872.

Hitchcock, Nevada D. *What a Reporter Must Be: Helps to Success in Newspaper Work.* Cleveland, Ohio: R. Hitchcock, 1900.

Holt, Michael. *The Political Crisis of the 1850s.* New York: John Wiley and Sons, 1978.

Houston, David F. *A Critical Study of Nullification in South Carolina.* New York: Longmans, Green and Co., 1896.

Hower, Ralph M. *A History of Macy's of New York, 1858–1915.* Cambridge, Mass.: Harvard University Press, 1943.

Hower, Ralph M. *The History of an Advertising Agency: N. W. Ayer & Son at Work, 1869–1939.* Cambridge: Harvard University Press, 1939.

Hudson, Frederic. *Journalism in the United States from 1690 to 1872.* New York: Harper and Brothers, 1873.

Jennings, Kenneth Q. "Political and Social Force of the New Jersey Press Association, 1857–1939." M.A. thesis, Columbia University, 1940.

Jervey, Theodore D. *Robert Y. Hayne and His Times.* New York: Macmillan Co., 1909.

Johannsen, Robert W. *Stephen A. Douglas.* New York: Oxford University Press, 1973.

Johnson, Gerald W., et al. *The Sunpapers of Baltimore.* New York: Alfred A. Knopf, 1937.

Josephson, Matthew. *The Politicos, 1865–1896.* New York: Harcourt Brace and Co., 1938.

Kehl, James A. *Ill Feeling in the Era of Good Feeling.* Pittsburgh: University of Pittsburgh Press, 1956.

Kibler, Lillian A. *Benjamin F. Perry: South Carolina Unionist* Durham, N.C.: Duke University Press, 1946.

Kielbowicz, Richard. *News in the Mail: The Press, Post Office and Public Information.* New York: Greenwood Press, 1989.

Kielbowicz, Richard B. "Speeding the News by Postal Express, 1825–1861: The Public Policy of Privileges for the Press." *Social Science Journal* 22 (January 1985), 49–63.

King, William L. *The Newspaper Press of Charleston, S.C.* Charleston: Lucas and Richardson, 1882.

Kirkland, Edward C. *Dream and Thought in the Business Community, 1860–1900.* Ithaca: Cornell University Press, 1956.

Klein, Maury, and Harvey Kantor, eds. *Prisoners of Progress: American Industrial Cities 1850–1920.* New York: Macmillan Publishing Co., 1976.

Klein, Philip S. *Pennsylvania Politics, 1817–1832: A Game without Rules.* Philadelphia: Historical Society of Pennsylvania, 1940.

Kleinpell, Eugene H. "James M. Comly: Journalist-Politician." Ph.D. diss., Ohio State University, 1936.

Kobre, Sidney. *Development of American Journalism.* Dubuque: Wm. C. Brown Co., 1969.

Lee, Alfred McClung. *The Daily Newspaper in America: The Evolution of a Social Instrument.* New York: Macmillan Co., 1937.

Leonard, Thomas C. *The Power of the Press: The Birth of American Political Reporting.* New York: Oxford University Press, 1986.

Lesesne, J. Mauldin. "The Nullification Controversy in an Up-Country District." *Proceedings of the South Carolina Historical Association* 1939, pp. 13–24.

"Letters to John Brazer Davis, 1819–31." Pp. 178–256 in Massachusetts Historical Society *Proceedings.* Volume 49. Cambridge: Harvard University Press, John Wilson and Son, 1916.

Lord, Myra B. *History of the New England Woman's Press Association, 1885–1931.* Newton, Mass.: Graphic Press, 1932.

Loth, David. *Public Plunder: A History of Graft in America.* New York: Carrick and Evans, 1938.

Lowe, Gabriel L., Jr. "John H. Eaton: Jackson's Campaign Manager." *Tennessee Historical Quarterly* 11, no. 2 (June 1952), 99–147.

Lyons, Louis M. *Newspaper Story: One Hundred Years of the Boston Globe.* Cambridge: Belknap Press of Harvard University Press, 1971.

Mandelbaum, Seymour J. *Boss Tweed's New York.* New York: John Wiley and Sons, Inc., 1965.

Marbut, F. B. *News from the Capital: The Story of Washington Reporting.* Carbondale: Southern Illinois Press, 1971.

Marquette, Arthur E. *Brands, Trademarks and Good Will.* New York: McGraw-Hill Book Co., 1967.

Marvin, Frederic R. "Editors and Newspapers: A Sermon." Portland: George H. Himes, 1883.

Maverick, Augustus. *Henry J. Raymond and the New York Press for Thirty Years: Progress of American Journalism from 1840 to 1870.* Hartford, Conn.: A. S. Halen and Co., 1870.

McCarthy, Charles. "The Antimasonic Party: A Study of Political Antimasonry in the United States, 1827–1840." Pp. 365–574 in *Annual Report of the American Historical Association for the Year 1902.* Volume 1. Washington, D.C.: Government Printing Office, 1903.

McCormick, Richard P. *The Second American Party System: Party Formation in the Jacksonian Era.* Chapel Hill: University of North Carolina Press, 1966.

McDonald, J. Angus. *Successful Advertising: How to Accomplish It.* Philadelphia: Lincoln Publishing Co., 1902.

McFarland, Gerald W. *Mugwumps, Morals and Politics, 1884–1920.* Amherst: University of Massachusetts Press, 1975.

McGerr, Michael E. *The Decline of Popular Politics: The American North, 1865–1928.* New York: Oxford University Press, 1986.

McJimsey, George. *Genteel Partisan: Manton Marble, 1834–1917.* Ames: Iowa State University Press, 1971.

Memoirs of Georgia. Atlanta: Southern Historical Association, 1895.

Mencken, Henry L. *Newspaper Days, 1899–1906.* New York: Alfred A. Knopf, 1941.

Morgan, Wayne, ed. *The Gilded Age: A Reappraisal.* Syracuse: Syracuse University Press, 1963.

Mott, Frank Luther. *American Journalism.* New York: Macmillan Co., 1940.

Muller, Ernest P. "Preston King: A Political Biography." Ph.D. diss., Columbia University, 1957.

Munson, Augustus J. *Making a Country Newspaper.* Chicago: Dominion Co., 1891.

Murray, Paul.*The Whig Party in Georgia, 1825–53.* Chapel Hill: University of North Carolina Press, 1948.

Nerone, John C. "The Mythology of the Penny Press." *Critical Studies in Mass Communication* 4, no. 4 (December 1987), 376–404.

Nevins, Allan. *The Emergence of Lincoln.* New York: Charles Scribner's Sons, 1950.

Nevins, Allan. *The Evening Post: A Century of Journalism.* New York: Boni and Liveright, Publishers, 1922.

New York State. Senate. Report of the Comptroller. 57th sess. 1835. S. Doc. 67.

New York State. Senate. Report of the Comptroller. 66th sess. 1843. S. Doc. 12.

Nichols, Roy F. *The Invention of the American Political Parties.* New York: Macmillan Co., 1967.

Nord, David Paul. *Newspapers and New Politics: Midwestern Municipal Reform, 1890–1900.* Ann Arbor, Mich.: UMI Research Press, 1981.

Nord, David Paul. "The Public Community: The Urbanization of Journalism in Chicago." *Journal of Urban History* 11 (1985), 411–441.

Northen, William J. *Men of Mark in Georgia.* Atlanta: A. B. Caldwell, 1910.

Nye, Russel B. *Society and Culture in America, 1830–1860.*New York: Harper Torchbooks, 1974.

O'Brien, Frank M. *The Story of the Sun.* New York: George H. Doran Co., 1918.

Olin, Charles H. *Journalism.* Philadelphia: Penn Publishing Co., 1906.

Orne, Col. Henry. *The Letters of Columbus Originally Published in the Boston Bulletin.* Boston: Putnam and Hunt, 1829.

Pegg, Herbert D. "The Whig Party in North Carolina, 1834–61." Ph.D. diss., University of North Carolina, 1932.

Philips, Melville. *The Making of a Newspaper: Experiences of Certain Representative American Journalists Related by Themselves.* New York: G. P. Putnam's Sons, 1893.

Pope, Daniel. *The Making of Modern Advertising.* New York: Basic Books, 1983.

Presbrey, Frank. *The History and Development of Advertising.* Garden City, N.J.: Doubleday, Doran and Co., 1929.

Prior, Granville T. "A History of the *Charleston Mercury,* 1822–52." Ph.D. diss., Harvard University, 1946.

Ratner, Lorman. *Antimasonry: The Crusade and the Party.* Englewood Cliffs, N.J.: Prentice Hall, 1969.

Register of All the Officers and Agents, Civil, Military and Naval in the Service of the United States. 1833, 1835, 1837, 1839, 1841, 1843, 1845. Various publishers.

Remini, Robert V. *Andrew Jackson and the Bank War.* New York: Norton, 1967.

Remini, Robert V. *Andrew Jackson and the Course of American Freedom, 1822–1832.* New York: Harper and Row, 1981.

Remini, Robert V. *The Election of Andrew Jackson.* Philadelphia: J. B. Lippincott Co., 1963.

Remini, Robert V. *Martin Van Buren and the Making of the Democratic Party.* New York: Columbia University Press, 1959.

Robertson, Ross M. *History of the American Economy.* 3d ed. New York: Harcourt Brace Jovanovich, 1973.

Robinson, Edgar E. *The Evolution of American Political Parties.* New York: Harcourt Brace and Co., 1924.

Rogers, Jason. *Newspaper Building.* New York: Harper and Bros., 1918.

Rorabaugh, William. *The Alcoholic Republic.* New York: Oxford University Press, 1979.

Rowell, George P. *Forty Years an Advertising Agent, 1865–1905.* New York: Franklin Publishing Co., 1926.

Rutenbeck, Jeffrey B. "The Rise of Independent Newspapers in the 1870s: A Transformation in American Journalism." Ph.D. diss., University of Washington, 1990.

Schellenger, Harold K. *An Era of Newspaper Organization: Development of the Buckeye Press Association, 1895–1908.* Columbus: Ohio Historical Society, 1939.

Schlesinger, Arthur M., Jr. *The Age of Jackson.* Boston: Little, Brown, 1945.

Schlesinger, Arthur M., Sr. *Political and Social Growth of the American People, 1865–1940.* 3d ed. New York: Macmillan Co., 1941.

Schlesinger, Arthur M., Sr. *The Rise of the City, 1878–1898.* New York: Macmillan Co., 1933.

Schlipp, Madelon G., and Sharon M. Murphy. *Great Women of the Press.* Carbondale: Southern Illinois Press, 1983.

Schroth, Raymond A. *The Eagle of Brooklyn: A Community Newspaper, 1841–1955.* Westport, Conn.: Greenwood Press, 1974.

Schudson, Michael. *Advertising, The Uneasy Persuasion: Its Dubious Impact on American Society.* New York: Basic Books, 1984.

Schudson, Michael. *Discovering the News: A Social History of American Newspapers.* New York: Basic Books, 1978.

Schultz, Quentin J. "Advertising, Science and Professionalism, 1885–1917." Ph.D. diss, University of Illinois, 1978.

Schuman, Edwin L. *The Art and Practice of Journalism: How to Become a Successful Writer.* Chicago: Stevans and Handy, n.d.

Schuman, Edwin L. *Steps into Journalism: Helps and Hints for Young Writers.* Evanston, Ill.: Correspondence School of Journalism, 1894.

Shanks, Henry T., ed. *The Papers of Willie P. Mangum.* Volume 1 (1807–32). Raleigh, N.C.: State Department of Archives and History, 1950.

Silbey, Joel H. *Political Ideology and Voting Behavior in the Age of Jackson.* Englewood Cliffs, N.J.: Prentice Hall, 1973.

Silbey, Joel H. *A Respectable Minority: The Democratic Party in the Civil War Era, 1860–1868.* New York: W. W. Norton and Co., 1977.

Sloan, William David, " 'Purse and Pen': Party–Press Relationships, 1789–1816." *American Journalism* 6 (1989), 103–126.

Smith, Culver H. *The Press, Politics and Patronage*. Athens: University of Georgia Press, 1977.

Smith, Culver H. "Propaganda Technique in the Jackson Campaign of 1828." *East Tennessee Historical Society Publications* 6 (1934), 49–61.

Smith, Page. *The Rise of Industrial America*. New York: McGraw-Hill Book Co., 1984.

Smith, William E. *The Francis Preston Blair Family in Politics*. New York: Macmillan Co., 1933.

Smythe, Ted Curtis. "The Reporter, 1880–1900: Working Conditions and Their Influence on the News." *Journalism History*, no. 1 (1980), 1–11.

Starr, Paul. *The Social Transformation of American Medicine: The Rise of a Sovereign Profession and the Making of a Vast Industry*. New York: Basic Books, 1982.

Steffens, J. Lincoln. "The Business of a Newspaper." *Scribner's Magazine* (1897), 447–467.

Stem, Thad, Jr. *The Tar Heel Press*. Charlotte, N.C.: Heritage Printers, 1973.

Stewart, Robert K. "The Jackson Press and the Elections of 1824 and 1828." M.A. thesis, University of Washington, 1984.

Swanberg, W. A. *Citizen Hearst*. New York: Charles Scribners' Sons, 1961.

Swensen, Rolf H. " 'An Age of Reform and Improvement': The Life of Col E. Hofer, 1855–1934." Ph.D. diss., University of Oregon, 1975.

Sydnor, Charles S. *American Revolutionaries in the Making: Political Practices in Washington's Virginia*. New York: Free Press, 1965.

Thayer, John A. *Astir: A Publisher's Life Story*. Boston: Small, Maynard and Co., 1910.

Tilley, Nannie. *The R. J. Reynolds Tobacco Company*. Chapel Hill: University of North Carolina Press, 1985.

Trachtenberg, Alan. *The Incorporation of America: Culture and Society in the Gilded Age*. New York: Hill and Wang, 1982.

Tree, Robert L. "Victor Lawson and His Newspapers, 1890–1910." Ph.D. diss., Northwestern University, 1959.

U.S. Congress. Senate. Committee on the Post Office and Post Roads, *Condition of the Post Office Department*. 23d Cong. 1st sess. 1834. S. Doc. 422.

U.S. Congress. Senate. Committee on the Post Office and Post Roads. *Condition and Proceedings of the Post Office Department*. 23d Cong. 2d sess. 1835. S. Doc. 86.

U.S. Congress. House. *Examination of the Post Office Department*. 23d Cong. 2d sess. 1835. H. Rept. 103.

U.S. Congress. House. *Report on Public Printing*. 26th Cong. 1st sess. 1841. H. Rept. 298.

Van Deusen, Glyndon G. *Thurlow Weed, Wizard of the Lobby*. Boston: Little, Brown, 1947.

Van Deusen, Glyndon G. *William Henry Seward*. New York: Oxford University Press, 1967.

Vinson, John C. "Electioneering in North Carolina, 1800–1835." *North Carolina Historical Review* 29 (April 1952).

Wallace, Michael. "Changing Concepts of Party in the United States: New York, 1815–1828." *American Historical Review* 74 (1968), 453–491.

Ward, Henry H. "Ninety Years of the National Newspaper Association: The Mind and Dynamics of Grassroots Journalism in Shaping America." Ph.D. diss., University of Minnesota, 1977.

Weed, Thurlow. *Autobiography of Thurlow Weed,* ed. Harriet A. Weed. Reprint ed. (New York: DaCapo Press, 1970).

Wendt, Lloyd. *Chicago Tribune: The Rise of a Great American Newspaper.* Chicago: Rand McNally and Co., 1979.

White, Leonard D. *The Jacksonians: A Study in Administrative History, 1829–1861.* New York: Macmillan Co., 1954.

Wiebe, Robert. *The Search for Order.* New York: Hill and Wang, 1967.

Wilson, Clyde N., ed. *The Papers of John C. Calhoun.* Volumes 10 and 11. Columbia: University of South Carolina Press, 1968.

Wingate, Charles F., ed. *Views and Interviews on Journalism.* New York: F. B. Patterson, 1875.

Index